'The important period of the Er
has not received much attention. Th
book fills the gap.' **Richard Pankhurst**

'This book is a must-read for anyone interested in
the modern history of Ethiopia.' **Ian Campbell**, author of
The Plot to Kill Graziani

IMPERIAL EXILE

'This is an important and dramatic story that deserves
to be better known.' **Philip Marsden**, author of
The Barefoot Emperor

'The first full account of how the Emperor spent those
crucial four years in exile in the UK.'
Professor Shiferaw Bekele, Addis Ababa University

IMPERIAL EXILE

Emperor Haile Selassie in Britain 1936-40

KEITH BOWERS

Copyright © Keith Bowers 2016

The right of Keith Bowers to be identified as the author of this work has been asserted in accordance with the Copyright, Designs & Patents Act 1988.

All rights reserved. No part of this book may be reproduced, stored in a retrieval system, or transmitted in any form or by any means, electronic, electrostatic, magnetic tape, mechanical, photocopying, recording or otherwise, without the written permission of the copyright holder.

Published under licence by Brown Dog Books and
The Self-Publishing Partnership, 7 Green Park Station, Bath BA1 1JB

www.selfpublishingpartnership.co.uk

ISBN printed book: 978-1-78545-087-7
ISBN e-book: 978-1-78545-088-4

Cover design by Kevin Rylands
Internal design by Andrew Easton

Printed and bound by CPI Group (UK) Ltd, Croydon CR0 4YY

CONTENTS

Prologue 6
List of key events 12
Introductory notes 14

Map of Ethiopia 16
Chapter One A Year from Hell 17
Chapter One Eyewitness In the Emperor's Footsteps: A trip to Dessie 35

Chapter Two Testing the Waters 38
Chapter Two Eyewitness The Bath Spa Hotel 62

Chapter Three The King of Kings 65
Map of Addis Ababa 66
Chapter Three Eyewitness A Visit to the Emperor's Palace 80

Map of Bath 84
Chapter Four Taking Refuge 85
Chapter Four Eyewitness Tales of a Princess 110

Chapter Five Murder Most Foul 114
Chapter Five Eyewitness The Mystic's Cave 127

Chapter Six Aiding and Abetting 129
Chapter Six Eyewitness Coffee with the Pankhursts 143

Chapter Seven Hitting Rock Bottom 147
Map of places visited in the UK 148
Chapter Seven Eyewitness Open Day at Fairfield House 171

Chapter Eight The Great Escape 174
Chapter Eight Eyewitness The View from Entoto 196

Chapter Nine Counting the Cost 199
Chapter Nine Eyewitness The Weekend Retreat 216

Chapter Ten The Final Curtain Call 220
Chapter Ten Eyewitness Inside the Guildhall 231

Epilogue 233
Acknowledgements 240
List of photographs 243
Chapter sources 246
Bibliography 254
Fairfield residents post-exile 260

PROLOGUE

The exile of the Ethiopian Emperor Haile Selassie in the city of Bath in the 1930s is a gripping human drama. There are a number of compelling reasons why I want to share this poignant story.

First, it deals with exile and separation – a universal human condition, which is becoming ever more prevalent in today's turbulent world. Second, Haile Selassie's enforced stay in Bath raises the perennial issue of how to deal with international aggression, and the attempts by the strong to dominate the weak. Third, the story of this exile experience gives a unique insight into a fascinating period of history both in Africa and Europe.

The life of a refugee is never easy. It can be often misunderstood and looked down upon. Being in exile is an intense and testing time for anyone, be they kings or commoners; rich or poor; western, African or Asian. Trying to understand the inner turmoil of a person separated from their homeland can help us to appreciate the full range of what it is like to be human and the importance of home. Those of us who have never been forced from our countries have escaped lightly. But pausing to consider such an experience can enrich our own lives and teach us something new about ourselves and others. The story of being forced into banishment, and then escaping from it, has been told in many cultures throughout history in myths, fairytales, songs and poems. The experience involves an intense range of emotions, and fluctuations in an individual's state of mind. Of course, getting inside the head of such an inscrutable and regal character such as Haile Selassie is not that straightforward. However, it is certainly possible to imagine many of the pressures and stresses he underwent.

This story of an extraordinary African monarch, who lived through extraordinary

PROLOGUE

times, provides a demonstration of the resilience of the human spirit. Haile Selassie was one of many exiles living in Britain in the 1930s as countless opponents of the fascist regimes in Italy and Germany had to flee for their lives. However, the Emperor's story is definitely among the more complex, intriguing and rewarding.

Haile Selassie ended up fleeing to Britain after the Italian forces of the fascist leader Benito Mussolini invaded his country in 1935 to help satisfy his colonial ambitions. The story has great relevance today. We are still witnessing big states bullying smaller ones, constant debates over how to organise collective security, and continued attempts by states and groups to impose what they regard as their civilising values on other countries and societies with different cultures and traditions. The Emperor was a symbol of national independence, which had been snatched away unfairly by Mussolini's invaders. Haile Selassie fled to Europe because he believed he could stir the conscience of the so-called civilised world and ask for help to repel an aggressor. He made an eloquent appeal to the League of Nations, the forerunner of the United Nations, but it fell on deaf ears.

The lukewarm response to Ethiopia's plight by the British government also revealed its condescending attitudes towards Africa. Some of these prejudices and ignorances persist to this day and the Emperor was one of the first African leaders to challenge the fundamental precepts and assumptions of colonialism. However, the Emperor's cause at the time was recognised and supported by millions of ordinary British citizens, keen to back an underdog. They recognised colonial bullying for what it was. Haile Selassie was a controversial character and there are still divided and hotly-contested opinions about his rule in Ethiopia. However, this book is not aimed at investigating any of the Emperor's alleged crimes and shortcomings, nor at providing a comprehensive assessment of his time in power. While some of his achievements as well as his mistakes are mentioned, my focus is not primarily political in nature.

This story also provides an engaging mingling of cultures between the privileged world of an Ethiopian monarch, and the genteel arena of Bath in the west of England. Here I have to declare an interest, which explains my passion and enthusiasm for this story. I live in Bath and have been on more than 50 trips to Ethiopia in the last 15 years. I love both places. I taught for several years at Addis Ababa University where the main campus is based in the grounds of the Gennete Leul, Haile Selassie's former palace.

Ethiopia is a surprising and beguiling country with its ancient Christian civilisation, its orthodox church with its many rites and sacraments, its hauntingly beautiful landscapes and more than 80 diverse cultures and languages. I have travelled to the eastern town of Harar where Haile Selassie grew up; to the volcanic lake area of Debre Zeit where he used to escape for weekends when in power; and to the northern town of Dessie where he manned an anti-aircraft battery when under attack by Italian warplanes. I have also visited three important religious sites of the Ethiopian Orthodox Church, which was so important to Haile Selassie: the northern town of Axum, the home of the legendary Queen of Sheba, and the claimed location of the Ark of the Covenant; the remarkable rock-hewn churches of Lalibela; and the Debre Libanos monastery, perched on the edge of a stunning river gorge.

DNA studies in the past few years have suggested that we all are descended from a group of migrant Africans who left the Rift Valley area of Ethiopia around 60,000 years ago. So the history of Ethiopia may be in some way the history of us all. Perhaps the fact that some of my DNA possibly originates from the country explains why I feel so at home there!

In turn, Bath has its hot springs expertly exploited by the Romans, its rolling hills, and its inspirational and exquisite Georgian architecture from the 18th and early 19th centuries. I have explored with great curiosity most of the city either on foot or by bicycle. I have marvelled at the beautiful wooded valley of Limpley Stoke and the unspoiled hills to the south of the city where one can walk undisturbed for hours. In this book I hope to capture some of the exciting essence of both places and make them come alive, especially for those not familiar with them.

Haile Selassie's separation from his homeland has all the ingredients of a great human story. It involves a tempestuous struggle of the soul against isolation and injustice against a backdrop of two incredibly diverse and magnificent civilisations. I am well aware though of the dangers of romanticising Haile Selassie's exile. It was a hard experience with few frills – a crucible of suffering, lament and longing. The Emperor's exile turned out to be no more than a brief interlude in his long reign, which began in earnest at his coronation at a glittering and sumptuous ceremony in Addis Ababa in 1930. However, he had held considerable power and influence for 14 years before that as regent and crown prince.

In trying to fully comprehend the exile period, it is important to understand where Haile Selassie came from and what impact the experience of separation had on him afterwards. Chapter One gives an account of the immediate events in Ethiopia leading up to his exile, and Chapter Three gives the full background of his early life and upbringing in his country. Chapter Nine examines how the Emperor's exile experience influenced his rule after he returned to Ethiopia. However, the main focus of this book is on what happened during the Emperor's enforced stay in Britain. Although the Emperor was ensconced in his handsome Victorian villa in Bath, his mind inevitably was mainly elsewhere – with his people, who were undergoing intense suffering.

The Emperor's enforced sojourn has enriched the history of Bath but is not that widely known or examined in detail. Many biographies have been written about the Emperor by authors both inside and outside Ethiopia, though few of them explore the Bath years in any significant detail. Some excellent articles have been devoted to

PROLOGUE

the activities of the Emperor while he was in the UK. But these focus more on what the Ethiopian leader did rather than his state of mind, and the impact of his exile on his emotions and personality.

My book will take a much more observational approach and will attempt to uncover the experience of what being in exile was actually like, rather than just focusing on what happened. It will concentrate on the bitter experience of separation from one's own country, especially at a time of great suffering and turmoil. The book therefore attempts to provide an accessible case study of the human condition of being in exile.

It is of course difficult for any of us to enter fully into the time when these core events took place between 1936 and 1940. We all have to try to suspend our knowledge of what happened to Haile Selassie at the end of his life when he was overthrown in a left-wing revolution in 1974. The image projected of him then as an out-of-touch old man, accused of heartless despotism, remains a very powerful one. But the main focus of this book is long before this time when the Ethiopian leader was in the prime of life, in his mid-forties.

A touching essay by the Palestinian intellectual Professor Edward Said reveals what it is like to be uprooted from one's own country. He says separation denies dignity, leads to miserable loneliness and that its essential sadness can never be surmounted. Said quotes the American poet Wallace Stevens, who said that being in exile was being forced to have permanently what he called the mind of winter. The French philosopher Simone Weil said that to be rooted was perhaps the most important but least recognised need of the human soul. A poem by an author called Paul Tabori says that exile is the long wait for the train that never arrives, the plane that never gets off the ground. And exile is a song that only the singer can hear.

The medieval Italian poet Dante, who himself was in exile, gives a very graphic but down to earth description of his experiences. In the *Paradiso* he says you have to leave behind what you love most: 'You have the bitter taste of someone else's bread, how salty it is; you also have to cope with the hard experience of going up and down someone else's stairs.'

This story of endurance is not just about one man from a traditional male society. Many women are part of the drama too. The Queen of Sheba is an important character in Ethiopian folklore. Empress Zewditu powerfully locked horns with Haile Selassie when he was Crown Prince. His wife Empress Menen shared his exile years, as did his two strong-willed and influential daughters, Princesses Tenagneworq and Tsehai. Tenagneworq had four daughters, who also made their mark on society. The towering international campaigner Sylvia Pankhurst looms large in this stirring story of exile.

The Emperor had an existence of epic proportions and could have easily been the basis for a character in a Shakespeare play. Such comparisons are often made but rarely justified. In the Emperor's case it certainly is appropriate as he lived a life infused with great drama and tragedy. Five of his seven children died before he did. He witnessed many betrayals and jealousies, and saw a host of family members and close friends killed in battle, or die prematurely through illness or accidents. He also battled against countless enemies and did not shirk from sometimes employing brutal and ruthless tactics to overcome them. Whatever his politics and record in power, Haile Selassie endured more suffering than many of us ever face or could cope with.

PROLOGUE

KEY EVENTS IN LIFE AND EXILE OF HAILE SELASSIE (Western calendar)

1892	Born in Harar as Teferi Makonnen. Haile Selassie is his baptismal name
1896	Ethiopian forces inflict a humiliating defeat on the Italian army at the battle of Adwa in northern Ethiopia
1906	Death of Makonnen Wolde-Mikael, Teferi's father
1910	Teferi becomes Governor of Harar
1913	Death of Emperor Menelik II. Lij Iyasu becomes ruler of Ethiopia
1916	Lij Iyasu deposed. Teferi becomes Regent and Crown Prince
1924	Teferi's Grand Tour of Europe
1928	Teferi crowned as Negus (King)
1930	Teferi crowned as Emperor of Ethiopia. Now known as Haile Selassie
October 1935	Italy invades Ethiopia
November 1935	Haile Selassie establishes military base at Dessie in northern Ethiopia
March 1936	Ethiopian army defeated in major battle of Maychew
April 1936	Haile Selassie retreats to Addis Ababa
2 May 1936	The Emperor flees Addis Ababa by train to port state of Djibouti and is evacuated by a British warship
5 May 1936	Italian army occupies Addis Ababa
11 May 1936	The Emperor arrives in Jerusalem after travelling to Haifa by sea
3 June 1936	He arrives in London after travelling by ship to Southampton
30 June 1936	League of Nations speech

KEY EVENTS

July 1936	The Emperor is based in London and also visits Scotland
August 1936	First trip by Haile Selassie to Bath to take the spa waters
September 1936	The Emperor leaves for London but later buys Fairfield House in Bath
October 1936	The Imperial family moves into Fairfield House
February 1937	Massacres in Addis Ababa after attempt to kill Graziani, the Italian Viceroy
December 1937	The Emperor breaks his collar bone in London in traffic accident
January 1938	Empress Menen and Ras Kassa leave Bath for Jerusalem
May 1938	The Emperor appears again at League of Nations but due to fatigue is unable to read his speech
September 1938	Death in Bath of Ethiopian Foreign Minister Heruy Wolde-Selassie
December 1938	Britain ratifies agreement recognising Italian occupation of Ethiopia The Emperor loses major court case against Cable and Wireless
August 1939	The Emperor writes to King George VI of England offering his services
September 1939	Outbreak of World War Two. Haile Selassie is still in exile in Bath
May 1940	Churchill replaces Neville Chamberlain as Prime Minister. The Emperor writes to Churchill offering his assistance
June 1940	Mussolini declares war on allies. The Emperor leaves Bath for Sudan
January 1941	Haile Selassie re-enters Ethiopian territory with British forces
5 May 1941	The Emperor enters Addis Ababa, five years after the Italians arrived
1954	Haile Selassie returns to Bath and is made Freeman of the City
1956	Death of Ras Kassa Hailu, the Emperor's most trusted adviser
1958	Fairfield House is given by Haile Selassie to the people of Bath
1960	Attempted coup against the Emperor in Addis Ababa
1962	Death of Empress Menen
1970	Haile Selassie makes an emotional visit to Italy
1974	The Emperor is deposed in a coup
1975	Death of Haile Selassie, murdered by revolutionaries
2000	The Emperor's body is buried in Holy Trinity Cathedral, Addis Ababa

INTRODUCTORY NOTES

Haile Selassie was a famous figure who attracted a lot of attention both during his long life and afterwards. A full summary of the sources used to tell the story of his exile in the UK can be found towards the end of this book. However, in addition to referring to the work of others, some of this narrative will be driven by my own contemporary eyewitness accounts of the key places associated with the exile period in both Bath and Ethiopia. This will give the opportunity to describe some of the rich and varied aspects of Ethiopian life and culture, which are not that widely known in the west.

Each of the ten main chapters is therefore followed by a brief supplement which contains my impressions of important locations or characters involved in the story of the Emperor's exile. This is an attempt to link the past to the present as well as to give a sense of place both in Bath and in Ethiopia.

Ethiopian names and places can be transcribed and spelled in a number of ways in English. Amharic is a phonetic language and these sounds can be represented by different English vowels and consonants. For example, Haile Selassie, Hayla Sellassie and Haile Sellassie are all in usage but I have plumped for Haile Selassie, the traditional international spelling of his name. Where possible I have tried to use the most common and widely accepted English versions of other Ethiopian names and places. I accept I may not have got everything absolutely right in all circumstances. Apologies in advance.

Ethiopians generally prefer to use Ethiopia rather than Abyssinia to describe their country. Abyssinia is a westernised term and is a corruption of the Amharic word, habesha, describing an Ethiopian person. For these reasons I will generally use Ethiopia in this book unless others referred specifically to Abyssinia in their notes or diaries, or the term was used in the name of an organisation. In the historical accounts there are some discrepancies in the dates of various events. Again I have tried to stick

INTRODUCTORY NOTES

with what the majority have used but accept there may be differences of opinion.

Many photographs are included in this book to give a clearer idea of the exile period. A full list of the photographs and credits can be found towards the end of this book. I have tried wherever possible to obtain high-resolution versions of the photographs used. However, some poorer quality photographs are displayed as their editorial and historical appeal means that a drop in production values is justified.

The historical events before, during and after the Emperor's exile are complex but it is vital to grasp some of the fundamentals in order to appreciate fully the vicissitudes of his experiences in Bath. My aim in this book is to give a helpful insight into the major landmarks in Ethiopian history without hopefully being overwhelmed by a torrent of detail. I am well aware of my limitations as a ferengi, the word Ethiopians use to describe foreigners. However, I have striven throughout to give a fair and accurate summary of the key events. The detailed reading list provides an invaluable resource for those who want to delve further into the background of this epic tale.

My fervent hope is that this book will be a valuable contribution to the rich histories of both Bath and Ethiopia.

IMPERIAL EXILE

CHAPTER ONE
A YEAR FROM HELL

On a late afternoon in early August 1936 a small, exotic and ascetic man with a well-trimmed beard and aquiline nose found himself on an express train from London to the spa city of Bath about 100 miles to the west. The passenger was the Emperor of Ethiopia, Haile Selassie, whose name means power of the trinity in Amharic, one of the country's main languages. The train he was travelling on was pulled along by a steam engine, belching its way noisily through the English countryside. The railway line from Paddington Station to the west of England was built in the 19th century by the British engineering genius Isambard Kingdom Brunel. It was truly a track fit for a king.

As he sped through the countryside, displaying its golden summer colours, the Emperor must have been glad for a few moments of quiet contemplation. He had just endured several months of hell, first unsuccessfully fighting fascist Italian forces in his beloved homeland, and then becoming a stateless refugee, forcibly ejected from his own country. He was exhausted, humiliated, and unsure where to turn next. In his mid-forties he should have been enjoying the prime of his life but it must have seemed anything but.

Friends and well-wishers had recommended Bath to him as a place to find solace because of its relaxing and healing spring waters. One of those advisers had an impeccable royal pedigree – the Duke of Connaught, the third son of Queen Victoria and Prince Albert. He said Bath was renowned for its quietness and good manners. In the days running up to his visit to Bath the Emperor had spent some time in Worthing, a fashionable resort on the south coast, which had played host to many members of the British royal family.

The Emperor's first view of the centre of Bath around 6.25pm would no doubt have lifted his spirits. The green rolling hills surrounding the city were impressive as was the meandering valley populated with spectacular Georgian houses, built in the distinctive Bath stone. But there was an extra bonus, especially for a man with such a deep faith in God. On the right side of the train, rising in majestic splendour, was the towering structure of Bath Abbey – a reassuring presence in the area for more than 400 years. Before that a huge Norman cathedral had occupied this site. And in the previous centuries a Saxon church had graced this strategic location next to the languid waters of the River Avon. Christianity arrived in Ethiopia before it came to the shores of Britain. For a man steeped in the religious history and traditions of his own country, a symbol of ecclesiastical stability such as Bath Abbey would likely have been a boon to his weary and tormented soul.

Bath Abbey dominating the landscape

The Emperor may not have known then that on this site in 973 AD Edgar had been crowned as the first king of all England. Haile Selassie had had his own coronation as Emperor in the Ethiopian capital Addis Ababa in 1930. The ceremony took place in St George's Cathedral, built by his predecessor Emperor Menelik II to celebrate Ethiopia's famous victory against the Italians at Adwa in northern Ethiopia in 1896. Italy had been seeking to extend its territory beyond its existing colony of Eritrea on the border with north-east Ethiopia. Its unexpected defeat at the hands of Menelik's troops was the first time western forces had been defeated by an African army.

CHAPTER 1

Haile Selassie was well aware of his own royal pedigree and his place in history. As a young man he had meticulously studied the *Kibra Nagast* or *Glory of Kings*, written in the 14th century AD. In these writings he could trace his own royal lineage back to King Solomon, the ancient monarch from the 10th century BC, said to have been blessed with great wisdom. Haile Selassie saw himself as the 225th king in the line of this Solomonic dynasty.

The Emperor certainly had the title to go with his royal credentials. He was officially known as His Imperial Majesty Haile Selassie I, Conquering Lion of the Tribe of Judah, King of Kings of Ethiopia and Elect of God. Emperor is an English word with no direct equivalent in Amharic but is accepted as a workable summary of Neguse Negest or King of Kings. In common speech the Emperor was also called janhoy or majesty.

A stained glass window in Holy Trinity Cathedral, Addis Ababa, depicting the meeting between King Solomon and the Queen of Sheba

Despite his perilous circumstances in 1936, the Emperor could draw some strength and self-confidence from having skilfully navigated the treacherous intrigues of the Ethiopian court to reach the pinnacle of power. He could also have taken inspiration from his original Ethiopian name, Ras Teferi Makonnen. Ras means prince or duke and Teferi means the man who is to be feared. It is from this name that the Rastafari, who regard the Emperor as a god, took theirs. Even by the early 1930s the Rastafari believed that the emergence of Haile Selassie in black Africa had fulfilled a scriptural prophecy about the arrival of a new messiah.

The *Kibra Nagast* tells the engaging traditional story of the love affair between King Solomon and the beautiful Queen of Sheba. She hailed from the mountainous kingdom of ancient Ethiopia, which means the land of people with burnt faces. According to the *Kibra Nagast*, Menelik I was the son born as a result of a passionate encounter between Solomon and the alluring queen. Menelik I is described as playing an influential role in Ethiopia's history by snatching something unique and invaluable from under Solomon's nose in Jerusalem – the Ark of the Covenant, said to house the written version of God's laws handed down to the prophet Moses.

To this day, many Ethiopians believe the Ark still rests in the northern Ethiopian town of Axum. This was the centre of an advanced civilisation for more than 800 years until it disappeared in the 10th century AD. The Axumite Empire, which also incorporated much of modern Yemen, established trading routes to other parts of the world, including India and Rome. Gold, emeralds and ivory were among the materials traded.

Local guides at Axum today even claim a secret tunnel was built from there all the way to the Red Sea, a distance of about 75 miles. Axum is one of the holiest sites in Ethiopia. The Ark is said to reside on a compound at the church of Our Lady Mary of Zion. It remains under permanent guard and no-one is allowed to see it, apart from the High Priest of Axum, an elderly monk who is charged with protecting and looking after the Ark until he dies. Successive guardians have been expected to name their successor while on their death beds.

By the time of his exile the Emperor had already demonstrated his trademark regal bearing to friend and foe alike, both at home and abroad. In August 1935 he had been interviewed in Addis Ababa by an intrepid journalist called George Steer, who was to help him greatly later during his exile in the UK. Steer described his encounter in these hallowed terms. In his despatch after the interview he said:

> *'Other people have remarked on the Assyrian perfection of his features, the delicacy and length of his hands, the serenity of his eyes and the great dignity of his bearing. The first thing that I noticed was the extreme rapidity of his mind. He spoke without hesitation and without any correction; quickly with the authoritative force of a logician. He had an immensely able mind, and he knew his own views to the last detail.'*

Steer said that throughout the interview the Emperor economised his gestures and sat perfectly straight in his seat. Only a jewelled hand moved a little from under his black cloak. Steer was mightily impressed. He described the Emperor as a man of great intelligence and completely self-controlled. His dogs lay at his feet for an hour and a half with what Steer described as the same motionless obedience.

CHAPTER 1

RESISTING THE ITALIANS

With this regal heritage, Haile Selassie believed himself to be specially ordained by God to perform solemn duties in service of his country. However, he could have been forgiven if on the 4.30pm train from Paddington Station he was actually not feeling that special. His year of hell had intensified after the Italian forces of Benito Mussolini invaded Ethiopia at the start of October in 1935. Mussolini was looking for an African colony to boost his prestige. The Italians had been smarting ever since the Ethiopians defeated them at the pivotal battle of Adwa at the end of the 19th century. Mussolini had announced the invasion to cheering crowds in Rome. He said that Italy had been patient with Ethiopia for 40 years. Now that patience had run out and he, Il Duce, was cauterising this festering wound.

Some Italians were quick to make public their condemnation of Haile Selassie. For instance, the Bishop of Brindisi in southern Italy described him as a half-savage king. However, although Mussolini saw Ethiopia as an enemy to be tamed, he had no personal animosity towards the Ethiopian leader. The British Foreign Secretary at the time, Anthony Eden, describes in his memoirs how Mussolini had told him personally that Haile Selassie was a cautious and educated man, but that the rases or princes were quite different. He said that war was their national pastime, a kind of necessary amusement. This was a typical propaganda line of the fascist regime, which argued that Ethiopia was not functioning as a nation state. Instead, the Italians claimed the territory was an unruly collection of warring factions, with widespread slavery still practiced. In Ethiopia at the time it is true that prisoners taken during internal battles were put to work with no wages in the households of the regional warlords who had conquered them.

The Italians believed the country now needed to be rescued by European civilisation. They argued that their colonisation would be an influence for good, as they would introduce a competent administration, end slavery, and build a modern infrastructure.

Several hundred thousand fighting men were to be dispatched by Mussolini to subdue the Ethiopians. The Italians had modern guns and aircraft, unlike the Ethiopian forces, which mainly relied on outdated rifles, and traditional weapons such as swords and spears. The Italians also recruited thousands of Eritreans and Somalis to fight alongside their army. They were known as askaris.

The diminutive Emperor was just five feet four inches tall or around 1.6 metres. Unlike many of his predecessors, he was no warrior. His skills lay elsewhere – in political strategy, devising legislation, developing policy, and courtly scheming. However, the Emperor still rushed to one of the battle fronts to lead his forces in person. Towards the end of 1935 he went first of all to the town of Dessie in the north where he established a forward base. George Steer was again hot on the Emperor's trail. He said that Haile Selassie went to war like a 'European gentleman, with his four-course meals, his wine cellar, his sola topi and walking sticks, his Arab horses and his motor cars.' His pet dogs were also taken along for the ride. One of the dogs was called Rosa and she was to end up having one of the most adventurous lives that any canine has had.

The Emperor relished practising firing his weapons and had a liking for arms of precision and accuracy. He was already a dab hand at firing an Oerlikon anti-aircraft battery. Observers were amazed by the Emperor's stamina and determination, especially for one appearing so physically frail. He was the complete opposite of the brawny and overbearing Mussolini.

However, the Emperor kept stressing he was no soldier and, despite his hard work and iron will, his critics say he was not able to come up with a compelling strategy to decisively influence events on the ground. From Dessie, Haile Selassie advanced further north – to Lake Ashangi and then to the town of Maychew. He donned his pith helmet, rode a white horse and studied the Italian forces through binoculars. All of this, of course, was a far cry from his normal sedate and administrative daily life in his palace in Addis Ababa. At Maychew he rested for a few days, thereby unwittingly allowing the Italians to build up their forces before what was clearly going to be a decisive battle.

For the first time since the Italian invasion, Haile Selassie was directly facing troops commanded by the leader of the Italian invading army, Pietro Badoglio. Before the fighting the Emperor held a traditional feast in a cave where warriors gorged themselves on raw meat and tej or honey wine. Eventually the Emperor made what is seen by many as a desperate and fateful mistake in attacking the Italians head-on in the hallowed tradition of previous Ethiopian kings. He had been encouraged by many of his supporters to remain true to this tactic of daring and bravery.

Badoglio himself wrote later that he knew that Haile Selassie would be forced into a direct confrontation because of the weight of history on his shoulders. In his account of the war Badoglio said that, although Haile Selassie had some good qualities, he did not possess any military acumen. The Italian general believed that the Emperor was at the mercy of squabbling rases, who were mainly out to protect their own interests and place in the pecking order. The general said that the Emperor failed to establish any discipline over them and wavered for too long between a head-on fight and guerrilla tactics.

In the ensuing pitched battles in Maychew the Ethiopian troops were massacred without mercy by a far better equipped army. The Italians had a great advantage because they had been able to intercept radio messages made by the Ethiopian high command. They also had full control of the skies. During the fighting the Emperor was seen risking his life by charging on to the plain in the height of battle. His Russian

CHAPTER 1

military adviser said that the Ethiopian leader's conduct had been irreproachable and he had machine-gunned the enemy with terrific effect. It was all to be in vain.

According to Italian estimates, more than 8,000 Ethiopians were killed with a total of only around 1,300 Italian casualties, killed or wounded. As they retreated, the Emperor's columns were attacked by Italian ground forces and artillery. But a major threat came from the air as Italian planes dropped bombs filled with poison gas – a war crime that was only admitted officially in Italy in 1996.

The Emperor had to witness some truly shocking sights. At one stage Lake Ashangi was littered with the floating corpses of hundreds of his men. Many Ethiopian soldiers, exposed to the poison gas, suffered grotesque burns and blisters to their faces, bodies and bare feet. Their lung tissue and eyeballs were also damaged. After a few days some of the victims began to lose pieces of flesh. The Emperor could only watch helplessly in the face of the Italian onslaught. None of his men had a gas mask. Even Haile Selassie himself suffered some injuries to one of his arms from the poison gas.

The Italians deployed what were called yperite bombs because they were similar to the ones used during the World War I battle at Ypres. The devices were filled with mustard gas and liquid, which was hard to wash off. The bombs were dropped by plane and exploded 250 metres above the ground. Two of Mussolini's sons were fighter-bomber pilots during the war with Ethiopia. One of them, Vittorio, described his missions as sport and fun. The Emperor wrote later that it was very distressing that the Italians should come with such newly-fashioned weapons to destroy the brave Ethiopian people.

The Emperor said that soldiers, women, children, cattle, rivers, lakes and pastures had been drenched continually with this deadly fine rain. In his view the Italians were attempting to kill off systematically all living creatures and pollute the water supply. Some Ethiopian soldiers, who had quenched their thirst in the local rivers, later twisted in agony on the ground for hours afterwards. The Ethiopians could only respond with their rudimentary weapons. They fought bravely where they could, according to the precepts of their warrior forebears.

Italian sources dispute that vast quantities of poison gas were used. In a biography of Mussolini, Nicholas Farrell says that only 974 mustard gas bombs were dropped and had little impact on deciding the outcome of the war. The decisive factors, according to Farrell, were that the Italians had a far superior war machine and the Ethiopians should have avoided pitched battles. In response to the allegations of war crimes, Italian military commanders also claimed that their forces were the victims of atrocities. They pointed to a stream of reports, which claimed that many captured Italians had been tortured and brutally butchered.

The journalist George Steer filed many dispatches in support of the beleaguered Ethiopian forces. He claimed that the Italians had attacked British, Swedish and

Dutch Red Cross ambulances. He believed this was being done to clear foreign witnesses out of the way because of what he claimed to be illegal methods of warfare being used by the Italians. For Haile Selassie, any debate at this stage about the cruelty or legality of Italian methods was of little use while he was on the ground in the thick of battle. He was also dismayed by the news that several of his rases had betrayed him and were fighting with the Italians. The Emperor was facing imminent disaster and had no option but to retreat further back towards the capital, Addis Ababa.

At the town of Korem the remnants of the Ethiopian army suffered more misery as Italian air raids continued relentlessly. The Emperor later painted a horrifying scene with corpses everywhere, in every patch of bush, wherever there was a hiding place or shelter. Many more dead bodies were out in the open and an intolerable stench hung in the air. Near the Imperial headquarters more than 500 corpses were decomposing. There were more dead than living and it was not possible to bury them all. This desolate place was described by the Emperor as a charnel house in which he had had to resign himself to living.

On the slow retreat south, the Emperor made a surprising detour to the historic orthodox churches at the town of Lalibela where he stayed for two days, praying and fasting. These churches were carved out of the rock in the 12th century by a powerful Ethiopian leader, Lalibela, a member of the Zagwe dynasty, who gave his name to the area. They are now recognised as a world heritage site, one of Ethiopia's foremost tourist attractions. The churches are an astonishing reminder of a thriving African civilisation nearly a millennium ago.

In this special place, resonant with religious and national identity, the Emperor sought solace, and tried to divine God's will for both himself and his country, now in great peril. Worldly methods had failed to halt the Italian tide. All that was left was to appeal to a divine power.

THE FLIGHT FROM ADDIS ABABA

After his spiritual retreat the Emperor rejoined his main columns marching south. More indignity and suffering were to envelop him once he reached Addis Ababa where a *Time* magazine reporter reported that he was seen wearing a bandage on his arm after the poison gas injuries. It was becoming clear that none of the Emperor's forces anywhere in the country could halt the relentless Italian advance. After he reached the capital he revealed to the British diplomatic representative Sir Sidney Barton that he had renounced the direction of affairs. The country would now be governed by a council of ministers. All of them realised it was impossible to defend Addis Ababa. In any case they were reluctant to fight there as many innocent civilians were likely to be killed. The Emperor and his closest supporters were fast running out of realistic options. They could surrender, retreat to the hills to fight an unaccustomed guerrilla war, or

CHAPTER 1

stand, fight and face likely death. None of these was palatable.

A further option was put on the table at a hastily convened council meeting. This was that the Emperor should make his escape from Ethiopia so he could appeal to the international community about the injustices meted out by the Italians. Ethiopia was already a member of the League of Nations and some of the Emperor's advisors urged him to go to plead his case in Geneva where the League was based. For the Emperor this plan was anathema. None of the 224 Ethiopian leaders before him had ever abandoned the country in the face of enemy attack. The Emperor was always keen to point out that his country had been free for more than 3,000 years. Now he faced the prospect of being regarded as a coward and deserter by his own people, and even possibly becoming an international laughing stock.

Accounts of the council's deliberations vary but it is recorded that the Emperor initially resisted the move to flee the country. He first of all agreed with a proposal to escape with all his forces to the western town of Gore and set up a base there to continue the resistance. But the majority of delegates at the stormy meeting urged the Emperor to leave. One of the main opponents to this plan was Takele Walda-Hawaryat, an ardent loyalist and the general manager of the municipality of Addis Ababa. He had not experienced firsthand the horrors of the northern front at Maychew and may have had a different point of view had he done so.

Takele was adamant that it was better to have a glorious death than go cap-in-hand to the European colonialists. One account even suggests that Takele threatened to draw his gun and was prepared to shoot the Emperor himself rather than see him slink away.

Another account says that Takele put the gun in his mouth to encourage the Emperor to commit suicide rather than escape. The courage and ferocity of many of Ethiopia's kings were legendary and well-known to patriots such as Takele. Eulogies were written to celebrate their great victories but a king martyred in battle was also revered as heroic and noble.

The League of Nations option was strongly put forward by Ras Kassa Hailu, a well-respected nobleman. He too had personal blood links to the Solomonic dynasty as he was Haile Selassie's cousin. He therefore could have pressed his own claim to the throne but chose not to. Instead the Ras remained loyal to Haile Selassie throughout his life and was by his side at every key moment. Faced with the imminent Italian threat, his view was that if the Emperor were killed or captured, that would be a decisive blow to the morale of the country and all resistance would come to an end. By going to Geneva the Emperor could argue his case from a point of legitimacy and could also give continued hope to the rebels. The Empress had already been planning to go to Jerusalem to pray for the country and she supported Ras Kassa's view.

The arguments of the Ras won the day and the Emperor embraced the League of

Nations option. He decided to appoint his childhood friend Ras Imru to take his place as commander of the remaining Ethiopian forces. In his written account of the debate the Emperor is very matter of fact about the decision to escape and typically betrays no emotion. He says simply that since they had to resolve thus, their advice had been accepted. It may well be of course that the Emperor had decided to take the League of Nations option from the start but manipulated events so that it appeared as if it was the idea of others.

Ras Kassa Hailu, a descendant of the Imperial House of Gondar, pictured before the exile years

The Ethiopian leadership had decided to put its trust in the principles of collective security rather than in weapons such as the gun or spear. There was no time to lose. The Italians were tightening their grip. The plan was for the Emperor and his family to be speedily transported by train from Addis Ababa to the port state of Djibouti on the Red Sea. Discussions had been going on for some time through Sir Sidney Barton about providing an escape route for the Empress. The British had already indicated they would help transport her to Jerusalem. After consultation with the French, the

CHAPTER 1

British made available a warship called *HMS Enterprise* to pick up the royal couple. The Emperor now wanted to go straight to Europe so he could immediately make his appeal to the League of Nations. His request provoked a blizzard of diplomatic messages between London and the *Enterprise*.

Even the embattled Emperor's closest supporters may have doubted whether they would ever see the return of their monarch. We will never know exactly what was going on in his mind but he certainly gave the appearance of a desperate man. Being pushed into exile is a daunting and terrifying prospect for anyone. Haile Selassie was not only trying to suppress his natural human emotions. He was also attempting to deal with the weight of expectation and duty he had placed on his own shoulders throughout his life. He had spent a lifetime being trained to hide his feelings but these cataclysmic events were simply overwhelming him. The journalist George Steer, ever on hand at a crisis, described how the Emperor looked very tired and worn. His usual calm dignity seemed at times to be tinged with despair. Steer said that vigour had left his face and, as the Emperor walked forward, he did not seem to know where he was putting his feet.

Once the fateful decision had been made, there were frantic preparations to enable the royal family to leave as soon as possible. Rapid decisions had to be taken about which of the Emperor's private and official belongings should be put on the train to Djibouti. This would have been a difficult conundrum at the best of times but, with the Italians breathing down their necks, it was a near impossible task. Among the tons of luggage hastily loaded onto the train were the Emperor's pet white and tan papillon dog Rosa and two of his precious lions. He had always loved these magnificent proud creatures, which were also the symbol of his rule.

A list was hastily drawn up with the names of advisers and servants who would also join the two trains being prepared to take the Emperor and his party. Among the passengers were the trusted foreign minister Heruy Wolde-Selassie and the Emperor's court chamberlain Kebede Tessema. Both men were the grandfathers of a prominent lawyer working in Addis Ababa today, Bekoure Heruy. He lives in the house built by Kebede Tessema and says his grandfather often told the story of how he was summoned at short notice to board the train to Djibouti.

Kebede was having lunch with his family after returning from the battlefield of Maychew. Suddenly a breathless official burst into the house after running from the palace. Kebede was ordered to leave right away without having time to finish his food. He left immediately without packing anything. At the palace he was given special orders to keep a close eye on a troublesome and powerful prince, Ras Hailu Tekle-Haymanot, who was from the Gojam region in northern Ethiopia. He was distrusted by the Emperor and the two men were to be lifelong rivals. The passengers and their special animal cargo boarded the train in secret during the hours of darkness. Kebede Tessema ended up being shackled in chains with Ras Hailu to make sure he did not escape and desert to the Italians.

In a ruse to neutralise any prying eyes the Emperor himself did not join the train until a few miles out of Addis Ababa at Akaki. The railway track to Djibouti had only been completed by French engineers about twenty years before. It was very different from Brunel's Great Western Railway line from London to Bath and beyond. The French-built line was narrow gauge and had to snake its way across some mountainous, sandy and boggy terrain. This line was familiar to Haile Selassie. A few years earlier in peaceful times he had been photographed in the desert alongside a steam engine during a hunting trip. But this time it was the Emperor and his family who were being hunted.

Travelling on the Addis to Djibouti railway line around 1930. The Emperor's son Makonnen is to his right and the Crown Prince is to his left in the light cloak

Their journey would have been terrifying with the prospect of Italian bombers emerging out of the sky at any moment. However, the Italians stayed their hand and allowed the Emperor's train to pass unscathed. Some men organised by Takele, still greatly opposed to the escape plan, tried to sabotage the train en route. The attempt failed. Before the train reached Djibouti, Kebede's partner-in-chains Ras Hailu was released as it was thought he would be a very disruptive presence in exile. As suspected, he turned tail and offered his services to the Italians. He was to be an influential collaborator for the next five years.

CHAPTER 1

Altogether, the train stopped for 11 hours while the Emperor conferred with his southern chiefs. He was seriously considering whether to change his mind about going on to Djibouti, no doubt horror-struck at the magnitude of what he was doing. However, it became clear that there were no realistic military options left and, with the Italians threatening to cut the line further up the track, there was no time for any more deliberations.

The evacuation had been far from regal and organised. Being so disoriented was a truly disturbing experience for the Emperor, a man used to exercising iron discipline and self-control. He would also have been desperately concerned about his wife and young family, and the uncertain future he was leading them into. While sitting peacefully on the train to Bath that August evening in 1936, the Lion of Judah could have been forgiven if his mind had strayed back to that hazardous train journey to Djibouti only three months previously. What memories and images came into his mind as he once again heard the sound of a train going over the tracks? Did he look out of the window at the sky above the English countryside half expecting to see the outlines of Italian bombers?

The Emperor's hasty retreat on 1 May 1936 had caused bewilderment and panic back in Addis Ababa as residents realised it would not be long before the hated Italians marched in. Some inhabitants began ransacking houses, stores and warehouses. John Spencer, an American adviser to the Emperor, was unnerved to find that the road to the train station was covered in an unbroken stretch of white. It transpired that the strange phenomenon was caused by feathers torn from hundreds of pillows and mattresses as looters went methodically from house to house searching for hidden valuables.

Spencer, who had no idea the Emperor had fled in secret, spoke of armed gangs roaming the streets, shooting indiscriminately at random passers-by. Other eyewitnesses described guards wandering around in top-hats, and looters selling glasses of champagne for next to nothing. The Italians did not intervene immediately to stop the mayhem. The lawlessness and anarchy displayed in the capital was a useful propaganda tool in their attempt to show to the outside world that Ethiopia was inhabited by savages.

Once the Italians arrived on 5 May 1936, they shot many people out of hand to restore order and prevent further ransacking. In his account of the war, the Italian general Badoglio described Addis Ababa as a sad spectacle. He said almost all the shops and houses had been sacked and burned. A storm of savage and devastating fury had passed over the city. Badoglio said the city now had no public services and was encumbered with human corpses, animal carcasses and the splintered remains of furniture and other household items. Mussolini, in a hand-written foreword to Badoglio's book, said the war had been waged in the true spirit of fascism – speed, decision, self-sacrifice, courage and resistance beyond human limits.

Chaos also descended when the Ethiopian fugitives on the train reached Djibouti, then a French colony. Ethiopians living there gathered on the streets in amazement and consternation. They could not believe the Imperial family was caught up in such a crisis. Many of them were weeping. The royal party was officially received by the French governor of Djibouti but this was an incongruous moment for diplomatic niceties. At the dockside it was already becoming clear that *HMS Enterprise* was not going to be able to accommodate all the people and belongings from the Emperor's party. In fact, the captain of the ship, Charles Morgan, had only been told to expect 12 passengers, not the 150 or so who had hastily been decanted from Addis Ababa.

Captain Morgan told the Emperor that the *Enterprise* was a working naval warship, not a passenger ferry, and they could only accommodate a maximum of 50 people. When this was announced to the anxious and dishevelled evacuees, they threw up their hands in horror and said it could not be done. In his report of the evacuation, the Captain said the reaction to his ruling was as if the throne room in the Papacy had gone up in smoke. At first, the Emperor flatly said it was impossible to comply but eventually agreed. He asked for more time to make the arrangements and promised to be ready from 5.30pm onwards.

The two beloved lions fell by the wayside as the Captain refused to take them on board but he did indulge the Emperor by allowing him to bring Rosa the dog. Two other extremely precious items of cargo were not left on the quayside – the Emperor's crown and the old war tent of his hero, Emperor Menelik, which he did not want to fall into enemy hands. All the bullion and cash ferreted out of Addis Ababa was also permitted on board.

The Captain said that the Emperor looked so weary and fragile that he felt a perfect brute for screwing him down over the arrangements for the journey. He immediately noticed what he called the Emperor's beautiful and delicate hands and said that his fingers were nearly twice the length of his own. Captain Morgan was well aware of the reports that one of the Emperor's arms had been burned in the Italian poison gas attacks. However, the Captain said he was glad to see that there was now no obvious sign of major disfigurement, though, as became clear later, the injuries were not insignificant and would take some time to heal fully.

It took several hours to sift through the various belongings. The Captain was astonished when the Emperor finally boarded at 5.29pm, one minute before the agreed deadline. The national anthem was played and the Emperor inspected a guard of honour. The Captain said he felt somehow that his personal Imperial cargo was almost at his last gasp and knew he was a very frightened man. He had a hunted look in his eye and he seemed only too glad to sit down as soon as the official presentations were over.

CHAPTER 1

SAILING UP THE RED SEA

The sight of the ship's gangplank being pulled up was no doubt sobering and chilling for the Imperial fugitive. His unwanted and unexpected exile had definitively begun. There was no turning back and little did the Emperor know that he was not to set foot on Ethiopian soil again for nearly five years. The Captain tried to lighten his passenger's mood by telling him that he was now as safe as the Bank of England. After final preparations were completed, the Enterprise set sail at 7.20pm. It had to travel at a speed of 22 knots to make up lost time to hit a planned rendezvous at the entrance to the Suez Canal.

Soon after the ship set sail, the Emperor was escorted to his quarters which the Captain had arranged for him. A sitting room had been prepared on the quarter deck with easy chairs, a carpet and a small table. Awning curtains were provided to maintain some privacy. The Captain led his protégé to the most comfortable chair and provided a cushion for him. The Emperor promptly fell fast asleep. After waking up, the newly-exiled leader regained his composure. He once again acted like the sovereign of Ethiopia.

Captain Morgan said that Haile Selassie's consideration, courtesy and, above all, his dignity left a deep impression on every officer and man in his ship. The skipper said there was something about the Emperor's smile that he could not resist. He wrote that you were always hoping that you would say or do something of which he approved so that you could see him smile.

Already the Emperor was caught in some international power play. The British government was keen to be seen to be helping a slighted and wronged ruler in need but they were also anxious not to upset Mussolini and destabilise Europe even more. They were terrified of driving him into the arms of Hitler, who was already becoming an enormous menace. Some voices urged Britain to avoid busybody diplomacy and think only of its own interests. In the face of such considerations, the British government ended up grudgingly doing the bare minimum to support the Ethiopian cause while pretending to do far more. During the Red Sea voyage the Emperor repeatedly requested that he be taken direct to the UK after dropping off the Empress in Haifa in British-mandated Palestine. But he was consistently turned down by the British authorities. These discussions set the tone for what became a decade of prickly diplomatic spats between the British government and the Ethiopian leader.

The crew of the *Enterprise* worked wonders in accommodating all their unexpected guests, many of whom had not seen the sea before. Officers gave up their cabins and slept in the gun room. Sanitary facilities were limited but most of the royal family members were granted the use of the Captain's private bathroom. Some of the Ethiopian entourage ended up sleeping on deck on camp beds. On one of his inspections the Captain said he found on the aft part of the ship a seething mass of humanity. They consisted of dressed and undressed officers, nurses, dressed and naked children, Abyssinian generals in full uniform, sentries, servants and Goanese stewards taking around iced-lemon squashes. The Captain said he could not believe he was on board a warship in the British Navy.

The Emperor's little dog Rosa also played her part in keeping up morale. She was put out of her master's quarters every night before bedtime and never moved until he returned for her. She would lie in the aft part of the ship and the crew used to tell her she was a very good little dog. The pet would just look up and wag her tail but she never moved. The Captain noticed that Rosa looked like she had lost sight in her left eye after she was injured when she refused to leave the Emperor's side in the heat of battle at Maychew.

News that the royal party was on board quickly spread throughout the region. Many other ships sighted the boat and drew near to get a close look at the royal menagerie. Many messages of condolence, support and encouragement were received as the ship steamed north. The Emperor was said to be greatly affected by one message which said that 'You have put your faith in the great white nations and they have let you down.' After the *Enterprise* reached the Suez Canal, the banks were crowded with onlookers. Police on motorbikes followed the ship from the shore to keep the crowds under control. At the mouth of the canal in Port Said, the Emperor lost his composure when he saw some Ethiopian supporters approaching the *Enterprise* in a boat decked out with national flags. Many of them were weeping. He wrote later that the sight of them, wiping away the tears with their handkerchiefs, awakened his own great grief and he was deeply moved.

When the ship finally arrived in Haifa, all of the Emperor's belongings had to be repacked, including some precious bundles of silver and gold bullion. Most of the booty had been hastily thrown into old boxes and dilapidated suitcases, which had now collapsed. While the work was being carried out, Captain Morgan was amazed to see the captain of an escort ship come on board, followed by an able seaman gingerly carrying a large hawk perched on a glove. A message for the Emperor was attached by string to the bird's leg. The hawk was taken immediately to Haile Selassie and he removed the message, which was written on stiff paper. He did not divulge its contents. The Captain could not believe how the hawk had found its way to Haifa. The bird was absolutely exhausted and the Captain even speculated whether it had flown all the way from Addis Ababa, 1,500 miles away.

For all his gallant exploits Captain Morgan was presented with a coronation medal by the Emperor. However, in his official report the Captain also revealed some less noble traits. He cheekily described the Emperor's teenage daughter Tsehai as quite 'a good-looker', and then said that the younger children, despite being 'savages', had been well-behaved and perhaps were very attractive.

CHAPTER 1

From Haifa the royal party went by train to Jerusalem, then under British rule. One of the Emperor's first acts was to visit the Ethiopian monastery of Debre Gannet based in Jerusalem. In a French newspaper interview the Emperor expressed his relief to come across an Ethiopian sanctuary where there was no smell of scorched buildings, and no corpses of priests barring the door. The Emperor spent two unsettled weeks in Jerusalem, staying initially in an ornate suite at the King David Hotel. He showed some reporters the raw burn marks on his hands and some in his entourage were very concerned about his generally weak and frail condition. One British official described the royal refugee as being in a bad temper. He said they would soon become mortally sick of what he called this ex-potentate. In a foretaste of the official snubs the Ethiopian leader was to receive in Europe, western diplomats avoided hosting official ceremonies for him. They shunned meeting him in person and sent their deputies instead.

The Lion of Judah was also greatly annoyed by the noisy slogans shouted by fascist supporters gathering outside his hotel. Above all, he was upset that seemingly little was being done to help him, though by this time the British cabinet had finally agreed that the Emperor could come to the UK. It felt it would have been impossible to refuse him entry, given Britain's support for the League of Nations and the fact that the Emperor had not formally abdicated. However, cabinet members did lay down three conditions. These were that he should come incognito, that his official entourage should be limited to around six people, and that he should undertake not to take part in the furtherance of hostilities while in Britain.

The Emperor would have become even more tetchy if he had caught sight of a letter written on 26 May 1936 by Eden to King Edward VIII. Although mainly a supporter of Haile Selassie, Eden looked as though he had to tread carefully not to ruffle the feathers of the King, who appears to have not been that keen to bail out his Ethiopian counterpart. Eden said he appreciated that His Majesty feared that Haile Selassie's visit may cause 'a certain inconvenience.' The Foreign Secretary also revealed that the Ethiopian leader had been thinking of going directly to a sanatorium in Germany on health grounds. However, Eden said the Emperor's health had improved and he would now definitely be visiting Britain. The letter added that Haile Selassie had signalled his intention to then go on to Geneva, and the Foreign Secretary anticipated that his stay in the UK would not be unduly protracted. How wrong he was.

One of the first acts of the Emperor's staff in Jerusalem had been to hide the silver and gold in a chamber of the Ethiopian monastery. British troops stood guard to protect this treasure trove, said to be worth hundreds of thousands of pounds in today's money. After a few days the Emperor moved from the King David Hotel to a luxurious villa on the top of a hill in a prosperous part of the city. His new position gave him the opportunity to scour his surroundings in case of any threats to his security. After a couple of weeks the Emperor left the Empress behind in Jerusalem with the younger members of the family, and a group of notables.

The next few years would see a succession of farewells and enforced separations with varying complications involving accommodation and schooling for the children and grandchildren. With his eldest children in tow, the Emperor returned to Haifa where he was taken on *HMS Capetown* to Gibraltar. The British cabinet had debated whether it needed to supply an official naval ship. However, it was decided that it would be necessary as there was a possible risk, however low, that the Emperor's vessel could be intercepted. He would therefore need some protection. It was always made clear that after Gibraltar the fledgling Ethiopian royal exile would not be provided with a naval ship for the final leg to the UK, despite his request for this to happen.

The British tactics were devoted to doing the bare minimum for the high-profile refugee. The Governor of Gibraltar was told in no uncertain terms by his masters in London that the royal visitor should not be entertained officially, though of course there would be no objection if he wanted to offer some informal hospitality. The Emperor had no choice but to comply with the British diplomatic games and at Gibraltar he was transferred to a normal civilian passenger ship, an Orient passenger liner called *RMS Orford*. The British government therefore ensured that the Emperor turned up on its shores as if he were a lowly commoner. The perfidious ways of international diplomacy were ever thus.

CHAPTER 1

CHAPTER ONE EYEWITNESS IN THE EMPEROR'S FOOTSTEPS: A TRIP TO DESSIE

In November 2013 I made the spectacular journey by bus from Addis Ababa through various mountain passes to the northern highland town of Dessie where Haile Selassie established his forward operating base against the Italian invaders moving down from further north. The trip on a new swish coach should have only taken around six or seven hours. However, it ended up taking ten hours because the bus driver was temporarily detained by police while we were en route. He had narrowly missed running over a local girl who had strayed on to the road while herding her goats.

Although she was physically unharmed, it had been a frightening experience for the young girl. As a result, her relatives were keen to gain some blood money for the driver's alleged recklessness. Such are the hazards of travelling around in modern vehicles in dramatic landscapes, largely unchanged for thousands of years. Haile Selassie would have followed the same twisting and turning route up to Dessie on its perch at the top of a steep hill, though the road would have been in a much worse state.

An earlier generation of Italians, who had settled in Ethiopia after the battle of Adwa, had already made an impact on Dessie. The town is on the main route north to Asmara, now the capital of independent Eritrea. The Italians had constructed some fine buildings in the town and established a piazza area or square. Haile Selassie chose the Villa Italia, the consulate, as his command headquarters. At the time of my visit the building was a little run down and seemed deserted. However, an educational institution specialising in new technology start-ups was going strong in some new buildings in the grounds.

The compound is on the forested slopes of Mount Tossa, with a sheer rock face immediately behind it. There are many trees surrounding the consulate, including pine, bougainvillea, mimosa and eucalyptus. The main house has a sweeping drive, similar to the one at Fairfield House, the Emperor's residence during his stay in Bath. Dessie means happiness in Amharic but the Emperor found little cheer during the tough three months or so that he spent in the town.

Although it was nearly 80 years since the Emperor established his base at the Villa Italia, there were still some unmistakable signs that he had been here. A lion is carved on some steps at the foot of a flag pole. An old large cannon lay rusting nearby.

Just after 8.45am one December morning in 1935 around ten Italian planes attacked Dessie in an obvious attempt to kill the Emperor. In a mission lasting one hour the planes dropped incendiary and explosive shrapnel bombs, killing 53 people and wounding around 200.

Following this attack the Emperor was photographed smiling in defiance while resting his foot on an unexploded bomb. The device could have exploded at any minute but the Lion of Judah appeared unperturbed and had no concern for his safety. He conveyed all the insouciance and arrogance of a lion hunter proudly displaying his prize. The photograph was a powerful propaganda statement, projecting his lack of fear of the encroaching Italian armies. In another raid around 20 planes caused widespread damage.

Haile Selassie wrote later that he feared his forces might be exterminated. He recounts how he fired away on his anti-aircraft battery but on that day the planes flew too high and so were too hard to hit. Later on in the campaign he was credited with one kill, an Italian S.81 bomber.

On the skyline up to the right from the Italian consulate compound is another angular hill. That vantage point is the former base of King Mikael of Wollo, one of Haile Selassie's rebellious leaders in the regions. From Mikael's hill one can see in all four directions, revealing why Dessie has always been very important to Ethiopian military thinking and strategy.

On the day of my visit some Ethiopian workers were restoring the huge aderash building where warriors would gather on the eve of battle to feast, drink and pledge their loyalty. Heads of oxen would have been hung on the walls. In an ante room I could still see where containers of honey wine had been stored. It would have been downed greedily by the boisterous, aggressive men about to depart for war.

The rest of Mikael's compound provided evidence of how Ethiopian noblemen lived around 100 years ago when Haile Selassie was a young man. A rudimentary court house was erected on site. Nearby was a special window from which miscreants would be hung for their crimes. In one abandoned room there was an early electricity generator built by Siemens, a German company. Haile Selassie too would have started life in such basic conditions. By the time he found himself on the train to Bath, some

CHAPTER 1

modern features such as paved roads and an electricity grid had been introduced in Addis Ababa. However, the capital was still nowhere near as developed as the western world he was about to enter.

King Mikael was the father of Lij Iyasu Menelik, who was briefly the ruler of Ethiopia in the early 20th century. He was forced out by powerful court factions, including those supporting Haile Selassie. The two men remained enemies and Lij Iyasu spent much of the rest of his life in prison. He died in mysterious circumstances shortly after the Italians entered Ethiopia in the autumn of 1935. The official cause of death was given as a form of paralysis. However, the workers who showed me around Lij Iyasu's house near the renovated aderash were all convinced, like many others in Ethiopia, that he was murdered on Imperial orders to preserve national unity. If Lij Iyasu had fallen into the hands of the Italians, they could have used him as a puppet ruler. Despite several detailed investigations by Ethiopian historians, no-one has yet come up with any definite proof either way about the cause of Lij Iyasu's death.

CHAPTER TWO
TESTING THE WATERS

The Emperor set foot on English soil in Southampton in early June 1936. Among the 15 tons of luggage were crates of gold bars and Ethiopia's old green Imperial treasure chest. There were also more than 100 cases of Maria Theresa thalers, the universal currency of silver bullion coins used in world trade since the 18th century. From Southampton the Emperor boarded a train and was given a tumultuous reception when he arrived at Waterloo Station in central London. He was welcomed by a host of supporters, including the suffragette campaigner Sylvia Pankhurst, the explorer Wilfred Thesiger and the omnipresent journalist George Steer.

Time magazine gave a vivid description of the Emperor's arrival in London. The magazine had already named him in January as its Man of the Year, a rare honour for an African statesman. The *Time* reporter said that among the cheering crowds were Chinese, Hindus, Arabs and black Africans, alongside English people of every class. Many of the well-wishers were waving home-made banners of support. Specially-decorated hat-bands, button-holes and badges were everywhere. Some in the crowd had been waiting for six hours.

As the train pulled in, the Emperor, wearing a black cape, could be seen sitting at a table decorated with flowers. His children, according to the beady-eyed *Time* reporter, were dressed in well-tailored, tweedy sports clothes and flannels. Other prominent people in the welcoming crowd were the black activist Marcus Garvey and Jomo Kenyatta, the future president of Kenya. Perhaps because of his well-tuned political antenna, the Emperor primarily focused on the official all-white reception committee of a League of Nations delegation and the private secretary to the British Foreign Secretary. He was a man called Oliver Harvey, an official who was usually sent to greet royal visitors when they were travelling incognito.

Marcus Garvey, however, believed the Emperor should have paid some attention

CHAPTER 2

to him, not the official delegation. He interpreted Haile Selassie's behaviour as a slight, feeling that he had been deliberately ignored. For many years afterwards he harboured a grudge against the Emperor and later described him in very unflattering terms. Garvey said he was a great coward who had run away from his country to save his skin and left millions of his countrymen to struggle through a terrible war that he brought upon them because of what he called his political ignorance and his racial disloyalty.

The official reception committee at Waterloo presented the Emperor with an engraved scroll lamenting the invasion of Ethiopia. In reply, Haile Selassie said he had come to England confident he would obtain justice there and exclaimed: 'May the British crown and people live forever.' The *Times* newspaper said that of the kings who had sought Britain's shores in their adversity, none had had a better claim to sympathy. The British government again vacillated. There was no official reception held. Its view was that the Emperor had come at his own request. He was therefore not accorded a state visit usually laid on for reigning monarchs. The *Times* also reported that the route from Waterloo station to the Abyssinian Legation was deliberately changed so Haile Selassie would not be cheered in the streets by the waiting crowds.

In a sign of the times, supporters of the British fascist leader Oswald Mosley gathered to protest at the presence of Mussolini's enemy in the UK. However, the government was powerless to prevent vast crowds gathering in support of the Emperor outside the Ethiopian Legation in Princes Gate overlooking Hyde Park. There were so many people that the police barriers were broken.

The Emperor was received in the Westminster Parliament some time afterwards by the Foreign Secretary, Anthony Eden. The Prime Minister, Stanley Baldwin, happened to be sitting on the terrace of the parliament building next to the River Thames. While taking some refreshment, he spotted the Ethiopian monarch in the distance. He felt it was too awkward for them to meet and so he dived behind a table to hide. His cowardly, evasive behaviour displayed the British government's ambivalence towards Haile Selassie all too clearly. Its distaste for him was reflected in the words of the Permanent Under Secretary at the Foreign Office, Sir Robert Vansittart. He ordered underlings to thwart any of the Emperor's diplomatic activity by heading off 'the little man.'

However, the Emperor did receive political support from some British politicians. The former Prime Minister, David Lloyd-George, protested about the UK's position on the Ethiopian/Italian war. He lamented that Britain would not do its duty due to the fear of getting a black eye. Later in a highly-charged debate in the House of Commons, Lloyd-George shook his fist at Baldwin and Eden, and called them cowards, poltroons and jellyfish.

A young journalist called Bill Deedes, who later became the editor of the *Daily*

Telegraph, had reported from Ethiopia during the Italian advance. Now in London he described how forlorn the Emperor looked when appearing before the press. Deedes chose to capture the mood by using some lines from Milton's epic poem *Paradise Lost*, including the memorable phrase, 'Majestic though in ruin.'

The writer George Martelli met the Emperor the day after he arrived in London at the Ethiopian Legation in Princes Gate. He described how a noisy crowd of journalists and others waited in a comfortably furnished sitting room with empty beer bottles strewn on tables. Many people jostled to catch a sight of what they described as the 'exotic beast' walking around in the garden in the June sunshine. Eventually Haile Selassie came over slowly onto the terrace and a dramatic hush descended. Martelli said that the Emperor had sphinx-like impenetrability and that, although politically the man was finished, he still had news value. Everywhere the Emperor went in London he was received warmly by locals who would surround his car and greet him in a friendly and respectful manner.

In the early days in London it was clear that Haile Selassie was restless and unsure of his next step. He was uncertain how long he should stay in the UK. He contemplated going immediately to Switzerland where he would have felt much more comfortable speaking in his fluent French. He would also have been close to the Geneva headquarters of the League of Nations. However, the Swiss government rejected any move by the Emperor to live there because it said it needed to foster peaceful co-existence and avoid conflict. The country's foreign minister said that he believed a great crisis would ensue if the Emperor settled in Switzerland.

Meanwhile, the British government continued to play its two-faced games. On the one hand, the government seemed willing to give the Emperor permission to stay longer in the UK, and the Home Office was instructed to give him some support. Eden too was able to give him significant help in the form of a freedom of customs concession. This meant that British officials in Addis Ababa would be able to move some of the Emperor's belongings from the Ethiopian capital to London. The concession was to prove invaluable in the months and years ahead. On the other hand, British ministers had already strongly outlined that the Emperor should not engage in any political activity which could embarrass the host government. He was urged primarily to consider himself as a private resident. One Foreign Office minute said its guest could become a nuisance and a danger if some moderation were not exercised.

A house further along the elegant row of Princes Gate was put at the Emperor's disposal during his early days in London. The property, at number six, belonged to Sir Elly Kadoorie, an Indian businessman who had made a fortune in Hong Kong in banking, rubber plantations, and other commercial interests. The house was also only a few doors away from the current location of the Ethiopian Embassy. Before the

Emperor arrived, London had been unseasonably cold. Ethiopian officials, concerned about the poor state of his health, had been worried that he might catch a chill.

Before ending up in Bath the Emperor lived an itinerant life. He travelled to Scotland and also rented for a short time a magnificent country house called Hazelwood House in the Hertfordshire town of Abbots Langley, around 25 miles north west of central London.

The Emperor was also invited to stay for a few days at Lincoln House on Wimbledon Common. His host was Sir Richard Seligman, a leading metallurgist and entrepreneur. Sir Richard's wife Hilda was a talented sculptor and she persuaded the Emperor to sit for her while she fashioned a stone bust of him.

The statue has stood for many years in nearby Cannizaro Park, an exquisite park of formal lawns, and informal pockets of woodland, including many maple trees. The bust is situated in an area where a tennis court used to be and is near the stylish former Cannizaro House, once used as a retreat by royalty.

THE GENEVA APPEAL

The main highlight of those first faltering weeks in exile was a trip to Geneva to carry out the mission for which he had left Ethiopia. It was a move which risked being misinterpreted by many of his own people as a sell-out. In mid-June 1936 he travelled by train to the Swiss city where he gave an incisive and memorable speech to the League of Nations. He was the first Head of State to address the assembly. The Emperor quietly took his seat a few rows back, having left his broad-brimmed hat outside the chamber.

When the Emperor rose to speak, he was barracked by a group of belligerent Italian journalists. They tried to drown him out by blowing whistles, stamping their feet and jeering. Some of them yelled 'Long live Il Duce!' The journalists had been put up to these antics by Mussolini in a bid to humiliate Haile Selassie and to express Italian anger that he had been granted a platform.

The piercing whistles had been provided by Il Duce's son-in-law, the Italian foreign minister, Galeazzo Ciano. He himself had participated in the invasion of Ethiopia during which he had been a bomber squadron commander. The Romanian delegate at the League of Nations, Nikolai Titulescu, was so outraged by the loutish behaviour of the baying mob of Italian journalists that he rose in his seat and cried: 'A la porte les sauvages!' or 'Get out you savages!' The Italian journalists were evicted in disgrace and held in prison for a time during which they indignantly demanded they be fed some spaghetti.

However, the Italian agitators were lauded in their own country. They later received prizes for what was described as their distinguished service to journalism. One of the journalists said that no other aspect of his career had brought him such support. By contrast, the outspoken Titulescu was dismissed from the service of the Romanian government. He went into exile himself and never returned to his native land.

The Emperor's famous appearance at the League of Nations

In his 17-page speech to the League of Nations delegates, the Emperor, dressed in a black cape to symbolise his mourning for his nation, attacked the Italian aggression against his country. He spoke in Amharic so he could, in his words, speak his mind from his heart and with all the force of his spirit. The audience of diplomats and politicians listened solemnly to the translations in English and French as he ran down his charge sheet against Mussolini's government. Then the Emperor addressed them directly: 'In brief, it is not only Ethiopia that is at stake but the decent way of life of the peoples of the world who have been thus affected and wronged.' In conclusion, this challenge was issued to the western governments:

'I ask the great powers, who have promised the guarantee of collective security to small states – those small states over whom hangs the threat that they may one day suffer the fate of Ethiopia.... What answer am I to take back to my people?'

Finally, he uttered the prophetic words: 'It is us today. It will be you tomorrow.'

Haile Selassie wrote many years later about this speech and said that there were not a few who considered his appeal as a joke. But in looking back he realised that he had been proved to be right. Some of the powerful nations that had scoffed then would endure hardships of their own as the Second World War progressed. As the Emperor

CHAPTER 2

soberly noted, the forces of the powerful came to naught. His comments in Geneva echoed a statement he had made shortly before escaping from Ethiopia. Then he had described himself as the last bastion of collective security, holding on until his 'tardy allies' appeared. But if they never came, then he said prophetically and without bitterness, that the west would perish.

Just a few days after Haile Selassie's mesmeric appearance in Geneva, the League chose to ignore everything he had said. They became even more reluctant to stand up to Italy. The League members called off their imposition of limited sanctions against Mussolini. They also refused to make a 10 million dollar loan to Ethiopia that the Emperor had urgently requested. Although Britain and its European allies were putting their faith in the policy of appeasement, that approach would prove to be misguided as the decade wore on. When it came to the crunch, the League had flinched and had supinely allowed one of its members to get away with it.

The League's attitude provoked widespread dismay among the Ethiopian diplomatic community in the UK. One of the officials at the Legation in London, Emmanuel Abraham, described later in his autobiography that it showed that there was no justice for the weak in this world. Haile Selassie himself could have been forgiven for feeling doubly betrayed. The western powers had refused to spring to his immediate rescue when the Italians invaded. They had also imposed an arms embargo a few years earlier when the Emperor was desperately trying to modernise his country's weaponry ahead of an expected Italian incursion.

As the Emperor's train pulled into Bath Spa Railway Station in August 1936, he may have still been brooding about the injustice of what had happened to him and his country. He had been abandoned and the only thing he could rely on was his faith in God.

EARLY DAYS IN BATH

With the Emperor on the train from London were two of his sons, 20-year-old Crown Prince Asfa-Wossen, and 13-year-old Makonnen, the Duke of Harar. His 16-year-old daughter Tsehai, which means sun in Amharic, was also on board. The Emperor had six children with Empress Menen. Tragically four were to die before him, including two of those with him on his first visit to Bath. The Emperor also had a daughter with Weyzero Altayach before he married the Empress. Her name was Romaneworq and she was also to die early in life.

According to the local newspaper, the *Bath and Wilts Chronicle and Herald*, a couple of Scotland Yard detectives had been travelling on the train with the Emperor and his small retinue of advisers. The newspaper, which loved having the royal family in town, delighted in calling Haile Selassie the negus, meaning king in Amharic. This was a demotion from his full King of Kings title, though presumably Neguse Negest was not as convenient for making a snappy headline.

Bath Spa Station today with a modern train entering its curved platforms. In Haile Selassie's time steam trains would have passed through the station

The royal party had brought forward their visit by a day to avoid large crowds but word had leaked out as several supporters were at Bath Spa Station waiting to greet the Emperor. The *Chronicle* said he was coming to Bath after a number of heart-breaking experiences, though they did not spell out details of the calamities that had befallen him.

It is not clear which route the Emperor took when leaving the station on his way to the upmarket Bath Spa Hotel in the east of the city. However, his first taste of Bath may have been to travel up Pierrepont Street and then along North Road over a bridge spanning the River Avon. Just upstream is one of Bath's many architectural wonders, Pulteney Bridge, designed in the late 18th century by the Scottish neo-classical architect Robert Adam. It is one of those rare river bridges in the world on which working shops are situated.

Pulteney Bridge spanning the River Avon

CHAPTER 2

Whichever route the Emperor took, the journey to the Bath Spa Hotel would only have lasted a few minutes. Just before arriving at the hotel, the royal party passed the tasteful facades of the Georgian houses in Sydney Gardens. The visitors quickly settled into the hotel and later on that first evening they were seen going for a stroll in the extensive grounds. Maybe they were reminded of the gardens of the Gennete Leul Palace back in Addis Ababa. In any case, the calmness of the balmy summer evening air in Bath was a great contrast to the hustle and bustle of London. The Bath Spa Hotel building was certainly suitable for such royal guests and bears some resemblance to the Emperor's own palace.

The Bath Spa Hotel today

On the day after his arrival in Bath, the Emperor received an official visit at the Bath Spa from the mayor, James Carpenter. They had lunch together and enjoyed the warm weather during the driest summer for 65 years.

The *Chronicle* breathlessly published what it referred to as an amusing diary story about the royal guests' first few days at the hotel. Among the Emperor's entourage was a family friend, Mrs Olive Muir, the wife of a naval captain. Before coming to Bath the Emperor had met the Muirs in Scotland. During his stay there he had been a guest of Lord Inverclyde at Castle Wemyss on the Firth of Clyde. The *Chronicle* said it was understood that Mrs Muir was being touted for a special mission on behalf of the Emperor but this was not specified.

One evening Mrs Muir and Princess Tsehai went to the hotel ballroom after dinner. Tsehai was asked for a dance by a white male guest and duly obliged. She was spotted by one of the Emperor's advisers and medical doctor, Dr Melaku Bayen, who was alarmed and angered at what he saw as a possible breach of Imperial protocol. The doctor, who spoke fluent English and had been carrying out translation duties, went up to the Princess and told her it was time for bed. Mrs Muir interjected, saying that she was acting as a chaperone and everything would be all right.

Dr Bayen was not a man to give up easily. He had been with the Emperor on the front lines in northern Ethiopia and was reported to have been the only qualified medical doctor among 100,000 fighting men. On some days he would perform up to 350 operations on the wounded, using surgical knives, scissors and other medical instruments sterilised in the flames of a primus stove. Now in a peacetime setting, he was apparently slighted by Mrs Muir's comments and he immediately scuttled off to inform Tsehai's father. However, when the Emperor heard the tale, he is said to have simply laughed.

The Emperor with the Mayor of Bath outside the Bath Spa Hotel. He is wearing a kabba, the traditional cloak worn by Ethiopian nobility, and appears to be holding a postcard in his hand

CHAPTER 2

Haile Selassie was keen to keep his visit to Bath low-key and asked for privacy. He took a completely different approach to that of royals and high society in the 18th century when Bath was the playground of the London court. Then the dandy Master of Ceremonies, Beau Nash, who helped to put Bath on the map, would rush to the north gate to meet any notables and people of rank. For a fee he would arrange for the bells of the Abbey to be rung to announce their arrival. He would also help the visitors draw up a list of what to do and who to meet. Such showiness was obviously not Haile Selassie's style, though his arrival did cause widespread interest in the city.

Bath certainly is no stranger to royalty. The city rapidly expanded in the early 18th century after Queen Anne made a number of visits to take the spa waters to heal her various ailments, including gout. Much of the court quickly followed and in the century afterwards a host of nobles, religious pilgrims, gentlemen and princesses were desperate to be seen in the city. Bath has also been the home of many other famous characters. Admiral Nelson lived there in the late 18th century and William Herschel, the intrepid astronomer, discovered the planet Uranus while living in New King Street. Bath was the place where a cross-country mail system was invented and from where the first Penny Black stamp was sent.

One of the porters at the Bath Spa Hotel introduced the Emperor to Earnest (Pop) Smith, a local leather manufacturer. The Emperor later placed an order for some bound copies of a prayer book of the Orthodox Church. The two were to form a firm and unlikely friendship. Later the Emperor gave Pop's daughter a silver brooch of the Lion of Judah on her engagement. In the coming months Pop Smith helped the Emperor to sell some of his jewellery to raise funds while living in Bath. He refused any commission, despite the Emperor's insistence. In the end, all Pop accepted was a first class return rail ticket to London and a free lunch. This was one of several friendships that the Emperor made among the city's business community, though some relationships were later put under strain when he struggled to pay his bills because of mounting financial pressures.

By the first weekend of the Emperor's stay, Princess Tsehai, who spoke good English, had already had her photograph published on the front page of the *Chronicle*. It was not often that such an exotic family was in town. Most people found the Emperor very polite and courteous. They would have had little idea of the horrors that he had recently gone through. All they saw was a skilful mask of cordiality and equilibrium.

Early on in his visit, Haile Selassie received a letter from the Empress giving various snippets of family news from Jerusalem. One vital titbit was some information about the latest exploits of his treasured little dog Rosa. The local press in Jerusalem had falsely reported that the dog had been run over and killed by a car, apparently leaving the Empress in tears and blaming an Italian driver for the mishap. She was able to reassure the Emperor that the pet was alive and well. The reply by the Emperor was made public as he sought to consolidate his image in the UK. He said he hoped to see the Empress soon. A report by the *Calvacade* magazine, published by the *Chronicle*, said that this was a reply to those who alleged that the Ethiopian leader cared only for a mistress and despised his Empress.

SEEING THE SIGHTS

Bath in the 1930s was an excellent venue to provide the temporary peace and quiet that the Emperor craved. It was a reserved and refined place with a proud heritage and no threats. The city was long past its breathless Georgian heyday of the 18th century when it had been caught up in a frenzied building boom and became the place to be seen at in the UK. Regency coastal resorts, such as Brighton and Eastbourne, were to become more popular by the early 19th century.

A few buildings of note had been built in 19th century Bath, including several churches and some fine Victorian mansions on the steep hill leading up to the location of what is now the University of Bath. But there was nothing to emulate the spectacular Georgian legacy – the Circus, the Royal Crescent or indeed the wide avenue of Great Pulteney Street, which is close to the Bath Spa Hotel.

The Royal Crescent in Bath, completed in the mid-18th century

Bath had a modest population in the 1930s of around 70,000 and had a solid industrial base. One of the most successful local companies was Stothert and Pitt, an engineering firm specialising in making dockside cranes which were exported all over the world. It had been involved in making high-explosive shells during World War I and then went on to contribute to the production of tanks in World War II. On the negative side, the appearance of the city had lost some of its sheen. In truth, it was a little run-down, grimy and dowdy. Bath had not been spared the country-wide economic crisis following the worldwide crash of 1929 and the resultant depression. Poor housing and some poverty were in evidence with ten per cent of the city's population suffering from tuberculosis.

Two years before Haile Selassie arrived, the Bath Preservation Trust had been formed to campaign to keep the city's heritage intact. The organisation is still going strong today. The Trust was responding to a number of initiatives to modernise the

CHAPTER 2

city. The historic Lower Assembly Rooms, which had housed dancing and card-playing in Georgian times, were pulled down in 1934 to make way for an improved traffic scheme as the motor car gained in popularity. Tension between the preservers and the modernisers was to continue for many decades to come. One city official said in the 1930s that Bath had been sleeping for 100 years. The British humorist H.M. Bateman sneered that the city could even be described as a temple to antiquity.

Bath was caught up in the national mood of nervousness about the instability in Europe and Hitler's increasingly aggressive moves for territory outside Germany's borders. It had only been a few months since he had moved into the Rhineland in March 1936 in defiance of the Versailles Treaty signed after World War I. No-one believed the German leader was going to call it a day after that. His unabated territorial ambitions were scaring everyone in the rest of Europe. The national mood in Britain had been gauged by a massive peace ballot held between the end of 1934 and the first half of 1935. Many votes had been collected while the tension between Italy and Ethiopia had been rising.

The results suggested that the people of the UK championed the cause of those who had been victims of aggression. In all, 11.5 million Britons took part in the poll. The vast majority of this sample, ten million, had agreed that if a member state of the League of Nations were to be attacked, then the other members should compel the aggressor to stop. The vast majority, 87 per cent, favoured the use of economic sanctions, though nearly 60 per cent were prepared to support military measures.

Many in the UK were soon to be dismayed by the reports filtering out about Edward VIII's affair with Wallis Simpson, who had been married three times. Already by August 1936, foreign newspapers were publishing stories about the couple taking a secret cruise in the eastern Mediterranean aboard the steam yacht Nahlin. The constitutional crisis was to develop into serious proportions over the next few months, upsetting many British people, who were greatly shocked by the scandal and disturbed by the instability caused. Given his own circumstances, this was a story that must have baffled the Ethiopian monarch.

Amid all these worries, Bath still had one massive card up its sleeve. The hot springs and spa facilities continued to draw visitors seeking healing and comfort. Even while he was on board the *Enterprise* naval ship in the Red Sea, the Emperor had been expressing a wish to go to a spa to help soothe his shattered mind and body. Now he had his chance. The ruins of the bath houses and temple built by the Romans were also a timeless attraction. During the 1930s there was a steady campaign to restore some of Bath's vigour. A new scheme was put in place to restore the Upper Assembly Rooms, which had also staged spectacular dances and card games in late Georgian times. This project would be completed by the end of the decade while Haile Selassie was still in town. It was also announced that modern buses would be introduced to replace the creaking tramway system, and there was a general push to develop revenues from tourism as the population became increasingly mobile.

Haile Selassie receives a warm welcome outside the spa baths. Princess Tsehai is behind him

On that first visit in the balmy days of August 1936, the Emperor soon ventured out to see the Royal Baths complex and took the first of several healing spa treatments. He wore a grey flannel suit and a dark blue cape, which was to become a familiar sight in the city. Traffic was held up in Stall Street on the approach to the baths which were incorporated into the imposing Grand Pump Room Hotel, built by the Victorians to revive Bath's spa industry. Haile Selassie described his welcome as wonderful and touching. It made a considerable impact on him, coming so soon after being treated so abysmally by the invading Italian forces. The welcome by Bathonians was a contrast too to the off-hand attitude shown by many members of the British government. The Emperor was obviously enjoying the attention, despite his request for privacy. Although he was offered the opportunity to leave the baths by a discreet exit, he chose to make his way out of the main entrance, happy to be seen by the crowds.

CHAPTER 2

During the month of August the Emperor visited the spa centre at the Royal Baths on at least eight occasions. He had a combination of treatments. One package was called Tivoli and cost seven shillings and six pence. A mud-based treatment cost nine shillings. Altogether he paid seven pounds two shillings and six pence during his various visits. The Emperor and his children also had the chance to see some of the other attractions Bath had to offer. They visited the Fortts factory in Manvers Street where the famous Bath Oliver biscuit was made. The recipe had been around for a couple of hundred years or so. The biscuit was promoted by a physician William Oliver as a low-calorie option for overweight sufferers from gout and rheumatism, who were patients at the renowned Royal Mineral Hospital. The hospital also provided treatment for many military victims of mustard gas attacks in World War I. How the Emperor must have wished that similar treatment could have been available for some of his own troops.

It would have been surprising if the Emperor did not have some uncomfortable flashbacks about the horrors he had seen and undergone while fighting the Italian invaders. Post Traumatic Stress Disorder was little known as a condition and such psychological traumas were not discussed openly. Now they are understood as being a normal human reaction to witnessing the brutal consequences of war. Any talk of struggling with psychological issues was seen as cowardly in those times, even more so for an elevated figure such as an Emperor. Nonetheless, the healing and comfortable warm waters of the spa baths would have helped him to soothe any hidden post-war demons he could have been wrestling with.

Overall, Haile Selassie appeared more interested in educating himself about practical processes and manufacturing than he was about absorbing the cultural aesthetics of the city. He visited the premises of Cedric Chivers, established experts in book-binding, and made a return call on the Mayor, speaking to him in French. They met at the Guildhall in the centre of Bath and the Emperor expressed admiration at the design of the 18th century banqueting room. Little did he know that two years later a meeting would be held there involving supporters of his mortal enemy Mussolini, and a toast raised there in Il Duce's honour.

No trip to Bath would have been complete without a tour of the site of the ancient Roman baths and temple to the goddess Sulis Minerva. This complex had been developed into a major tourist attraction, following some key archaeological discoveries towards the end of the 19th century. After these excavations life-size stone statues of various Roman Emperors were erected at the edges of the baths. These figures stared down silently on Haile Selassie as he made his tour, mixing with the rest of the visitors. The Emperor admired the ingenuity of these early Italians in establishing the baths but, of course, he had nothing but contempt for the current political leadership ensconced in Rome.

The Emperor on his tour of the Roman Baths. Prince Makonnen is on the left of the picture, captured by the *Chronicle*

Around 2,000 years ago Romans in Bath who believed themselves to be the victims of injustice invoked the wrath of the goddess against their enemies. They wrote curses on lead tablets and threw them into the sacred spring by the temple in the hope the goddess would do her worst in vengeance. Many of the maledictions were inspired by the theft of treasured possessions such as clothes or jewellery. One wonders what the Emperor, a victim of the outrageous theft of his country, would have been tempted to write in a modern-day version of those curses.

More than a million litres of hot water bubble up at the sacred spring every day. It takes just eight seconds to fill a bath at this rate of flow. The water originally fell as rain on the slopes of the Mendip hills near Bath around 10,000 years ago and drained into an underground lake two miles beneath the surface. The hot liquid is then slowly forced upwards where it emerges at a constant temperature of around 45 degrees Centigrade.

Haile Selassie, his emotions buffeted around like a shuttlecock, may have been reassured by this humbling force of nature. The sight is bound to have reminded him of his own capital of Addis Ababa, which was also founded on the site of a number

CHAPTER 2

of hot springs. The Emperor also loved another thermal waters site in a more remote part of southern Ethiopia – Wondo Genet, which was surrounded by rich indigenous forests, breathtaking vistas and teeming wildlife.

The sacred spring today in the Roman Baths complex

The Pump Room above the ancient baths site was a favourite location in two of the novels by Jane Austen, who lived for several years in Bath in the early 19th century. She disliked many things in the city, then coming to the end of its Georgian expansion. She was annoyed by the glare given off by the sun on the pristine stone buildings and made fun of the superficiality of society chatter and gossip. The Pump Room was the main place for upstanding members of society to see and be seen, a kind of court but with no political power.

Today a string trio or a pianist regularly plays classical music throughout the day, though there is no mention as to whether any musicians performed for Haile Selassie. It is also possible to drink some of the sulphurous hot spring water. It contains more than 40 minerals and is said to be beneficial for health.

As soon as word spread that the royal visitor was in town, tours were arranged from London to see him. The Pump Room was a popular spot to try to get a glimpse of the Ethiopian monarch. One rumour was that his dark beard had turned grey, due to his harrowing experiences at the hands of the Italians.

No mention was made in the *Chronicle* as to whether the Emperor was taken to see the two main architectural jewels of Bath – the Royal Crescent and the Circus. However, it would have been odd if these sites had not been pointed out to him. The Crescent is shaped in an exquisite half ellipse. All of its 30 Georgian houses are designed in perfect harmony and proportion. The Crescent derives its royal title because the Duke of York and Albany stayed there at the end of the 18th century.

The Circus consists of three equal crescent sections making up a perfect circle. Some believe that it was modelled on the Coliseum in Rome, though the facades face inwards rather than outwards.

Some impressive guests have lived in the Circus. They include the portrait artist Thomas Gainsborough, who painted the great and the good in the 18th century, and the indefatigable explorer Clive of India. Both the Crescent and the Circus were designed by the versatile architect John Wood and his son, also called John. They were both avid students of the Italian architect, Andrea Palladio. Their work influenced many of the other architects who designed the swathe of Georgian buildings in Bath. Palladio in turn had been inspired by the buildings created during the classical Greek and Roman civilisations. Those with an attuned sense of irony would have undoubtedly mused about the incongruities of the Emperor's presence in a city with so many Italian influences.

Addis Ababa was only around 50 years old when Haile Selassie came to England and so he and his government were not as focused on preserving old buildings as the people of Bath. Although many structures in the country were flimsy and short-lived, Ethiopia did boast some architectural heritage to be proud of. In the holy city of Axum there are some ancient giant stelae or obelisks, dating back to the fourth century AD when they were built as markers for the graves of rulers. The Italians were to cause more outrage and offence when they shipped one of these obelisks back to Italy as a symbol of their victory in 1936.

Just north of Lake Tana, the source of the Blue Nile, lies the ancient capital of Gondar where several Ethiopian rulers made their home. Tourist guides rave about the area as a kind of magical Camelot, the court of the mythical British King Arthur and his knights of the round table. The Ethiopian King, Fasilides, built an impressive 17th century castle in Gondar. Every year to this day thousands of pilgrims flock to the Fasilides baths to celebrate Timket, the vibrant festival in mid-January marking epiphany.

In the 18th century Empress Mentaweb, who was also known as 'berhan mogasa,' or 'glorifier of light,' also built a spectacular castle in the royal enclosure. On the whole though, many Ethiopians do not revere bricks and mortar in the same way as ardent conservationists in Bath and elsewhere in the UK. In Ethiopia most people tend to care more about the religious and historical significance of particular locations rather than the specific buildings erected there.

He may have emerged from an ancient dynasty but the Emperor proved to be no slouch at playing the public relations card. In those early days in Bath he happily obliged for photographers for the *Chronicle* while on a visit to a Post Office exhibition staged at the Octagon Chapel. He saw how modern telegrams worked and sent one to the

CHAPTER 2

director of the exhibition. One priority for him was how he could most effectively keep in touch with his embattled forces in Ethiopia, which had now retreated to the town of Gore as arranged. Later in August 1936 the Emperor was reported as having received telegrams from some of the resistance fighters there.

The Emperor looking relaxed in a photograph in the *Chronicle* at the Post Office Exhibition at the Octagon Chapel in Bath

His daughter Tsehai continued to be a hit with locals and sent her own telegram at the exhibition, saying she had enjoyed her visit very much. As word spread that the Emperor and his party were inside, several hundred people gathered outside hoping to see them. Again the royal guest was offered the chance to leave through a rear entrance but he was happy to stroll out into the thick of the well-wishers, knowing he would receive a sympathetic response. The crowds were 20 deep in places and blocked the road. The police were doing their best to keep order. A cheer went up as the Emperor left. Many hands patted his car and, because of the crush, some did not even catch a glimpse of the foreign visitor.

It is interesting to speculate about why Haile Selassie attracted such crowds. Perhaps his presence was a distracting novelty amid the humdrum routine of daily life in Bath. Maybe Bathonians were displaying an early obsession with celebrity. If these events had occurred in our Twitter and Facebook age, you can be sure a host of selfies would have been taken with the Emperor as a kind of stage prop in the background. Royalty has always been a great draw for the British public and regal sightseeing is more fun and agreeable in warm summer weather. Perhaps people were intrigued and keen to see for themselves what an Ethiopian monarch would look like in the flesh. Britain in the 1930s had a relatively small African population and Bath was no exception. This was some time before the wave of immigrants to the UK from former British colonies in Africa, south Asia, and the West Indies. The royal party would therefore have been a rare and prized sight.

Another rapturous welcome for the Emperor outside the spa building as captured by the *Chronicle*

The people of Bath quickly recognised that the Emperor loved children and dogs, which was bound to make him popular. Another reason for the gathering of the enthusiastic crowds was that they simply wanted to support the Ethiopian monarch. They could see that he had been the victim of a gross injustice. Whatever their motivations, the warmth of these hordes must have been a boon to the beleaguered Emperor. It is possible that some in the city harboured resentment over a refugee from Africa being praised and lauded. Racist and jingoistic attitudes did exist at this time in Britain but there was not much evidence of any overt anti-Emperor sentiment. However, the Foreign Office did receive a formal complaint ahead of an event to be held by the Mayor of Bath to entertain the Emperor at a garden party in Parade Gardens by the River Avon. The complainant believed that too much official fuss was being made of the Emperor.

CHAPTER 2

The British government once again showed its contradictory attitude towards the Ethiopian refugee. The Mayor received an official letter from the then Home Secretary, Sir John Simon, asking him to call off the event. However, a small unofficial note was also enclosed, saying that, as Mayor, he was free to do as he liked. The reception therefore went ahead and all the guests enjoyed eating strawberries and cream in the sunshine.

The Emperor naturally was interested in the religious life of Bath and asked to see St Stephen's Church, perched mid-way up the steep Lansdown Hill. The 19th century church, with its lantern tower and corner pinnacles, is a much-loved landmark. It was also another reminder of home as there is a St Stephen's Church on the corner of Meskel Square in the centre of Addis Ababa. Haile Selassie also travelled to nearby Bristol Cathedral and saw the spectacular Clifton suspension bridge over the Avon gorge. Were these tourist activities a superficial distraction from his woes? Or did the sight of several churches remind him of his faith in God, which had been sorely tested over the last few months?

WRAPPING UP THE VISIT

There was still no decision by mid-August 1936 about when the Empress would leave Jerusalem and rejoin her husband. However, news did emerge about Princess Tsehai. It was announced that she was intending to move soon to London to start work as a nurse in the Great Ormond Street Children's Hospital. She had always had a dream to become a nurse, though her new career also greatly helped the Emperor. Nothing is designed to win the hearts of the British more than to see someone putting themselves out to help sick children. The Princess asked to be treated like anyone else on her arrival at the hospital and proudly donned the red and white striped uniform. She was paid the modest sum of £20 for her first year. Sadly, this popular and spirited young Ethiopian Princess was to die just six years later due to complications during pregnancy, yet another crippling blow for the Emperor.

The royal party appeared to be enjoying the restful sojourn in Bath but it was not possible to escape the constant reminders of the instability in Europe. News from the Spanish civil war was depressing with accounts of the brutal shelling of San Sebastian. In a chilling echo of the Ethiopian battlefields, there were also reports of poison gas being used. Haile Selassie could not escape from war and suffering. He was also humiliated in mid-August when it was announced by the occupying Italian forces that the Emperor's private estates around Addis Ababa had been seized and would form the basis of agricultural colonial properties to cultivate coffee, sesame seeds, grain, wool and hides.

On 18 August the Emperor was reported to have interrupted his time of leisure in Bath and taken the 8.37am breakfast car train on a brief trip back to London, travelling first class. He went there to consider looking for a house, as living in hotels was proving to be too expensive. The Emperor told the press that he had already spent a large part of the money he had brought with him in the struggle for independence in his country and he now had to economise as best he could.

The lack of money was to be a niggling feature of his entire exile in the UK. The Emperor said he did not intend to settle for any length of time in England as he was still dreaming of a return to Ethiopia. However, Putney Heath in south-west London was said to be on his mind as a possible location to buy a property. Bath at this stage was not a public option for putting down any roots, though it may have been already crossing his mind as a possibility.

The Emperor was invited to attend Bath races on the top of Lansdown Hill on 21 August. Locals had already figured out that he loved horses and enjoyed going out for long rides. Although he turned down the invitation it was thought some of his party would attend. But they too withdrew. The reason cited by the local newspaper was that it was a day of fasting, which is frequent in the life of the Ethiopian Orthodox Church. Over the course of the year there are around 180 obligatory fasting days, including every Wednesday and Friday. Priests fast for up to 250 days a year. On fasting days worshippers eat fewer meals and totally abstain from meat, fat, eggs and dairy products. The Emperor strictly observed these fasts all his life, as do many Ethiopians today. The race day at Lansdown proved to be unseasonably cold. The royal visitors may have been told one of the jokes doing the rounds at the time – that summer in England begins on 31 July and ends on 1 August.

Newspapers all over the UK carried snippets of news about the Emperor and his family. At the end of August the *Northern Daily Mail* ran a tongue-in-cheek diary item highlighting what it referred to as one of the strangest receptions he had received since his arrival in the UK. The Emperor had travelled to Hampton Court near London, the former palace of King Henry VIII, who himself had a titanic struggle with powerful figures based in Rome when he refused to acknowledge the authority of the Pope. After lunching with some Egyptian diplomats, the Emperor went to the pool to watch some of them go swimming. Suddenly hundreds of swimmers in bathing costumes burst into applause with chants of three cheers for the Emperor ringing around.

At the start of September there was some news to lift the spirits of Bathonians and the country at large. It was reported that the *Queen Mary* was the first ship to cross the Atlantic in less than four days. The liner made it with just three minutes to spare. Here was some rare news celebrating human endeavour and achievement amid all the gloom of the rise of fascism in Europe.

An invitation was extended for the Emperor to attend the Bath Horse Show a

CHAPTER 2

couple of days later. It was a genteel occasion as far removed from the charnel houses of Lake Ashangi and Maychew as could be imagined. It had only been a few months since the Emperor paraded around the battlefield on a white horse. His presence as a guest of honour at the show proved to be a big draw and there was an unprecedented demand for tickets. The show at Lambridge on the edge of town attracted all the best horses in England. The crowd in the grandstand all rose when they spotted their famous visitor. A special Negus tent was erected by the enclosed ring so the Emperor could watch the horses in comfort. He was guarded by special commissionaires, and especially enjoyed the show jumping and the events lined up for children.

An enterprising reporter from the *Chronicle* was sent to the Bath Spa Hotel to see if he could winkle out any information from the Ethiopian leader about his plans for the future. The main question was whether he intended to return to Ethiopia to try to regain his crown. The sleuth from the *Chronicle* did not get very far and came back pretty much empty-handed. He was reduced to reporting merely that he had seen the Emperor in close consultation with one of his special advisers, Ras Kassa, on the terrace at the hotel. It was Ras Kassa, of course, who had been one of the leading voices urging his leader to flee Ethiopia. The reporter was not able to give any insight as to whether the Ras was having any cause to regret his decision.

News about the royal party's immediate movements did emerge quite soon afterwards. It was announced they would be leaving for London in early September. They had intended to stay for three weeks but had extended their trip by a week. The *Chronicle* was delighted to announce that Bath now had a feather in its cap because the Emperor liked the city and was delighted by the warm welcome he had received. Ras Kassa said that one day the Emperor would be back in the city of the Roman baths. The Emperor was impressed by Bath's beauty, its proud history, its friendly people and curative waters. He said he had never felt better anywhere else in England.

His assessment was in keeping with other comments about the English character that he made at different stages of his life. He had his quibbles with some leading members of the British government but his respect for ordinary Englishmen and women was genuine. Perhaps the Emperor was impressed by the English concept of keeping a stiff upper lip at times of adversity. He may also have admired the English bureaucratic mind, which had been running a vast empire across the world for a couple of centuries.

The popular English writer Rudyard Kipling summed up the British stoical character when he wrote about the importance of dealing with the two impostors of triumph and disaster in just the same way. These were sentiments that would certainly have been appreciated by the Ethiopian exile. As for Bathonians, it was becoming clear that a kind of chaste love affair between them and the Emperor was gathering momentum.

The Ethiopian leader had already been in exile for around four months by the end of his enjoyable stay in the city of Georgian architecture. His recuperative spell had provided some short-term balm for the various traumas he had experienced in the past year.

However, it would surely have been dawning on him by now that he could be away from his own country for a considerable time to come. Maybe even some doubts were already creeping into his soul that he might never return to the land of his birth. The odds were continuing to stack up against him. The Italian forces were tightening their grip in Addis Ababa, and the European powers in which he had placed so much faith were lukewarm in their support at best. Furthermore, the Emperor was wrestling with the far-reaching consequences of his decision to flee. He knew that some of his subjects might never forgive him for what was, in their eyes, a complete betrayal of them and the Ethiopian nation. He could not help but be haunted by the reports of the widespread suffering of his people as the Italians brutally imposed their will on Ethiopia, shooting prisoners out of hand.

One prominent member of the Emperor's entourage, a giant of a man called Balahu, was reported to be among the victims. Balahu was seven feet five inches tall and had been singled out by the Emperor to be his personal umbrella carrier and then drum major of the Imperial band. He came to the Emperor's attention when he appeared before him at a sitting of the supreme court, charged with murdering a man in a dispute over a woman. Haile Selassie was so impressed by Balahu's height and bearing that he paid blood money to the relatives of the victim and incorporated him into his service.

It was galling for the Emperor to imagine the occupying troops strutting around his own capital. The Italian high command had made its headquarters in his palace at the foot of the imposing and beautiful Entoto Mountain. All of us would shudder at the thought of our enemies making themselves at home in our private space. One story being circulated was that the conquering Italian general Badoglio had commandeered the Emperor's throne and had turned it into a cradle for his pet dog.

The press reports that the Emperor was already thinking of looking for a house in England showed that he was starting to accept the reality of his precarious position. He needed to put down at least some temporary roots for himself and his young family. There was also the additional complicating factor that in the short-term he was simply running out of money, an embarrassing predicament for the King of Kings. Separation from one's own home and country, particularly when it is enforced, can be corrosive to one's state of mind. Quite simply, the Emperor would have been missing everything about his life in Ethiopia: the familiar weather patterns; the accustomed rhythms of the working day; the reassuring sight of known landscapes, food, sounds and living space; and prized possessions, including books, pets and paintings. The Emperor's very identity had been snatched away from him. He had schemed hard and long to reach the pinnacle of power but everything was now under threat. He was

CHAPTER 2

nowhere near to finishing the objectives he had set out for his kingdom. Yes, he had introduced the country's first ever constitution in 1931 but he wanted to do so much more to modernise his country, including boosting education and the economy.

Although he had a small trusted band of loyal followers around him in the UK, he had lost a lot of his aura as the Lion of Judah. He was the conquered, not the conquering. He was not quite a nobody yet but perhaps had already begun to feel that he might become one, consigned to irrelevance and impotence. He stood to lose an enormous amount. He had been the biggest fish in the relatively small Ethiopian pool. Now he was a small figure in a large global pool without much influence. The harsh reality was that he was already turning into an outcast and even at this early stage it was becoming difficult to see how he could reverse his fortunes.

Living with uncertainty can be very wearing, especially if one's pre-exile life and identity were as well-defined as the Emperor's was. The English word exile comes from Latin. 'Ex' means 'from' and 'salire' means 'to leap out of.' The Ethiopian leader was certainly ripped out of one existence and dumped into another in the blink of an eye. It was not quite out of the frying pan and into the fire, more a case of being thrust into a world of cold ashes, devoid of joy and optimism. No-one can adequately prepare to cope with the testing and ferocious pressures of exile.

However, Haile Selassie had already proved that he was extremely resilient. He had built up a reputation for biding his time and being an expert manager of his own emotions. He gave little away by his inscrutable features. But you have to go back in time to understand the extent of how prepared he was to deal with the exile experience. The key lies in his extraordinary upbringing when his character and modus operandi were forged.

CHAPTER TWO EYEWITNESS THE BATH SPA HOTEL

The Bath Spa Hotel was perfect for the reserved and private Emperor. An advertisement from the 1930s described the property as the quietest hotel in Bath. The hotel began as Vellore House, a distinctive residence built for a gentleman. The first owner was General Augustus Andrews, who had served in the British army in India. The architect was John Pinch the younger. In the early 19th century he built several desirable properties in this area at the foot of Bathwick Hill. Vellore House was later sold to the Rector of Bath Abbey, who had a large family including a wife and seven daughters.

The property then served as a boys' school until 1912 when it became a fashionable hotel. The advertisement for the Bath Spa boasted of 100 bedrooms and 60 bathrooms with hot and cold water. It had a lift, radiators, nine acres of manicured grounds, and even an orchestra. The advertisement provided no information on how much the rooms cost. The royal party took over one wing and the living room was on the ground floor. There was also a study in which the Emperor worked during the day and well into the evening. With him were his three children, his trusted adviser Ras Kassa, and two assistants.

The British news magazine *Calvacade* published some inside information about the Emperor's daily routine. It described how he rose to pray during the night for his nation. In the mornings he would go through his mail. On fasting days he would just have bread and water for breakfast. On other days it was mainly Bath water and fish. The Emperor was said to have astonished guests when, according to *Calvacade*, he ordered a dozen eggs for himself and his family for dinner. The magazine said the Emperor spent much of the evening plotting how he could return to Ethiopia. Other guests were delighted to be able to see the royal party strolling round the grounds,

CHAPTER 2

which contained a grotto and some magnificent cedar trees. The Emperor would then spend the rest of the evening writing until midnight.

Today the hotel has an Admiralty Room, a reference to the fact that the building was requisitioned by the Admiralty in the run-up to World War Two in the late 1930s. Bath was seen as a secure yet convenient location to hold secure and confidential meetings. The city became an alternate base because London was becoming too dangerous as war loomed with Germany. Churchill, who was in charge of the British Navy at the start of the war, was a frequent visitor to the hotel while Haile Selassie was still living in Bath. The Emperor would certainly have loved the intrigue and the complicated planning involved in marshalling the Royal Navy. Britain did not quite rule the waves any more as the days of empire were drawing to an end, but its navy was still impressive. It is intriguing to speculate whether these two leaders ever met in Bath in the early days of the war. Their paths did definitely cross after Churchill became the war time prime minister. Before then Churchill's attitude to the Ethiopian question had been somewhat contradictory. He had always deplored the cruelty of Italy's invasion but was also on the side of those who urged caution about not inflaming Mussolini and shepherding him into Hitler's arms.

The elegant Kennet and Avon Canal near the Bath Spa Hotel

In public Churchill supported the principles of the League of Nations but in private backed Italy. He made clear his dislike of sanctions at the start of October 1935. He said it would be a terrible mistake to smash up Italy and would cost Britain dearly. On the other hand Churchill always seemed to have a good opinion of Haile Selassie, describing him at an early stage as the only enlightened Abyssinian prince.

The Bath Spa Hotel is across the road from Sydney Gardens, which date back to the novelist Jane Austen's day. One of her houses in Bath was at the opposite end of the park and she loved to go and watch the firework displays held there. In its first incarnation Sydney Gardens was a commercial pleasure park and there was an entrance fee. When the railway and canal came to Bath, they both cut across the gardens, much to the delight of the owners. They were paid handsome prices to enable the trappings of modern life to disturb their land and insisted that they be constructed in keeping with the local Georgian style. It is possible that Haile Selassie walked around these gardens on his evening strolls and at the very least he would have seen them while being driven into Bath or coming into the city on the train.

CHAPTER 3

CHAPTER THREE
THE KING OF KINGS

The future Haile Selassie made his way into the world near the important eastern town of Harar where his father Ras Makonnen Wolde-Mikael was the governor. The Ras had been a commander at the famous battle of Adwa and so commanded huge respect throughout the country. He was described as a man who wielded a great deal of power in a quiet way. The war hero was also the first cousin of Emperor Menelik II and so was part of the Solomonic dynasty. Menelik regarded Makonnen so highly that he had designated him as his heir. Both men were members of the powerful Shoa aristocracy originating from a central province in northern Ethiopia.

Makonnen's new son was born in 1892, high up in a mountain village about 25 miles from Harar, which had a large Muslim population. His mother had gone there to escape the many diseases and other problems caused by four years of great famine. During these years 90 per cent of all cattle throughout Ethiopia are estimated to have disappeared. Not long after the new baby was born, the area was deluged with heavy rains, seen by many as a good omen. The local population was very superstitious and witchcraft was also prevalent. Because of the propitious arrival of the rain, the future Emperor was already marked out as a man of special destiny by those in the Harar area. The society he was born into was feudal, religious and agrarian.

Even at the beginning of his life Teferi faced serious challenges. He was the only child that his mother Yeshemebet carried to full term. None of his mother's nine other pregnancies were successful, though Makonnen had had another son by another woman. The other son died as a young man, leaving the young Teferi as the undisputed heir to his father's title and lands. Teferi's mother died when he was just two. She was barely 30. It now fell to his father to look after him in early childhood. His father did not marry again so the young Teferi had no maternal influence in his life. This experience undoubtedly made him emotionally tough and self-reliant

IMPERIAL EXILE

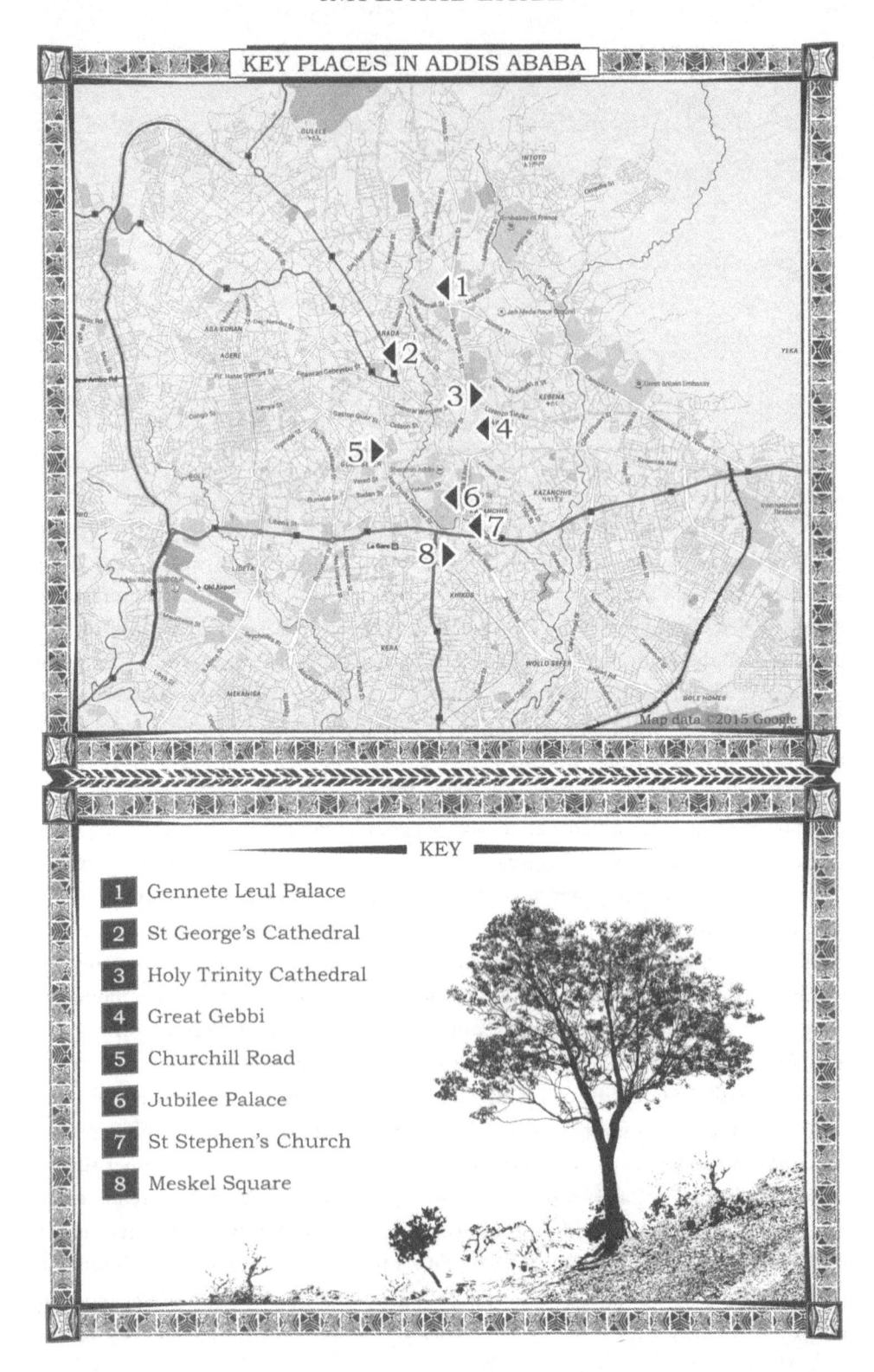

KEY PLACES IN ADDIS ABABA

KEY

1. Gennete Leul Palace
2. St George's Cathedral
3. Holy Trinity Cathedral
4. Great Gebbi
5. Churchill Road
6. Jubilee Palace
7. St Stephen's Church
8. Meskel Square

CHAPTER 3

but of course he missed out on the loving and nurturing support a mother brings.

Teferi clearly adored his father. He tells a touching story in his writings about how his father tended to miss his meals because he was grieving for his wife. No-one in the household dared approach Makonnen and tell him to come and eat, apart from Teferi. On occasion Makonnen would answer his call and it gave Teferi great joy and pride to watch him eat. Teferi also wrote that Makonnen's main thought had been to please God in every manner and that he wanted to conduct himself by following his example.

The young Ras Teferi

GROWING UP IN HARAR

Harar is not far from the coast and is an ancient place where Arab traders came to do business with the highland Ethiopians. It has its own language, Harari, and is also a centre for growing chaat – a mild narcotic leaf which today is prized through Ethiopia, Somalia and across the Red Sea in Yemen. Chaat looks a bit like privet leaf and is very bitter to the taste. Some aficionados chew the leaf ceaselessly so it turns into a great ball in one side of their mouth. They end up looking a bit like hamsters. The leaf is sought after partly because it enables chewers to have some moments of great concentration. Modern-day students love consuming chaat just before exams. However, the stimulant also causes depression and sadness. Chewing chaat had no appeal for the Emperor. He avoided addictive substances such as alcohol and tobacco.

Harar is also famous for its city walls and its hyenas. Today tourists can try their luck emulating a local man who feeds hyenas with lumps of meat on the end of a wire stick, kept in his mouth while the creatures chomp noisily away. The French philosopher and poet Arthur Rimbaud lived in Harar for a number of years and was a friend of Ras Makonnen. The Frenchman was the first European to do business in the town and helped develop the exporting of coffee, which is widely grown in the area.

Jaded tourists struggling with the hot sun in Harar can seek respite in a villa housing a museum dedicated to his life in Harar. Rimbaud died young, aged 37. It was the year before Teferi emerged into the world.

The young Teferi was small and slight but it quickly became apparent that he had a strong intellect. His father was very keen on his country extending links with the modern world and Europe. He therefore entrusted much of Teferi's education to a French Catholic Capuchin priest, Monsignor André Jarosseau. Naturally the young child was also schooled in the complicated ways and theology of the Ethiopian Orthodox Church. The Monsignor said that he raised Teferi as if he were his own son. Over the years the two of them kept in touch. They were said to have exchanged around 500 letters until the Monsignor's death in 1941. Father Jarosseau had long flowing hair and a beard, and one western visitor to Harar said it made him look like an Italian saint.

Teferi spent a lot of time learning and playing with his cousin Ras Imru Selassie, who was to be a lifelong friend and confidant. Haile Selassie left Imru in charge of the rump of the Ethiopian army after escaping from the Italians many years later. By the age of six both boys could recite all the psalms in Ge'ez, the ancient liturgical language of the Orthodox Church. Ge'ez also forms the basis of Amharic, the language of the court and the establishment. Teferi could speak other indigenous Ethiopian languages, including Tigrinnia, Harari and the languages of the Gurage and Oromo peoples.

Teferi was also taught French by Dr Joseph Vitalien, a prominent physician from Guadeloupe. He soon became fluent in the language, which he used in countless diplomatic situations for the rest of his life. He also learned to speak several other international languages, including Arabic and some Italian, German, Latin and English. Such a range of linguistic ability would obviously be of some help to him in the dark days of exile – feeding his regular and eclectic reading habits, keeping up with international developments, and also dealing with a variety of formal and informal contacts.

The boys took to their other studies enthusiastically, and absorbed philosophy, world history and geography. They focused on history and the law, studying the *Kibra Nagast*, the glory of kings, and the *Fetha Nagast*, the law of kings, a 13th century work focusing on ecclesiastical law and civil administration. Teferi maintained he had an upbringing like the sons of ordinary people and there had been no undue softness like many other princes received.

Teferi's father was often away on military and other duties in Addis Ababa, a journey which took up to a month by slow march. The travelling time was reduced to just a day when the French-built train line opened a few years later. Now courtesy of the national carrier, Ethiopian Airlines, you can fly to Addis Ababa from the nearby town of Dire Dawa in just an hour. The Emperor was born into a distinctly medieval age but by the end of his long life he saw many of the modern benefits the 20th century had to offer. Makonnen also led the way in travelling abroad. He went twice to Europe on special missions for Emperor Menelik and visited Italy, France and

Britain. He attended the coronation of Edward VII in 1902 following the death of Queen Victoria. The governor of Harar was to pass on the travelling bug to his son, who was enraptured by the stories his father told him about modern, sophisticated Europe.

Although Teferi was brought up in a remote area, his mind was already a seething mass of knowledge. He devoured countless books and tomes, all fuelling his curiosity about the world. His deep faith and interest in spiritual matters were already forming. With his father often preoccupied by his various duties, the young Teferi was also looked after closely by another Catholic, Abba Samuel. Teferi described him as someone who strove for the enjoyment of the soul, not the flesh. He also said that in goodness and humility he gathered knowledge from anyone, just like a bee. Despite this influence from the Catholic faith, Teferi never deserted the Orthodox Church, which was to remain his bedrock for his whole life.

In those early years in Harar, Teferi's character was forged from his education and from his place in society. He could not help but be a product of the era in which he was born and grew up. Like other rases and princes, he was caught in the intricate system of human relationships in the hierarchical Ethiopian society. With someone of his precocious talent and background, it was not long before Teferi began to make a contribution to the complex society around him. At the tender age of 13 he was created a dejazmach, which means leader of an army, and is equivalent to the title of a count in English. Teferi was put in charge of a mountainous region not far from Harar. He was on his way.

THE COURT

Just a year later, in 1906, Ras Makonnen died. The death of a cherished father is a terrible blow to any son but especially to one still in the early stages of adolescence. Dysentery or typhus was mentioned as cause of death but there was the lingering suspicion, never proven, that he may have been poisoned by a rival. Such were the internecine politics of Ethiopia at the time. The Ras was taken ill while on a journey to Addis Ababa. Incapacitated, he turned back but was forced to rest at a place called Kullubi when his condition worsened. The young Teferi was summoned from Harar to be at his bedside. His father could not speak because of his illness and Teferi sat the whole day by his side until the end came. Teferi was now an orphan and became a solitary, self-contained figure.

Shortly after his father died the young dejazmach went to Addis Ababa, accompanied by local dignitaries and several thousand soldiers. In the capital, Emperor Menelik was openly distraught as preparations were being made for a commemoration ceremony for Ras Makonnen. Menelik astounded his courtiers by suddenly leaping up from his throne and weeping when he saw a portrait of his dead cousin. By tradition the royal family did not reveal their emotions in public, but on this occasion the Emperor could not contain himself. After the mourning period, Emperor Menelik took Teferi under his wing. He was keen to show his young relative the ropes of power and privilege. Teferi sometimes travelled with Menelik's entourage. He could see for himself the trappings of regal authority as the royal carriage was pulled by eight white horses. Around 500 men led the way on foot, dressed in white tunics armed with rifles and swords. Teferi respected Menelik all his life. He understood and approved his moves to begin uniting Ethiopia by subduing the various warring factions in different parts of the country.

Teferi also attended Menelik School, a special lyceum set up to educate the elite of Ethiopia. Here he had the chance to mix with his clever and ambitious contemporaries, many of whom were to become his allies and rivals. Teferi was deemed too young at 14 to take over the governing of Harar straightaway and was given some administrative responsibilities instead, in Selale to the north of Addis Ababa. Menelik greatly admired the young Teferi. He said his charge had the qualities of a hawk and was sad that he would not live long enough to see him pounce in earnest.

At this time Addis Ababa still functioned largely as a medieval society with cruel and brutal laws to keep everyone in order. People routinely had their feet, ears or hands chopped off for even minor crimes. The biblical injunction of an eye for eye was offered as revenge to relatives of those harmed or killed by unruly city dwellers. A bizarre practice known as leba chai was also rife. This was designed to identify robbers and stolen property. Leba chai literally meant 'following a thief' and involved giving a youth a drink mixed with powerful hallucinogenic drugs. The hapless individual was then tethered to a rope to keep an eye on him as he wandered around aimlessly in a stupor. Wherever he eventually collapsed was considered to be the home of a thief. Many people were wrongly accused because of such a mystical and unscientific approach, open to much manipulation.

The young Teferi immediately took to the life of court intrigue. He loved the detail of arcane policy, the manoeuvring of the various power-seeking factions, and the constant scheming involved in the giving and withdrawing of Imperial patronage – known as shumshir in Amharic. In later life Teferi had this process of musical chairs down to a fine art as he was able to recall a myriad of names and individuals whose fates he personally controlled and moved around to fit in with his grand design. The former Imperial librarian Hans Wilhelm Lockot believed that many people underestimated the Emperor's amazing memory. He said he was able to store away personal information in his brain about thousands of people, including their positions, functions, tribal connections and family relationships. Later in life his ministers were in awe and terror at such displays of intelligence, and, according to the historian Christopher Clapham, often tumbled like mice before the Emperor.

CHAPTER 3

Menelik suffered a debilitating stroke in 1909. The resultant power vacuum ensured that court conspiracies reached fever pitch. Following the death of Ras Makonnen, the old leader now had no immediate male heir but he identified his grandson Lij Iyasu as his successor should he succumb to his health problems. Menelik said that any man who opposed Lij Iyasu would be cursed. The life of anyone who raised his hand against him would end in failure, any sons would be cursed as black dogs, he would suffer a miserable death and nobody would know his grave. The young Teferi kept himself in the mix while the intrigue rumbled on. In 1910 he was appointed to his father's previous position as governor of his home town of Harar, though he had to give a pledge not to challenge Lij Iyasu's growing authority.

Teferi now turned his attention to finding a wife. He became interested in a woman called Menen Asfaw. She was to become one of the rocks of his life, especially in the exile years in Bath. Menen was involved in a failing marriage to a much older man and was the niece of King Mikael, who lived on that strategic hilltop in Dessie. She was therefore the cousin of Lij Iyasu, who encouraged the liaison for political reasons. Many Ethiopians in this era married when they were very young. Divorce was relatively common and easy, so many people were married two or three times. Menen is reported to have had at least two husbands and four children before meeting Teferi. The six children Teferi and Menen brought into the world proved to be one of the great joys of the Emperor's life, though they also brought him tragedy and heartache. Zenebeworq died at the age of 15, three years before Teferi set foot in Bath.

Teferi wrote that after his appointment as governor and his marriage to Menen he lived happily for about a year: 'But thereafter, since in this world joy and sadness always alternate, my joy began progressively to turn into sadness.'

His analysis of the human condition was apposite throughout his life, though in exile in Bath there were to be far more sadnesses than joys.

TAKING THE REINS

Menelik eventually died in 1913 and Lij Iyasu officially took over as leader, sparking off more tension with his rival Teferi. In the uneasy period that followed, Teferi had the first of two close brushes with death. He was involved in a boating accident while out on Haramaya Lake near his home town of Harar. The boat unexpectedly sprang a leak. The passengers frantically tried to scoop out the inrushing water with their hats but it was no use. The boat capsized, tipping all the passengers into the water. Abba Samuel, who had kept a close eye on Teferi as a child in Harar, drowned while trying to save his young charge from perishing. The Abba, which means father, had exhausted himself keeping Teferi's head above water until help arrived. Seven people altogether died in the tragedy. Today Haramaya Lake has largely disappeared due to erosion, population increase and other environmental factors.

IMPERIAL EXILE

The palace coup against Lij Iyasu was staged in 1916. He was seen as lacking the moral fibre to be a serious leader but his enemies may have exaggerated his weaknesses and ignored his achievements. However, it is certainly true he had a violent and cruel temper. Teferi was later to record that the blood of many had been flowing during his rule. Lij Iyasu's opponents also portrayed him as a wastrel and playboy, and condemned him for what they claimed was his abandonment of the Orthodox Church for Islam. The daughter of Menelik, Zewditu, was installed as Empress in Lij Iyasu's place. Teferi emerged as regent and the crown prince, singled out as the future Emperor. He claimed that he did not instigate the plot to depose Lij Iyasu but had supported the decision only at a later stage. Teferi's preferred modus operandi was always to work behind the scenes, manipulating events to his advantage.

Lij Iyasu's attempts to protest against his dismissal were quickly overcome. But his father Mikael mounted a severe challenge to the authority of the new regent. His army of around 100,000 men marched towards Addis but Teferi managed to muster a loyal force of a broadly similar size to meet him. The two forces clashed in a bloody battle at Sagale near Addis Ababa and Mikael was defeated. The crowds in Bath, who were so desperate to catch a glimpse of the Emperor 20 years later, would have had no idea that he had emerged from such a bloodthirsty and precarious background. In effect, Teferi's long reign in power began after his great victory.

In 1918 Teferi had his second close brush with death. In August and September Addis Ababa was subjected to a flu epidemic in which more than 10,000 people died. Teferi succumbed to the infection and fell gravely ill. His condition became so critical that he received the last rites of the Orthodox Church but somehow he managed to pull through. He said later that he had been spared by the greatness of God.

THE GRAND TOUR OF 1924

In the early 1920s Teferi was very busy consolidating his power and influence, though he was still waiting patiently to emerge as the undisputed ruler of Ethiopia. In domestic policy he was able to bring some progressive influence to bear on laws and policy. He ended the barbaric punishments involving the chopping off of limbs and also instituted some reforms to reduce the amount of slavery. On the international scene one major achievement was Ethiopia becoming a member of the League of Nations. This decision signalled Ethiopia's intent to be a modern state and developing the pro-western stance of progressives such as Teferi's father, Ras Makonnen. Britain strongly opposed Ethiopia's membership as it believed the country was not ready. Ironically, Italy was a supporter of the move after overcoming some initial reluctance.

In 1924 Teferi decided to embark on a grand tour of a number of countries, including several important European powers. He took with him a host of advisers and influential politicians. The hope was they could implement back home what they

CHAPTER 3

had discovered about modern methods and technology. One of the main aims of the tour was to push Ethiopia's ambition of gaining access to a port on the Red Sea. The trip forms quite a large section of the first volume of Haile Selassie's autobiography. Out of the total of 312 pages, 44 are devoted to the expedition, which lasted more than four months. The young leader for once was very enthusiastic in his language when describing these events. Clearly it was a journey which left a tremendous lasting impression. The party went first to the Holy Land and saw Nazareth, Cana and Bethlehem. They also saw the Egyptian pyramids and the Sphinx. Then it was on to Paris via Marseille where Teferi said they saw amazing things. In a curious prelude to events a decade later, the royal group visited Rome and were praised to the hilt. The Ethiopian visitors appeared on an upper balcony with the Italian king, Victor Emmanuel, to salute all the people in the crowd in the square beneath. Teferi wrote that all the assembled masses began shouting joyfully with one voice: 'Long live Italy! Long live Ethiopia! Long Live His Highness Crown Prince Teferi!' Even the normally deadpan Teferi cannot resist a note of sarcasm about this spectacle. Writing at a time when Italian invaders were swarming unwelcome across his country, he commented on this previous reception in Rome: 'When they think of this today, how extraordinary must this appear to them.'

Teferi also had an audience with the Italian strongman and his eventual nemesis Mussolini. This was the only time they met, though the encounter obviously made a huge impact on the Regent. Several decades later Haile Selassie gave an interview to the French newspaper *Le Figaro* during which he said he had found Mussolini physically impressive. He spoke of Il Duce's powerful face, his enormous eyes, his projecting jaw, and his voice with its always changing inflections. The Emperor said the Italian leader was theatrical and took advantage of everything. The Pope also granted Teferi an audience in the Vatican, prompting renewed whispers that the Regent was too close to the Catholic Church.

Teferi also waxed lyrical about London. He listed a number of places he especially liked, including the Tower of London, Buckingham Palace, St Paul's Cathedral, St Thomas's Hospital, the High Courts of Justice, Windsor Palace, and the Houses of Parliament. He said they were a perpetual memory engraved in his heart. However, in a foretaste of what he was to find in England a decade later, he discovered that some in English society were ambivalent about the young Regent in their midst. The welcome he received was not as ecstatic as elsewhere in Europe. King George V did not come to meet him at the railway station and the Prince of Wales was not available either as he was attending the Olympic Games in Paris.

Instead Teferi, already eight years into his role as Regent, was met by the Duke of York, the future George VI. It was later revealed that the Regent was not happy by this slight, though of course he did not show it publicly. His state of mind was indicated by his long-time friend and associate Dr Charles Martin, who was later to be the Ethiopian representative in London at the time of the Regent's exile. In his diary, Dr Martin said that Teferi complained about his snub by the British royal family and said it had been a complete contrast to his reception in France and Italy.

The Regent was not completely ignored. He was formally welcomed at Buckingham Palace the next day and was given a separate luncheon a day later with a farewell audience just before he left. However, there was an unseemly row about Teferi being awarded the Grand Cross of the Order of Bath, the highest honour for European royalty and other important individuals. One critic said that this award would be cheapened by being conferred on someone who, after all, was only the heir apparent to the throne of an uncivilised and primitive country. During his trip the Regent was reported to have been dejected by the lack of warmth he encountered from British officials during policy discussions, including those about obtaining a permanent port. The Regent said they had treated him with evasion, superior politeness and official caution.

The English press were fascinated by the African visitor. The *Daily Express* marvelled at Teferi's shiny elastic-sided black boots. The *Guardian* eulogised about the man with an 'extraordinarily handsome face… a fine hawkish nose, and large, gleaming eyes.' The *Times* was also positive, praising what it called his devotion to modernisation. One of its reporters noted how, during his visit to the Tower of London, the Ras-regent had carefully examined the execution block, a headsman's axe, and a model of a woman on the rack. It also scoffed that the rest of the group had been pleased the most by instruments of torture and weapons, 'casting them and their leader in a barbaric and bloodthirsty light.'

The *Observer* drew attention to Teferi's policy of sending young Ethiopians to Europe for special training. Another journalist remarked on the Regent's already apparent gift for 'hastening slowly.' He said his favourite expression was 'time is needed.'

Teferi liked the sincerity, clarity and honesty of transacting business and making purchases in Britain. He was also impressed by the country's sense of duty and its elite schools. In his autobiography the Emperor would again let his guard slip and made an incisive critique about British officialdom as opposed to the British character. He said he greatly admired the goodness of people in terms of their innate character and habit rather than their political motivation. The press also loved Teferi because he gave two lions as a gift to the British King. Altogether he had brought six kings of the jungle on the trip to offer as presents to various European leaders. In return the British King presented the Regent with the crown of Teodros, who had died in a battle with British forces in 1868. After the UK, Teferi visited Greece where he was struck by the antiquity of Athens.

Then it was on to home where Teferi was given a tumultuous reception as he arrived at the train station in the capital. Guns captured at Adwa were fired in salute. Later a huge feast was held in the large palace hall, well lit by electricity, a symbol of the new age. Around 20 modern cars were also ordered to be imported into Ethiopia for use in the government service, and a new road to the town of Jimma was commissioned. The royal delegation had not got very far with its dream of securing a Red Sea port but they had certainly had a lot of fun along the way. The Regent liked what he had seen of modern technology and development in the west, and filed it all away in his calibrating mind for future use.

THE CORONATION

Four years after his tour of Europe, Teferi faced momentous challenges. Empress Zewditu, under pressure from the forces of conservatism, attempted to oust Teferi from power. In support the Commander of the Imperial Guard tried to stage a mutiny but it was stopped in its tracks when Teferi deployed Ethiopia's only tank, a Fiat 3000. He turned the tables so much that the Empress was forced to agree to make him King, or Negus, of Ethiopia, effectively her ceremonial equal. It was an extremely unusual arrangement in the history of power politics in the country. Teferi now was very close to achieving the ultimate prize – ruling on his own as undisputed leader of Ethiopia. Throughout his stay at the court he had had a number of significant military and diplomatic victories in which his customary patience and cunning came to the fore.

When he was crowned King in October 1928 he faced yet another threat. A large army supporting a conservative leader called Balcha Safo arrived on the outskirts of Addis Ababa in a show of support for the Empress. However, Balcha's army deserted after being bribed. They were unwilling to sacrifice themselves for their commander, who was seen as crazy and headstrong. Balcha himself surrendered and was forced to undergo the ritualistic humiliation of publicly carrying a large stone on his shoulders to show his contrition.

Now there was only Empress Zewditu between the Negus and complete control of Ethiopia. Her former husband Ras Gugsa Wole took matters into his own hands and raised an army to threaten Teferi but he was defeated and killed. The decisive intervention this time came not from a tank but from a Potez reconnaissance plane, which had spotted Gugsa's secret manoeuvres. Two days later the Empress slipped into a coma and died. She had been suffering from diabetes and the official version is that she passed away due to natural causes. However, again tongues started wagging and there was a suggestion that she may have been poisoned. Others believed that she had collapsed and died of grief after hearing of the violent death of her former husband.

Whatever the truth, the way was now clear for the Negus to announce to his country and to the world that he was the undisputed sole ruler of Ethiopia. The 225th king in the Solomonic line was ready to take his place on the Ethiopian throne. He promoted himself from King of Ethiopia to King of Kings or Neguse Negest. He also assumed his baptismal name, Haile Selassie, or Power of the Trinity. This strong and forceful name helped to convey the message that he had been anointed by God.

Teferi decided that his accession to Emperor was going to be marked by a huge formal ceremony. He was not that showy or effusive in his daily working life but he did not want to stint on projecting his newly-acquired ceremonial power. He now saw himself as the state incarnate. The coronation ceremony took about seven months to plan. The new Emperor believed that the coronation would also be a tremendous opportunity to carry out some important diplomatic work with developed nations. Important treaties were at stake with other governments and the League of Nations. The Emperor also pointed out that civilised countries also made time for coronations.

As if to prove the point, he bought the state coach of the former German Emperor Wilhelm II for the coronation ceremony. Harnessed to the carriage was an impressive team of Lipizzaner stallions from the Spanish riding school of Vienna. The Imperial vestments, the crown and the orb, the Imperial Sceptre, ring and sword were all specially made out of gold and diamonds. A top-class goldsmith from Regent Street in London was commissioned to produce a number of coronets studded with pearls for the royal princes to wear. All the other rases were provided with golden headgear. The wives of the princes were given golden diadems. Military commanders wore striking headgear made out of lions' manes.

Before the ceremony, Addis Ababa was spruced up with the colours of the Ethiopian flag, green, yellow and red, displayed on many streets. The police were given spanking new uniforms. Strenuous efforts were made to clean up the piles of rubbish, animal mess and smelly drains. But it was something of a losing battle as the ramshackle city was still primarily agricultural and rural. Even in modern day Addis Ababa, with its vast array of impressive and gleaming multi-storied hotels and shopping malls, one can still frequently see herds of sheep, goats and donkeys being driven through the streets.

In the 1930s the capital was derided by many foreign visitors for only having one generator, few street lights, one asphalt road and one decent hotel called the Imperial. As George Steer was to discover, even in the Imperial there was no-one to clean your room, and guests had to bring along their own houseboy. Another journalist, Leonard Mosley, described Addis Ababa as a shanty town with a few wedding cake trimmings. The irreverent British journalist and writer Evelyn Waugh was also on hand to pour scorn on the coronation. Waugh said the place was full of spies, who were busying themselves trying to force everyone to use the Emperor's new name, Haile Selassie. Anyone who still referred to him as Teferi was threatened with a heavy fine. Waugh reported that among the world-weary European residents of Addis various jokes were

CHAPTER 3

doing the rounds. He said the new title of Haile Selassie was corrupted to 'highly salacious' or 'I love a lassie.'

On the eve of the coronation a significant ceremony was held to reveal a dramatic statue to honour Menelik. The representative of Britain, the visiting Duke of Gloucester, took part in a ceremony to unveil the statue showing the doughty Emperor on his horse. The tribute was placed in front of St George's Cathedral where the coronation was to be held. The statue is there today, near a terminus for the new light railway mass transit network. Haile Selassie was clearly showing that he saw relations with Britain as important. Buttering up a possible useful future ally would not go amiss. For his part, the Duke of Gloucester presented the Emperor with a pair of stylish sceptres inscribed in Amharic.

The striking statue of Menelik on his horse

Ironically the cathedral of St George was built by an Italian architect, Sebastiano Castagna. He had stayed on in Ethiopia after being taken prisoner in the battle of Adwa. The ceremony was infused with elaborate religious imagery. The man in charge was the Egyptian Archbishop Abuna Qerillos, the highest official in the Ethiopian Orthodox Church. Alongside him were six bishops, dressed in hooded white capes. The coronation began on the evening of 2 November and contiued right through to shortly after noon on the next day. Empress Menen was fully involved, the first Emperor's wife to have done so. Many of the proceedings took place in a special tent attached to the outside of the cathedral. Haile Selassie was resplendent with his bushy beard, carrying an orb and sceptre. He was dressed in a purple and gold robe, and sitting on a crimson throne. After much chanting, prayers and the singing of psalms, he was anointed with sacred oil.

Crowned as King of Kings

It was then time for the grand finale. The Archbishop placed a crown studded with jewels on Haile Selassie's head. Three Ethiopian planes saluted the new Emperor as he was about to go back inside the cathedral to attend a final ceremony of Mass. Fortunately their Imperial mission passed off without mishap, though they flew alarmingly low. In the previous fortnight, as the young explorer Wilfred Thesiger wryly noted in his diary, the Abyssinian air force had managed to crash two planes.

Finally at 12.30pm it was all over. A visiting British naval band played the newly-composed Ethiopian national anthem and a 101-gun salute was fired. The Emperor passed through the crowds in the church yard and then was taken by carriage for a two-mile journey through the streets to the Imperial palace. In the procession behind him were members of the royal family, envoys and visiting western diplomats. Hundreds of men on horseback and troops dressed in military uniform also joined the march past. There was reportedly no cheering or hand clapping; only ululating. Incredible footage of this procession can still be seen via YouTube.

CHAPTER 3

In the evening a dinner party for more than 100 guests was held in the palace reception hall. The guests were seated around a u-shaped table, and used gold cutlery and ornamental plates. European food formed most of the menu but there was also Ethiopian fare with an assortment of wat or sauce and the staple food injerra. This is a spongy pancake-like substance made from teff grain, which is highly nutritious and naturally gluten-free. In a moment of Waugh-type pathos the guests were treated to an unintended spectacular firework display of showering rockets and roman candles after the inexperienced guards accidentally managed to set off the whole stock at once.

True to form, Haile Selassie did not register any of his personal emotions when he wrote about the coronation. He had never been one for spontaneity but now he adopted an even more impassive public persona. It had been an arduous and twisting road for the young man from Harar to reach the pinnacle of power. But at the age of 38 he had arrived.

Along the way he had gained much experience and knowledge which would stand him in good stead for the tribulations of exile in Bath. He had had a privileged upbringing with a thorough education and had been well-schooled in court diplomacy. His faith had been strengthened by surviving his two near-death experiences and he had acquired a supportive wife, who had borne him six children, greatly enriching his life.

The Grand Tour of 1924 had given him some exposure to modern life and diplomacy, and his coronation had given him legitimacy and confidence in his role. His character had been tried and tested, and he had developed an array of subtle and highly effective psychological tactics against opponents. In the face of great pressure and internal threats to his life, he had shown himself calm and able to deal with a crisis.

On the other hand, he now had a lot to lose and there were many things that he would miss greatly by being away from his country. He faced having everything snatched from him just when his reign was gathering momentum. Being in exile was probably something he would never have contemplated facing. He would have read little that would help him deal with the unknown. The pulverising shock to his system during the year of fighting against the Italians had also destabilised him massively. Now the biggest test of his life so far was going to stretch him to the limit.

CHAPTER THREE EYEWITNESS A VISIT TO THE EMPEROR'S PALACE

The first Imperial palace in Addis Ababa, which means new flower, was created by Emperor Menelik shortly after he founded the capital. It was called the great gebbi or compound, and was built on the top of a bluff near the city centre. Today it serves as the official residence and office of the prime minister. Guards high up in wooden sentry boxes peer out onto the road below from Meskel Square to the parliament building up the hill. As part of forging his own identity, the Emperor founded a series of his own palaces even further up the hill in an area called Siddist Kilo. They were established on a large section of land his father had owned since 1887.

Teferi restored his father's old house and built a new palace called Amsalle Gennet or 'Image of Paradise.' He also built another palace which many years later housed the law library at Addis Ababa University, next to the modern Faculty of Journalism and Communication where I taught for five years. In an ironic twist, this palace in the late 1920s also served as the residence of the Duke of Abruzzi, cousin of King Victor Emmanuel III of Italy. The biggest building project Teferi undertook on his father's land was the construction of the Gennete Leul Palace, meaning 'Paradise of His Highness.' It took 800 workers around eight months to finish. The house is built with stone and was modelled on an English country residence. The Palace was opened for the visit to Ethiopia by the Swedish Crown Prince, Gustav Adolf, in early 1935. There was a banqueting hall on the ground floor, some bedrooms on the second floor and some space for the Emperor's study. The furniture was reported to be decorated with wood-carved royal lions. Outside in the compound, several real lions could be seen. Some were kept in cages, others were allowed to roam or bask lazily in the sun. On one occasion five lions escaped from the compound, mauling several sentries, one of them to death.

CHAPTER 3

The lavish furnishings inside the house were provided by the British firm Waring and Willow. The Emperor did not have long to enjoy his new home and seat of power before the Italians took it from him. Mussolini's troops just marched right in and were billeted there. The beloved pet lions were shot because they were a symbol of royal power. The victorious Italian general Pietor Badoglio made his headquarters elsewhere, at the Italian Legation.

The stone palace building is still standing today as part of the university compound. The house looks down over some attractive gardens with flowers and trees. In the centre is a fountain known affectionately by students as the kissing pool. It is so-called because, in more sedate times, courting student couples would come here to sneak a cheeky kiss or two. Leading off from the kissing pool is a small shaded path where things got a little more serious. This is nicknamed by some students as 'beg tera' or 'sheep market.' The explanation is quite simple. Here, frisky couples would kiss and cuddle under a blanket.

The kissing pool in the grounds of Addis Ababa University

As their bodies lay intertwined, their combined four legs would poke out beneath the blanket, thereby resembling the four legs of a sheep. The former Palace is now home to the Institute of Ethiopian Studies, and a cultural and ethnological museum. One of the first exhibits as you go into the museum contains displays of various fables and stories, involving indigenous animals such as lions, monkeys, baboons and hyenas. Haile Selassie's kingdom was exotic and had little in common with the UK and Bath. The spectacular natural wonders of Ethiopia include its imposing mountains with the highest peak in the Semien Mountains, Ras Dashen, stretching upwards to more than 15,000 feet. Elsewhere there is the natural splendour of the Rift Valley lakes, and mighty rivers such as the Awash in the east, the Omo in the south and the iconic Blue Nile, which has its source in Lake Tana in the north.

The Thames in London and the River Avon in Bath may have their charms. But they are puny in scale compared to these tremendous rivers, which help drain the Ethiopian highlands, known as the water tower of the Horn of Africa. Although Haile Selassie was impressed by the buildings and monuments in Britain, he must have found the landscape a little dull and generally uninspiring, monochrome and insipid. Britain in the 1930s was largely made up of a white population with relatively little diversity of cultures and religions. This would have appeared strange to someone ruling a complex and extensive mix of races and cultures. In the Ethiopian highlands there are peoples such as the Amharas with their impressive and energetic shoulder-shaking dance known as the iskista; the northern Tigrayans, who bob and weave in a more restrained dance going round in circles, and in central areas live the Oromo, whose dances involve many violent leg movements and jumping.

A range of indigenous music instruments accompanies the various dances – the krar which is something like a harp; the one-stringed masinko played with a bow; the washint or flute; and the magnificent deep-toned begana played mainly by men and women of rank. In the lowlands of the south-west there are some completely different ethnic groups: the Mursi, whose women wear huge protruding lip plates; the Hamer, whose teenage boys prove their manhood by jumping over groups of bulls; and the Bodhi tribe, whose men feast for months on blood and milk to bulk themselves up like sumo wrestlers so they can take part in fierce fighting competitions. In the south-east are the desert Somalis, and in Afar in the north-east lies the unstable volcanic region of the Danakil Depression. The area is below sea level, and bubbles and gurgles alarmingly. It was in Afar that archaeologists discovered the tiny skeleton of one of the most ancient early humans or hominids ever found. She was nicknamed Lucy because at the time her discoverers liked listening to a Beatles song, *Lucy in the Sky with Diamonds*. Lucy's Amharic name is Dinkenesh, which means 'You are marvellous.'

Christian belief may have taken root as early as the 1st century AD. Priests at the countless Orthodox churches jealously guard a variety of mystical scrolls, and elaborate, desirable, silver crosses of all shapes and sizes. Although there are many Orthodox Christian believers in Ethiopia, Muslims have formed a significant part of the population since the 7th century AD. Various spirit beliefs also abound too.

The population of Haile Selassie's kingdom was around 15 million. Today it has shot up to around 90 million, the second largest population in Africa after Nigeria. The number of Ethiopians is predicted to reach a staggering 170 million in 2050. It was this diverse and complex land that Haile Selassie ruled from his new Gennete Leul Palace before coming to Bath. There were still some unruly and rebellious

CHAPTER 3

princes throughout the country but slowly the Emperor was already imposing his will on them and centralising control. The intellectual and emotional challenges in keeping such a complicated show on the road were likely to have appealed greatly to the rigorous, analytical mind of the Emperor.

When the Emperor first heard that Italian troops were billeted in his palace, he must have been disgusted to the core. Worse was to follow as Rodolfo Graziani soon replaced Badoglio as the overall Italian commander. He decided to move out the troops from the palace and set up his administrative headquarters there. Graziani's decision was not only a further indignity for the Emperor but it proved to be a fateful move of far-reaching and devastating consequences as we shall see later in Chapter Five as the story of the Emperor's exile unfolds.

IMPERIAL EXILE

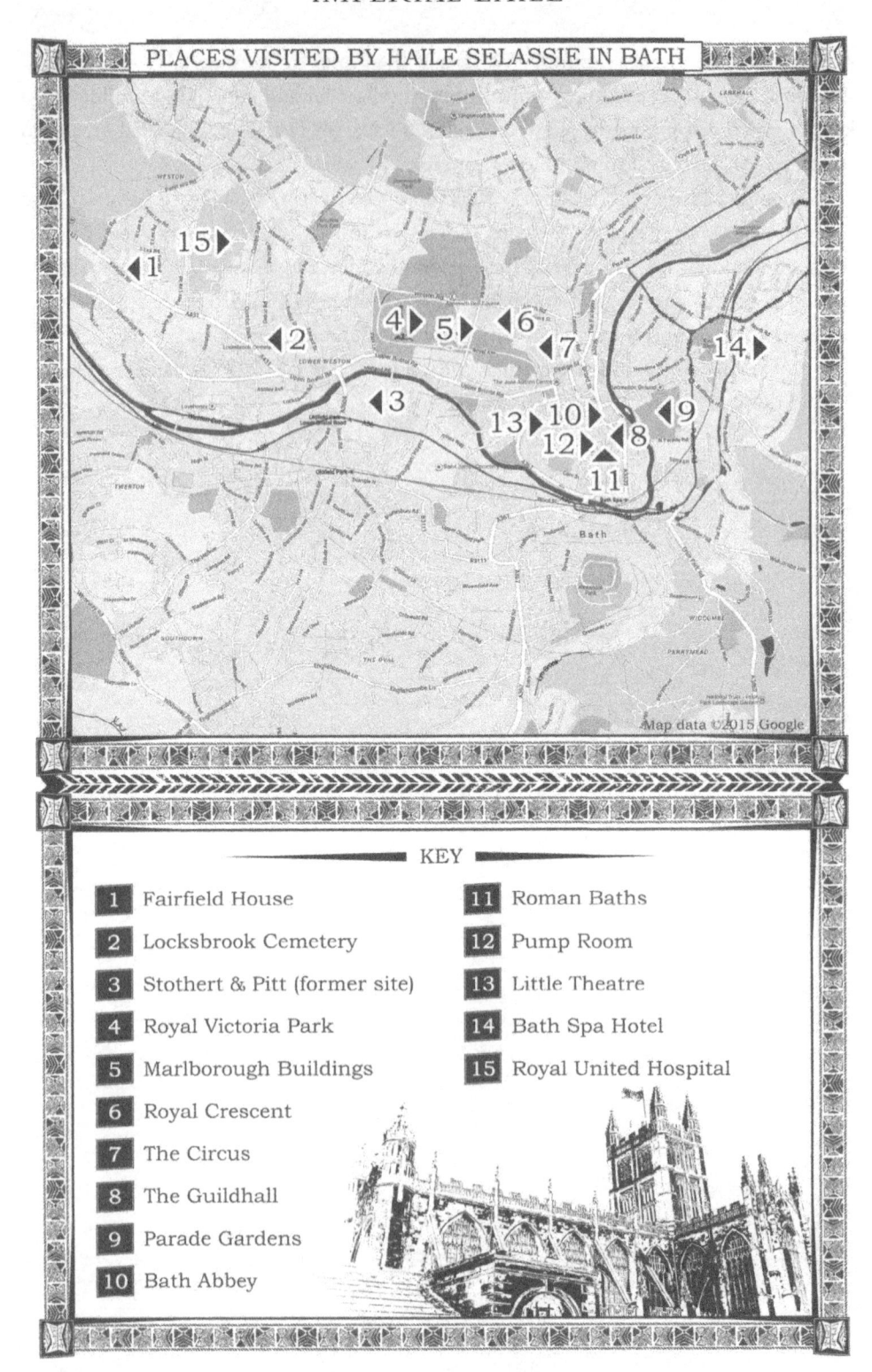

PLACES VISITED BY HAILE SELASSIE IN BATH

KEY

1. Fairfield House
2. Locksbrook Cemetery
3. Stothert & Pitt (former site)
4. Royal Victoria Park
5. Marlborough Buildings
6. Royal Crescent
7. The Circus
8. The Guildhall
9. Parade Gardens
10. Bath Abbey
11. Roman Baths
12. Pump Room
13. Little Theatre
14. Bath Spa Hotel
15. Royal United Hospital

CHAPTER 4

CHAPTER FOUR
TAKING REFUGE

When Haile Selassie and his party left Bath in early September 1936 after their month of recuperation and sightseeing, they made it known they would be back one day. That turned out to come much sooner than the residents of Bath had thought. Within a few days the *Chronicle* was eagerly reporting that Haile Selassie had bought a house in Bath, though that was at first denied by an Ethiopian spokesman. However, it was certainly true that the Emperor was house-hunting in earnest, though everyone was left guessing as to the location.

It was now becoming urgent for the Emperor to put down some roots for the sake of his family and possibly for his own equilibrium and sanity. He had liked what he had seen during his initial courtship with Bath, and now in a sudden move wanted to make the commitment more binding. However, he clearly would still rather have been in his own country. Although he had not been officially banished by the Italians, he could not return as he would face likely death or imprisonment. He had chosen to leave but it was clear now he was fully in exile, effectively barred from his homeland.

Having accepted the reality of his situation, he made the pragmatic choice of settling in Bath, known as the Queen of western England. It seemed to be the best of all the English options. It was far enough away from London to be relatively free from the critical gaze of the British Foreign Office. Bath was still accessible enough to the capital by train if the Emperor needed to engage in some surreptitious politicking or lobbying. Another advantage was that property was cheaper there than in London, an important consideration for the cash-strapped Emperor.

Bath with all its royal connections was a suitable abode for someone of his pedigree and rank. Everywhere you go in Bath you are reminded of its links to the monarchy – the Royal Victoria Park, the Royal Crescent, the Royal United Hospital. If it was good enough for the Imperial Romans and Queen Anne in the early 18th century, then it seemed to be good enough now for the ruler of Ethiopia. He would have been struck by the fact that the coat of arms of the city of Bath featured a lion, as part of a commemoration of the coronation of King Edgar in the 10th century.

Altogether around 500 symbols of lions are present all over Bath, a great encouragement to a ruler who called himself the Lion of Judah. Two bronze kings of the jungle stand guard at the entrance of the Royal Victoria Park in Bath, and lion symbols appear on numerous door knockers around the city. In another shared ceremonial link, both Ethiopia and England have St George, the slayer of dragons, as their patron saint. The memory of his father's respect for the British king Edward VII could also have been a strong influence.

A lion statue standing guard at Royal Victoria Park in Bath

The Emperor may well have heard that two French leaders, Louis XVIII and Napoleon III, also spent some time in Bath when they were exiled from their own country. The two of them came from rival dynasties. Louis XVIII spent 18 years in England when he was forced to escape from France during the reign of Napoleon Bonaparte. For some of the time he resided in some style at the splendid and aristocratic Hartwell House in Buckinghamshire with 100 courtiers. Napoleon III spent time in London while plotting to see if he could reclaim the throne of his uncle, Napoleon Bonaparte. Both Louis XVIII and Napoleon III stayed in houses on the wide, fashionable thoroughfare of Bath's Great Pulteney Street, close to the Bath Spa Hotel.

Napoleon III would often lodge in the Sydney Hotel, now the Holburne Museum, and also lived at number 55 Great Pulteney Street. Louis XVIII stayed at number 72 when he visited Bath in August 1813. He was accompanied by his niece Marie Thérèse,

CHAPTER 4

the daughter of Louis XVI and Marie Antoinette, and they were said to be well-received. If the Emperor knew their stories, he would have been encouraged by the fact that both returned to their countries after their exiles and reigned over their citizens.

Holburne Museum, which was a hotel in the late 18th century

The more modern story of King George II of Greece may also have provided Haile Selassie with some encouragement. The Greek monarch was forced into exile in 1923 and lived for many years in Romania. In 1932 he came to Britain and spent a lot of time living in the exclusive Brown's Hotel in London. Towards the end of 1935, less than a year before Haile Selassie was forced into exile, King George was able to return to Greece and reclaim his throne.

While weighing up his options, Bath to the Ethiopian exile appeared elegant and classy, though not ostentatious like the south of France where Edward VIII and his American consort would soon choose to live during his self-imposed exile. The Emperor had also found the spa waters to be very agreeable, and he appreciated the warm but respectful welcome he had received from Bathonians. One of his embassy staff in London was quoted as saying that the Emperor simply liked Bath and the air in the city. However, the spokesman said there was absolutely no political significance in the Emperor taking a house in the UK.

Because of his French education and language skills, it is perhaps surprising that the Emperor did not seem to have given serious consideration to setting up his base in France. He had enjoyed his trip to Paris in 1924 and would have felt more at home in the culture. However, he had been greatly dismayed by the decision of the French Prime Minister Pierre Laval in early January 1935 to withdraw its traditional protection from Ethiopia. The decision came after a series of negotiations between Mussolini and the French. It removed a major obstacle preventing Il Duce from invading Ethiopia and the Emperor believed he had been betrayed.

A few months later the French government had also shocked the Emperor when the British minister Samuel Hoare came up with a pact with Laval to prevent war by carving up Ethiopia, giving a big share to Italy. Their proposed plan collapsed due to widespread political opposition, especially in Britain. The Emperor completely distrusted Laval but could maybe afford to be a little more sanguine about the British position, which was more ambivalent. Britain also had a huge respect for its monarchy, whereas the French had abandoned theirs long ago.

Choosing to settle in England was more a decision of the head than the heart. Although the British government may not have been completely trustworthy from the Emperor's point of view, England still had a powerful military and diplomatic presence in the world. It also had a number of colonies in north-east Africa, including Kenya and Sudan. England therefore may instinctively have seemed the best bet for helping him regain his throne. Haile Selassie had clearly admired British know-how in his 1924 visit and had been entranced by London as a seat of technological and commercial excellence. He had also made some very influential and useful contacts in the few weeks he had been in Britain in the summer of 1936. Remaining in the UK was clearly a massive decision, involving many complicated and unknowable factors. However, it was a time of extreme crisis and the Emperor needed to make up his mind quickly. He was in uncharted territory and whatever he decided would have involved an element of risk. The die was now cast. Bath it would be.

FAIRFIELD HOUSE

After the cataclysmic events of the previous few months, the King of Kings had now been reduced to the humdrum task of looking for somewhere to live. The word had been put out among those in Bath who dealt discreetly with the buying and selling of properties for dignitaries. Within a few days, the company of Fortt, Hatt & Billings alerted the royal house-hunters to a Victorian mansion, Fairfield House, in Newbridge Hill in the west of Bath. In mid-September the Emperor took the train to Bath again so he could view the property. He immediately decided to buy it and the news was officially released. The *Chronicle* proudly proclaimed in a headline that the allurement of Bath had triumphed.

Fairfield was set in around two acres of land and was a graceful villa, ironically built in an Italianate style sometime in the 1840s. It provided the privacy the Emperor craved, with its high walls and imposing hedges made out of trees and shrubs. Despite its pleasing appearance, the property was not from Bath's finest period of architecture and nowhere near as prestigious and chic as the house the Emperor had stayed at in

CHAPTER 4

Princes Gate in London.

However, Fairfield was in a quiet, respectable area on the Kelston Road and had quite a lot to offer. Some fine reception rooms were situated downstairs and five principal bedrooms were on the first floor. There were also a considerable number of other rooms in the attic and the basement, including a strong room and a wine cellar. A cottage stood separately in the grounds with a garage and there was a sizeable garden. Fairfield had belonged to a widow, Mrs Campbell-White, who had died abroad. She had no obvious connections that could be considered embarrassing to the Ethiopian royal family. Indeed, her husband had once been Lord Mayor of Belfast, a respectable position in the British hierarchy. The deal was reportedly done for the relatively modest amount of £3,500, around £220,000 in today's money. However, given the spiralling inflation in property prices in the UK, that sum would only buy you a modest one bedroom apartment in Bath today.

Fairfield House at the time it was bought by Haile Selassie

Fairfield House was mainly surrounded by fields. One reason why the Emperor may have liked the house is that the view from the front overlooking the Avon valley reminded him of the hills of Harar where he grew up.

Empress Menen had already been alerted to the decision to buy in Bath and soon the *Chronicle* reported she had left Jerusalem. She was sailing to Europe on the French liner Compiègne. With her were the couple's third son Sahle Selassie, their eldest daughter Tenagneworq and a retinue of nine. The Emperor's new residence needed some work to make it fit for an Imperial family. A host of carpenters, plumbers, painters and decorators descended on Fairfield.

Amid all this activity Haile Selassie was involved in some urgent diplomacy as the League of Nations again considered Italy's occupation of Ethiopia. Serious questions were being raised as to whether his country still had the right to be a member of the organisation. Italy was refusing to attend the League's meetings while Ethiopia's membership was still recognised. The Emperor let it be known that, according to his information, two thirds of his country was now under Mussolini's control. One of his spokesmen was also forced to deny a rogue report in circulation suggesting that the Emperor was about to formally abdicate his throne.

The Emperor caused an international sensation when he suddenly decided to fly to Geneva to prevent Ethiopia's delegates from being excluded from the League's business. He and six Ethiopian officials, all wearing bowler hats, took off in a specially chartered plane from London around lunchtime. At this time in Britain headgear was a mark of social status and bowlers were seen as practical and fashionable hats worn by English gentlemen of distinction. The Ethiopians were making a statement as they travelled to Geneva. On this occasion, the deposed Ethiopian leader was not allowed to make a formal speech but he was keen to embarrass the major powers and bring international prominence to the League's latest deliberations, which eventually ended in deadlock.

The Emperor with his wife Empress Menen at Bath Spa Station after her arrival in the UK

The Empress arrived at the port of Folkestone in late September 1936 after having travelled overland through France from Marseille. Rosa the pet dog had to be sent back to France for some time as the correct papers had not been filled in. Soon afterwards the Empress made her first visit to Bath, her unexpected new home. The

CHAPTER 4

Chronicle was on hand to take a picture of her arriving at the station. The express train from London was crowded, and the Empress and her entourage leaned out of the windows as they drew into the station. She was the first to get off. The royal party was driven to the trusty Bath Spa Hotel where they had lunch.

In the afternoon they went to inspect Fairfield. The Empress had not accompanied Haile Selassie on his Grand Tour of 1924 so she was seeing England for the first time, at a moment of great personal stress. It is not recorded publicly what she thought of either Bath or Fairfield House. However, members of her family today say she found it very difficult to live in the UK and that every day was a struggle. She spoke little English and throughout her stay in Bath was not seen in public that much, especially as she was often in poor health. Despite her tribulations, her relatives say today that her support for all the family cannot be overestimated. Without her the Emperor's time in exile would have been even more miserable than it turned out to be.

The *Chronicle* was in an upbeat mood about the Imperial family putting down roots in Bath. The paper reported that the decorative work at Fairfield was nearing completion and thought it would not be long before the Ethiopian contingent could move in. According to the paper, there was every reason for thinking that the Empress would find the air, amenities and surroundings of Bath as agreeable as her husband had done.

After the Fairfield House refurbishment had been completed, the large double drawing room downstairs was a presentable location for the Emperor to receive visitors. The dining room with a pantry was also downstairs, and there was a morning room and a telephone room or small office. Fairfield's telephone number was Bath 7489. Crucially, however, with the English winter on the horizon, the big rambling house was heated by just a few fireplaces.

The number of people living in Fairfield fluctuated after the royal exiles moved in later in the autumn. The Emperor had a large extended family, who were often on the move for educational or political reasons. The best estimate is that over the next few years between 20 and 25 people at any one time stayed at the house and the cottage in the grounds. The community at Fairfield was made up of some of the Emperor's children and grandchildren, some priests, advisers and servants. These included a steward, waiter, cook, chauffeur, a gardener and a butler called Jesus. The various children and grandchildren were looked after by a live-in English governess or nanny. Space was limited and it probably felt claustrophobic for some of the household. Around a dozen of the workers and servants lived in cramped conditions in the cellars.

After the Emperor moved in, he was keen to take possession of some of the family's belongings, which were being transported from Addis under the freedom of customs notice arranged by the sympathetic Eden. They did not have too long to wait. The shipment arrived in London in February 1937, having been given final permission to leave by Mussolini himself. The consignment included some fine rugs, local artefacts and upmarket cutlery, which would grace the dining and drawing rooms. Everything was transported free of charge by the P and O shipping company. Although the downstairs became reasonably elegantly furnished, the upstairs was described as being relatively spartan. At Fairfield there was no elaborate throne, just regular chairs to sit on.

THE NEW ROUTINE

The Emperor moved swiftly to recreate some of the court and palace atmosphere he had been used to in Addis Ababa. The staff were encouraged to look down and pass their ruler silently if they happened to meet him in the corridor. When he was running the country from the Gennete Leul Palace, the Emperor was used to working for between 12 and 16 hours a day. He kept to a similar punishing schedule in exile, despite all the hardships and dislocation he was to endure. The Emperor rose at 5am and worked until lunch. He then rested for two hours and played with his children and grandchildren. He admitted that spending time in conversation with his family was his one and only relaxation.

The Emperor managed to fit in a stroll every day in the grounds of Fairfield and often went into town. Bath residents reported seeing him out with Rosa with perhaps one or two assistants walking a few paces behind him. He was understandably suspicious of the English weather and was often seen carrying an umbrella, rain or shine. He would often walk at the same hour to the post box with letters for other exiles, diplomats and other contacts. One of his regular haunts was in the area of the magnificent Marlborough Buildings, on the edge of the Royal Victoria Park.

Marlborough Buildings today

In the evening the Emperor worked in his study again until dinner at 8pm. The rest of the evening was spent reading and writing. He said he would often continue studying until after midnight. The Emperor revealed later that his reading in the evening was

CHAPTER 4

mainly about ecclesiastical matters, and biographies of leaders such as Lincoln and Napoleon. Both of these leaders had experiences which the Emperor could relate to. Lincoln was the American president who had been prepared to fight a civil war over slavery. The continued presence of slaves in Ethiopia had been constantly criticised by the western powers and was clearly an issue with which the Emperor was wrestling. He had made some progress in abolishing slavery but had been running into resistance from some of his traditional princes.

Napoleon clearly fascinated Haile Selassie. On his Grand Tour of Europe in 1924 he had been to the battlefield of Waterloo where Napoleon was finally defeated in 1815. Like Haile Selassie, the French leader was small in stature and was keen on introducing laws to centralise his authority. He was also a man given to hard work and the Emperor liked the fact that Napoleon had a bee, the symbol of industry and toil, on his coat of arms. In another link between the two men Napoleon also experienced exile, and saw out his days on the windswept and barren island of St Helena in the middle of the Atlantic.

Further insight into Haile Selassie's reading habits is given by Hans Wilhelm Lockot, whose role as head of the Imperial National Library gave him a special insight into the Emperor's love of books. Lockot says that the Emperor particularly admired seven men and their writings. Napoleon was one of them. Another was Frederick the Great of Germany. The Emperor especially liked Frederick's maxim that the king is the first servant of the state. Like Haile Selassie, Frederick loved animals. The Emperor also appreciated the values espoused by the Prussian king, including independent judges, incorruptible civil servants and a disciplined army. Napoleon and Frederick were the top two as far as Haile Selassie was concerned. The other five authors he admired were: the genius of political manipulation Niccolò Machiavelli; the great bishop and theologian Augustine of Hippo; the spiritual visionary Thomas à Kempis; the French revolutionary writer Voltaire and finally, the German playwright and philosopher Johann Wolfgang von Goethe.

That first autumn in Bath gave a reminder of the precarious times the Emperor was living in, even while based in the relative backwater of western England. Against the backdrop of increased tension with Nazi Germany, a local committee for air raid precautions made its first recommendations in November. The plan called for volunteers to become street wardens, though the construction of elaborate bomb shelters was not considered practicable. A few days later came the dramatic news that Edward VIII had abdicated. His subjects across the country were shocked. However, the ascension of the new King George VI greatly cheered the citizens of Bath, who turned out in force on the streets to greet the news. Troops with fixed bayonets were on hand to maintain order just in case. At a boxing tournament in the Pavilion opposite Bath Cricket Club, the *Chronicle* reported that a thousand spectators sang the national anthem with great fervour. The Emperor, sitting in his mansion a few miles away, would have greatly approved of this display of royal sentiment.

CASH FLOW PROBLEMS

An audit of the Emperor's financial position had been carried out in August 1936 while Haile Selassie had been on his original reconnaissance visit to Bath. The investigation had been done by Charles St John Collier, Governor of the Bank of Ethiopia. The amount of cash brought from Ethiopia was reported as half a million French francs and 200,000 Maria Theresa thalers, worth around £17,000. But just how much was this apparently fabulous fortune really worth? Comparing the purchasing powers of sums of money in different eras is complicated and inevitably an inexact science. Nonetheless it is an exercise well worth doing. Various comparison tools exist today and results can vary, depending on which factors are taken into account, including general inflation, consumer prices, wages, manufacturing output and quality of life.

By taking a rough average of results using consumer price inflation, the simplest yardstick, the thalers in the Emperor's hoard were equivalent to around £1 million pounds today. The French francs were worth around 350,000 euros or £250,000 in today's money.

Altogether that meant the Emperor had, very roughly, around £1.2 million at his disposal in the early frenzied days of exile. At first glance it would appear to be a considerable amount of money, but not that much when taking into account that the Emperor had to move a large royal household at short notice. This meant dealing with countless unexpected expenditures in an acute emergency, including extensive travel and accommodation costs and other logistics.

In the Bank of Ethiopia audit it was reported that the Emperor also owned a property in the Swiss town of Vevey and had a trust fund for his children valued at £54,000, more than £3 million in today's money. However, this fund was inaccessible because of the strict rules under which it had been created. Collier said that the available cash should help the Emperor keep his head above water for the time being. But he noted that his style had been unduly extravagant, living in expensive hotels and attended by a variety of hangers-on. It was Collier who had advised the Emperor to buy a house to conserve his cash reserves. Collier also supervised the formation of Fitzmichael Trust Company to take over available assets of the Ethiopian governments, including its share in the National Bank, the Djibouti rail and salt companies.

Even though the Emperor had taken the advice to purchase a property, his outgoings in the autumn of 1936 were still considerable. He had to continue to juggle the various needs of his far-flung family, and many other exiles from Ethiopia were clamouring for financial help. By the end of the year the Emperor was openly struggling with cash flow problems. His hoard had virtually vanished. As a result,

CHAPTER 4

he found himself in the embarrassing predicament of having to sell off some of his assets. On 22 December 4,500 pieces of silverware had to be put up for sale. They were sold in just two hours. The sale raised the precise sum of £2,527, or around £160,000 in today's money. Not a bad haul for 120 minutes work. The *Chronicle* said the Emperor received no special prices as silver was sold by the ounce and, as the paper gravely noted, sentiment counted for little among buyers. One royal cup engraved with a crown realised 12 shillings an ounce and a prize cup embellished with the Lion of Judah was sold at 10 shillings an ounce. The two cups fetched £10 and £18 respectively.

The enterprising *Chronicle* reported a few weeks later that a silver canteen in fine condition had been spotted for sale in the window of a jeweller in Old Bond Street in central London. It noted that each piece was embossed with the crest of the Emperor and was heavily gilded of continental design. There were 12 table spoons, 36 table forks, 36 table knives, 12 cheese knives, 12 dessert spoons, 12 fish knives, 12 pastry spoons and 12 ice spoons.

A massive source of funds was in theory available in the form of the Imperial Crown, safely locked away in the Tower of London. It had been secreted out of Addis Ababa as the Italians approached the capital. The crown was incredibly valuable with its diadem of diamonds, sapphires and rubies. But, desperate as he was, selling the crown was certainly a step too far in the Emperor's thinking. In addition to these silverware sales, the Emperor initiated some very public legal actions to try to retrieve some money he claimed was owed to him. One court case involved suing a merchant in Liège for £14,000, or around £880,000 in today's money. This was the sum that the Emperor said was due to him for sale of coffee grown on his personal plantations in Ethiopia. The sum included a compensation of around £3,000 for losses sustained through the devaluation of the French franc.

One big case involved taking on Cable and Wireless for money that the Emperor believed, as the rightful and lawful Ethiopian head of state, he should have received for telecommunications services. Cable and Wireless were not refusing to pay up. Its view was the money should now instead be paid to whom many saw as the new ruler of Ethiopia, King Victor Emmanuel of Italy. This case was to rumble on for a couple of years, seriously draining the Emperor's tight finances even further because of inflated legal costs.

Another titanic legal battle was waged over the assets of the Bank of Ethiopia, which had been liquidated by the occupying Italians. Substantial holdings of the bank were held by the Bank of Egypt, and the Emperor initiated legal moves to gain access to these funds. The constant legal battling took a heavy toll on his emotional resources. Many years later the Emperor described how the financial pressures on him had led to him leading what he called a meagre existence.

Nonetheless the Emperor still maintained his dignity and was careful about his image. He turned down a proposal by a British company to make a film about his recent experiences with the projected title of *Fly by Night*. He also revealed in his autobiography that he had also rejected a very generous financial inducement to attend the Texas Centennial Exposition in the United States. The Emperor made it crystal clear he was not for sale, despite his fragile finances.

THE AUTOBIOGRAPHY

Early on during his stay in Bath the Emperor took the decision to write his memoirs. In the mornings at Fairfield he would dictate his thoughts in Amharic and notes would be taken by his close advisers. The book covered the period from the Emperor's birth in 1892 to the start of his exile from Ethiopia. Several speeches and other official documents are quoted verbatim. It therefore would appear that some of the Imperial archives had been hastily gathered up in the mad dash to Djibouti.

The question arises as to why the Emperor embarked on this project, a rare enterprise for any monarch, let alone a Solomonic king. Was it simply to while away the time and try to give some purpose to his disjointed life? Perhaps he was desperate to record his achievements, thinking sub-consciously that he would not have any further opportunities to carry out any more initiatives in his country. Did he want to simply put the record straight, or remind himself where he had come from? It is possible the Emperor also wanted to justify some of the more controversial aspects of his reign in suppressing opponents.

As always, he was also keen to express his faith and trust in his creator, even though he was unable to fathom what had happened to him in his year from hell. In the preface he asked why God had made all the Ethiopian people, from the ordinary man to the Emperor, sink in what he called a sea of distress and why God had made the Italian people up to its King swim in a sea of joy. The Emperor then beseeched God to save his nation.

This first part of the autobiography was eventually published many years later in 1973. The original drafts went through considerable revision at the hands of a committee of advisers. In some accompanying notes to the English translation, Professor Edward Ullendorf said the autobiography was bound to be an apologia pro vita sua or defence of his life. He wrote that the Emperor expressed himself with a lofty disdain for specifics, with all the oracular trappings of a papal pronouncement. The book is largely devoid of emotion and is more of a catalogue of the actions and decisions of the Emperor. He always jealously guarded his inner thought processes. Towards the end of the volume, the Emperor talks simply about his admiration for what he called the tenderness and kindness of the British people. He had especially been touched by the rapturous reception he had received at Waterloo Station when he had first arrived. He was to finish dictating the record of his life in a few months.

CHAPTER 4

However, on legal advice it was decided not publish the memoir while the Emperor was in the UK, probably because of the fear of provoking the Italians or upsetting his British hosts.

Haile Selassie's attempt to write about his life and introduce a working pattern he was familiar with was in keeping with the actions of many exiled people. The desire for routine burns very brightly, and writing gives a sense of power and independence. Professor Said, in his essay on exile, noted that it was not surprising that so many exiles were novelists, chess players, political activists and intellectuals.

Another 20th century exiled Emperor to write his autobiography was Kaiser Wilhelm II of Germany. After losing support of the German army he was forced into exile in Holland in 1918. Four years later the Kaiser published the first volume of his memoirs in which he defended his record and denied he had been responsible for the outbreak of the First World War in 1914. He also quickly established a daily routine that he was to stick to for the rest of his life. He was a voracious reader, like Haile Selassie. The deposed German leader also had his share of cash flow problems. He was reduced to selling some of his first wife's pearls when inflation spiralled out of control in Germany in 1923, thereby lessening the value of his savings and holdings.

The Kaiser also bought a fine property but this was much grander than Fairfield. He lived in a manor house, which had originally been a 14th century castle. The country residence in the village of Doorn still had a moat. The Kaiser's day began at 7am with a brisk walk, after which he fed the ducks bobbing around on the moat waters. Unlike his Ethiopian counterpart, the Kaiser never returned to his homeland, even though he long harboured hopes that he would. He spent the next 20 years in aimless irrelevance, chopping down trees and indulging his passion for hunting. Haile Selassie certainly knew some of the Kaiser's story. At his coronation he had purchased the state coach used by the Kaiser when he had been crowned in 1888. The Kaiser died in despair and impotence without seeing the restoration of the monarchy in his country. His fate could easily have been shared by Haile Selassie.

THE BLESSINGS OF CHILDREN

One of the priorities for the Emperor and Empress in their first few months in Bath was to sort out schooling and education for the various children and grandchildren living in Fairfield House. Family was very important for the Emperor. Despite his official stiff formal persona, he obviously loved his children and grandchildren with great affection. They were generally to be a source of joy amid the gloom and sadness. His love for his family also sprang from his desire to be an example to a nation where familial obligations and duties were considered to be very important, and provided the bedrock for Ethiopian society.

An insider's glimpse into the children's world is provided by Ruth Haskins, the assistant nanny at Fairfield shortly after the royal family arrived. I met her in September 2015 when she was 96 years old and living in a residential home about ten miles to the south-west of Bath. Her abiding memory of the Emperor is that he was very kind to her and always tried to involve her in the activities of the family. Ruth was 16 when she started work at Fairfield and has given a number of interviews over the years about her time in the house. She looked after seven children and grandchildren in all, plus a boy priest. She said they all spoke perfect English and were lively and good fun. However, they had to be quickly educated about multiplication tables, British nursery rhymes, and children's stories. The children were allowed to be noisy in their nursery and on occasion in the garden, but had to remain quiet in the rest of the house. According to Ruth Haskins, the downstairs of the house was very grand with chandeliers, gilding and French furniture.

Most of the children who lived at Fairfield. On the left is Prince Sahle Selassie, the Emperor's youngest son. All the others are his grandchildren, the offspring of Princess Tenagneworq and Ras Desta: Hirut, Amaha, Aida, Seble and Iskender

Many years later Ruth Haskins recalled her time at Fairfield in an article in Bath's newspaper the *Chronicle*. She described her embarrassment one day when she saw the Emperor by chance with two attendants following him on Newbridge Hill near Fairfield House. As protocol dictated, she bowed to him. Her gesture was spotted by passengers travelling in a passing bus, who found it amusing and roared with laughter. Ruth carried on her way, her cheeks burning red with embarrassment.

On another occasion Ruth accompanied the royal family when they went

CHAPTER 4

on what was meant to be a private visit to Bristol Zoo. When they arrived they discovered news of their attendance had leaked out and large crowds had gathered to catch a glimpse of the famous local visitors. The royal family was met by the Mayor of Bristol dressed in full regalia with the zoo superintendent in a morning suit. As police struggled to hold back the crowds, the trip had to be abandoned. Ruth declared ruefully that the locals had come not to look at the animals but at them. There were similar scenes when the children in the Fairfield household were taken to the swings in the Royal Victoria Park in Bath, just down the road from Fairfield. But such a large crowd swarmed around them that they had to abandon that outing as well.

The young governess also described how she was meant to be paid 15 shillings or the equivalent of 75p a week. In the event she says she never received any wages, despite frequent reminders. Her mother gave her the money for the bus. Ruth eventually left after a few months as her mother felt she had been working too hard and had no social life. Ruth promised not to release any details of her work at Fairfield House and did not talk publicly about her experiences until after the Emperor had died.

Ruth Haskins tells a moving story in an interview for an HTV television documentary in 1999. On one occasion she saw the Emperor start crying as the household was listening to a gramophone record, which had noises of shouting and gunfire during a battle. She said that tears rolled down his cheeks and dripped onto the back of his hands, stretched out on his knees while sitting down. The injuries caused by poison gas attacks had not yet cleared up and Ruth Haskins said the sight of Haile Selassie's tears dropping onto his pock-marked hands was very sad and something she would never forget. Years later, the Emperor would occasionally tell some of his family about the distressing effects of the gas, which also caused vomiting and diarrhoea.

Doris Benson, who was close to the Imperial family, told the BBC in a radio documentary in 1987 that she often saw the Emperor pacing up and down alone in the garden, looking sad and abstracted. She said it was not difficult to imagine what his thoughts were and that he was always fretting for news from Ethiopia.

Hilary King was friendly with the grandchildren at Fairfield and would often go to play with them there, even introducing them to pillow fights. She told the HTV documentary-makers that going there was not like turning up at a normal residence. Instead of being greeted by the family of the house, a servant would appear when they knocked on the door. Without saying a word, he would gesture them to move to the correct section of the house. In an interview for the BBC radio documentary Hilary also recalled once taking lunch with the Emperor and his family. She had been warned to only speak to him if he communicated with her first. Because he was usually a man of few words, the lunch mainly passed by in excruciating silence. The only sound Hilary can remember is the embarrassing screeching of her knife when trying to cut her vegetables on her gold plate.

Visitors to Fairfield must also have been intrigued by the Ethiopian calendar and different ways of keeping time. To this day Ethiopia uses a calendar based on the Julian system and not the Gregorian calendar used in the west. It is yet another indication of Ethiopia's otherness, unique culture and identity. One trader in Bath was left baffled when one of the Emperor's staff asked for an order to be completed in several moons time. There are 13 months in an Ethiopian calendar year, not 12. Christmas in Ethiopia falls two weeks after yuletide in the western world. New Year is not celebrated on January 1 but around the end of the rainy season on September 11, a date now overshadowed internationally by the terrible terrorist atrocities in America. As for timekeeping, the start of a new 24 hour period is not midnight but 6am. Dawn starts around this time all the year round as Ethiopia is not that far north of the equator. In the Ethiopian method of timekeeping, 7am is therefore one o'clock in the morning, six hours behind the western system. 10am in the west is 4am in Ethiopia and so on.

Several of the children and grandchildren did not live at Fairfield the whole time as they attended boarding school. The *Chronicle* published two touching accounts of how the Emperor took care of his granddaughter Princess Aida Desta when she first went to school. He travelled with her to St Claire's School all the way down to Penzance, at the south-west tip of England. Princess Aida was just ten and was the eldest daughter of Princess Tenagneworq. The paper wrote:

> 'The little Princess presented a pathetic figure as she gravely bowed to her grandfather when taking leave of him and the emperor kissed her on both cheeks. The Negus was attired in his familiar blue cloak and bowler hat. The girls of the school cheered lustily and then surrounded the forlorn little princess, who already appears to have captured all hearts.'

Ethiopian flags were hoisted all over the school and thousands watched the royal party arrive. The modern school building and grounds today look very similar to those of Fairfield House.

The *Chronicle* was again on the case when the Emperor went to pick Princess Aida up at the end of term in July 1937. Haile Selassie's car, which had a silver crown on the bonnet, was involved in an accident in Exeter High Street on the way to Penzance. The front wing of the car, which was being driven by his Ethiopian driver, clipped the back wing of a vehicle parked outside a church. Shoppers quickly

CHAPTER 4

recognised Haile Selassie, who was in a passenger seat with one of his sons, and surrounded the vehicle. The police took some particulars and the car drove away to spontaneous cheering, which the Emperor smilingly acknowledged.

The royal traveller then broke his journey at Okehampton in Devon where he had a vegetarian lunch at the White Hart Hotel. There was more cheering when he arrived at St Claire's School in Penzance. The Emperor planted a tree to mark the coronation of the new king of England and was a guest at the annual school speech day. The *Chronicle* reported that the Princess came running when he arrived. After a formal bow to her grandfather, he took her in his arms and greeted her affectionately. The Dean of Exeter said the Emperor had been able to maintain a shield of personal and Imperial honour, battered but unstained.

The Princess certainly made an impression in the area. Following her death in 2013 the *Western Morning News* ran a feature article about her time in Penzance. It prompted a widespread response with many local people sharing their memories, including a couple of readers who said the Princess had no side, and no airs and graces. This enthusiastic response by readers is typical whenever nostalgic articles about the Ethiopian exiles are published today by local newspapers in the UK.

The Emperor also spent some time at the Abbey Hotel in Great Malvern where Princess Aida's sisters, Princesses Hirut and Seble, were later to go to school. He would become a frequent visitor too to King's College in Taunton, which was attended by his youngest son Prince Sahle Selassie, and his grandson Amaha Desta. Amaha would later show his athletic prowess by running the 100 yards in 16 seconds, a school record in under-ten races.

Family life in Fairfield settled into its formality and routines, though even the serious-minded Emperor could relax on occasion. He sometimes joined in the games of tennis and ping-pong at which he was said to excel. It begs the question as to how he approached a game of table-tennis. Did he always play competitively or just for relaxation? Did he always seek to win or did he allow his family to beat him sometimes? If he lost, how did he deal with defeat? Did he go on the offensive with bold attacking strokes or try to grind down his opponent in a war of attrition by merely returning the ball without taking any risk? Playing against an Emperor must also involve some tricky rules of etiquette. Do you always let him win and always compliment him on his shots, be they good, bad or indifferent?

Strange as it may seem, the Emperor never lost his love of games. In his mid-seventies he once surprised everyone around him when he challenged his cousin and childhood companion Ras Imru to an impromptu game of billiards. The gauntlet was thrown down during a visit to the governor's palace in Asmara, the capital of Eritrea. The ping-pong guru of Fairfield House took off his formal jacket and removed a billiard cue from its bracket with a flourish. The group of onlookers watched in amazement as the shirt-sleeved Ethiopian ruler moved lithely around the table, smiling and clearly enjoying himself. Ras Kassa's grandson Asfa-Wossen Asserate was one of those dumbfounded by the spectacle. Looking back now, he says this is the only time he ever saw the Emperor drop his guard and behave as a normal human being.

Makonnen, the Duke of Harar, the Emperor's second oldest son, became something of a celebrity in the Bath area. He appeared in a photograph in the *Chronicle* in November 1936, posing happily with fellow pupils at the local St Christopher's School. During his teenage years Makonnen shone at sports and broke the record for the quarter mile sprint. He always loved sports and continued to excel when he left St Christopher's for Wellington College in Berkshire at the end of 1938.

The Duke of Harar showing off his athletic prowess at school in Bath

The Duke also got himself into the paper when he was photographed sitting in a new Morris car which had been delivered to the royal household in Fairfield. Although too young to take the car on the roads, he was given lessons on how to drive it by John Gait from Bath Garages.

CHAPTER 4

Seated in style. The Duke of Harar clearly enjoying himself. John Gait is next to him

The Duke was to throw himself into local life and later toured local pubs on a motorbike with a friend, who said he smoked like a chimney. He would even hide a bottle of whisky in his room at school. The Duke liked to dress well and often sported a Harris Tweed jacket, flannel trousers, and a sports shirt. He especially loved wearing a cravat, and, like many teenagers, knew how to have a good time. On one occasion Makonnen went to watch a film at the Beau Nash Theatre in Bath. According to a school friend, he was so taken with one of the usherettes that she was soon sitting on his knee.

Life at Fairfield therefore was perhaps not that disagreeable for younger members of the Imperial family. Makonnen and his elder brother Crown Prince Asfa-Wossen also enjoyed listening to gramophone records. Their favourite disc was *There's a Small Hotel*, a popular American jazz song composed in 1936 by Richard Rodgers with lyrics by Lorenz Hart. The song was based on a couple's trip to a hotel either in New Jersey or California. It was part of a Broadway musical and was later recorded by Frank Sinatra in a Hollywood film. Away from his musical interests, the Crown Prince spent some time in Bristol and attended Liverpool University where he was visited on a number of occasions by his father. Young Iskender, one of the Emperor's grandsons, also contributed a sense of fun and mischief to the Fairfield household. He had a pet budgie, which was taught to sing *God Save the King*. The bird would often pipe up with the anthem at 6am, driving some of the staff to distraction.

Throughout his stay in the UK Haile Selassie remained a figure of fascination and even became part of the cultural scene. He was a popular choice for people taking part in the numerous fancy dress competitions up and down the land. His stylish capes were admired and even talked about in women's fashion pages. Everywhere he went people asked the Emperor for autographs. He usually obliged, signing his name in Amharic script. The Emperor was also in constant demand to speak at various functions, and open church fêtes and bazaars. He wrote a lot of letters, received many social invitations from influential people, attended fund-raising events, and granted a host of newspaper interviews.

The social whirl. At an unspecified function in Bath

The issue of Italy's occupation of Ethiopia was debated frequently at public meetings, and in newspaper opinion columns and correspondence pages. The Emperor was a celebrity and was undoubtedly one of Britain's most famous exiles. He moved relatively freely around the country and needed to rely only on low-level security from the British police. During his exile the Emperor stayed at a number of upmarket hotels and stately homes belonging to the landed gentry. Even today Haile's Selassie picture or a special plaque commemorating his visits still adorn the walls of a number of hotel lobbies, especially in the west and south-west. On several occasions the Emperor made contacts among some of Britain's literary and artistic community. He was to admire many aspects of British culture throughout his life.

CHAPTER 4

In the early part of his stay in the UK Haile Selassie also attracted the attention of two renowned sculptors who fashioned eye-catching busts of the Imperial exile. One of them was Jacob Epstein, who described the Emperor as having noble handsome features, lit by melancholy. His bold bust in bronze attracted rave reviews. The other sculptor was from Yugoslavia, Sava Botzaris, who also produced a striking and much-admired sculpted head of the Emperor. Botzaris said the Ethiopian leader had a holy face. The head was described as being of heroic proportions, three times the actual size.

The Emperor on one of his early visits around Bath

AT HOME

Although some awkward problems were already surfacing, the first few months in Fairfield House had seen the royal family create some much-needed stability for themselves. However, there was no room for complacency. The Emperor was constantly concerned about how his forces were holding up against Italy's move to consolidate its powers. He would have heard that Balcha, the man who had been forced to carry a stone in contrition across Addis Ababa after rebelling against the Emperor a few years previously, had died at the age of 80 in a machine gun battle with Italian troops. In a terrible incident elsewhere two of the sons of his close confidant Ras Kassa had been murdered after they had been tricked into surrendering at the town of Fiche north of Addis Ababa. They had been promised in a deal with the local Italian commander that they would not be harmed but this turned out merely to be a ruse. Instead they were quickly executed. Another of the Ras's sons was tied to a tree and shot after being discovered hiding in a cave.

Ras Kassa was a man of great faith but even he must have struggled to comprehend and absorb this news. Only one of his four sons was now alive – Asserate, who was based with him at Fairfield and went on to study at Monkton Combe, a nearby prestigious school. One wonders what the Emperor could say to Ras Kassa about his bereavements as they went for their routine walks in the garden of Fairfield House.

In mid-December 1936 Haile Selassie also received some bad news about his trusted childhood friend and commander Ras Imru, who had been left in charge of the remnants of the official Ethiopian forces. The Ras had been forced to move from his new base in Gore under pressure from Italian troops. Ras Imru's forces were chased to the south-east where he had surrendered. He was sent into exile in Italy where he was imprisoned until he was released by allied forces in the autumn of 1943. Hearing of Ras Imru's surrender was a sobering moment for the Emperor. It would have reopened the sensitive question of whether it was right to have fled to Djibouti. He is likely to have pondered deeply whether he would have fared any better if he had stayed in his country.

The Emperor in unfamiliar surroundings in Bath

One small diary item in the *Yorkshire Evening Post* revealed how touchingly pathetic the Emperor's predicament had become. The paper reported that *National Geographic* magazines had continued to be sent on subscription to the royal palace in Addis Ababa. However, in December copies began to trickle back to the UK with the stark

CHAPTER 4

message written in English on the envelope: 'Gone Away.' It was a rare example of fascist understatement.

The *Chronicle* was in optimistic mood around Christmas of 1936, the first the Emperor was to spend in Britain. The paper said it was the happiest festive season for years. There was no snow and wages were on the up. But there was no escaping the worrying backdrop of instability in Europe. The Pope gave a Christmas message in which he spoke about his fears for humanity and warnings of a new terrifying reality in Europe. The Ethiopian royal exiles did not celebrate Christmas on 25 December but two weeks later, according to the custom of the Ethiopian Orthodox Church.

January appeared to be a more positive month for the Emperor and his family. On the 14th of the month a notice appeared in the local press that a special At Home event was going to be held at Fortts in Milsom Street to be hosted by the royal couple. Tickets cost two shillings and six pence with afternoon tea provided. It was billed as a chance for the people of Bath to show some sympathy for the Ethiopian cause.

The royal couple pictured in Bath, probably in the grounds of Fairfield House

By now the Emperor was badly missing the support and trappings of the Orthodox Church. In early 1937 it was reported that he had decided to build a chapel in the Fairfield grounds. Many years later the Emperor revealed the full story about his dream of building his own church. He said the royal group was distressed that they could not utter their pleas to God in a properly constituted chapel. The Emperor sent a letter to an Ethiopian priest based in Jerusalem, saying they required a consecrated stone so they could create a place of worship and that it was necessary to listen quietly until he knew his creator's decisions. The stone arrived just before Good Friday and was sanctified on Easter Sunday. It was laid in the greenhouse in the grounds of Fairfield House. The glass windows of the greenhouse were whitewashed to maintain some privacy. The chapel was to be a source of great solace and inspiration for the Emperor. On Maundy Thursday he would wash the feet of his servants in the chapel, following the example of Jesus Christ. A sprig of rosemary would be added to the water.

The At Home event was duly held in central Bath on 22 January and the *Chronicle* published a photograph with the royal couple receiving people in line. Everyone passed by in single file with dignified bows. Two hundred people paid their two and six for afternoon tea. The event sent out a strong political message, even though on the surface it appeared quite low-key and insignificant. The *Chronicle* was in great form, headlining its report: 'Negus: I want justice.' The Emperor spoke of a most hideous crime which had been committed, but said everyone was hurrying to shake hands with the criminal Mussolini. The paper weighed in itself, suggesting that the banqueting room where the event was held had turned into a palace and the court of the Negus. It said the occasion reminded them of Belshazzar's Feast, a reference to events described in the Old Testament Book of Daniel when King Belshazzar encouraged his followers to drink wine from cups and vessels stolen from the Temple in Jerusalem. During the feast the revellers praised the gods of gold, silver, brass, iron, wood and stone. After such blasphemy Belshazzar was shocked to see a mysterious message written by a chilling unknown hand on the wall. The *Chronicle* speculated what should be inscribed on a modern-day wall about the war between Italy and Ethiopia. It suggested it should be 'put not your trust in princes or in any child of man.' The paper pointed out that it had had only been six years since the chief magistrate of Bath and fellow citizens had gone to Rome as friends of Italy.

The Emperor spoke from a dais with Ethiopian colours draped behind it. He said he had made friends wherever he had gone in Bath and was thankful for the welcome and the privacy he had been shown. A string quartet then played the Ethiopian national anthem, which moved the Empress to tears. Mayor Long said that the city could now claim the couple as citizens of Bath. He condemned the Italian aggression and the League of Nations. He also pledged aid to Ethiopian refugees in Sudan and Kenya. Amid all the solemn speechmaking, there was the opportunity to talk about the favourite topic of conversation in Britain – the weather. The Mayor felt sure that the Emperor had come to Bath because of its beauty and salubrious climate. The

CHAPTER 4

Emperor had a different view, saying he had been only expecting one enemy, the English climate. However, he was grateful that so far the winter had been mild and the enemy had not put in an appearance yet.

The next day things began to change as the River Avon rose seven feet above normal due to heavy rains. Within a couple of weeks snow was reported and sledging was in full swing at Charlcombe on the edge of the city. The winter was only going to deteriorate, putting a lot of pressure on the royal exiles in the largely unheated Fairfield House. Worse news though was to come from Ethiopia itself as the calendar ticked over into February 1937.

CHAPTER FOUR EYEWITNESS TALES OF A PRINCESS

The comfortable and prosperous residential area of Annandale in Virginia, just across the Potomac River from Washington DC, would appear to be an unlikely venue to discuss what happened in the inner sanctum of Fairfield House in the 1930s. However, it was in the late fall of 2014 that I found myself there on the trail of one of the few people still alive who had been in the house at that time. I was coming to see Princess Seble Desta, the third daughter of Princess Tenagneworq and Ras Desta. I had been given her contact details by her younger sister Princess Sophia, whom I had met earlier in another unlikely setting – the Pret à Manger cafe next to Marks and Spencer in Kensington in west London. Sophia herself had been too young to live at Fairfield and spent a lot of the time as a very young child living in Jerusalem.

The Virginia weather had turned cold and windy as I arrived at the landmark of a distinctive white-panelled chapel. I then made my way amid the falling orange and russet leaves to a nearby large house in a cul-de-sac where Princess Seble was staying with one of her daughters. The residence was comfortable and well-appointed, a world away from the higgledy-piggledy old stone villa at Fairfield.

The Princess had a unique child's view of the events of her grandfather's exile. She was part of the hasty escape from Addis Ababa to Djibouti and also can remember going down into the cellars at Fairfield during air raid warnings in the early part of World War Two. I ended up having two meetings in America with the redoubtable Princess. She was polite and friendly but also sprightly and sharp. After all these years she was understandably still anxious to protect the memory of her grandfather. Most of the time she referred to him as His Highness but occasionally would mention him as grandfather. She also revealed that she affectionately sometimes called him grandpa when they were in the enclosed and cloistered setting of Fairfield. Her comments reveal something of the private man behind the usually impenetrable mask of his regal persona.

CHAPTER 4

The Princess had recently been facing tough times as two of her sisters had died in the previous couple of years or so. One of them was her eldest sister Princess Aida, who had made that sentimental journey to St Claire's school in Penzance with her grandfather. In the few months prior to our meetings the death had occurred of her second eldest sister, Princess Hirut or Ruth in English. The two princesses had played hide and seek together in the nooks and crannies of Fairfield. Princess Seble can still remember vividly the dramatic evacuation from Addis Ababa. She was only around five years old at the time but such a disturbing experience is not easily forgotten. The young members of the family were told to pack quickly some small items. Princess Seble wanted to take all her favourite dolls and can remember asking repeatedly where they were going and why. It was only when she was told firmly that she was allowed to take just one doll that she realised something serious was going on and that they were all in danger.

The Princess did not go to live in Fairfield immediately and was left behind in Jerusalem when her grandmother Empress Menen first departed for Bath. She can still recall the narrow streets of Jerusalem and had her first exposure to the English character as she attended an English-speaking school. At home the Princess mainly spoke in Arabic, not English, and forgot a lot of her Amharic. Once in Fairfield, the Princess was encouraged by her grandfather to use English and Amharic, though he too could speak Arabic. The Princess found England impressive and can remember travelling on the train to Bath from London. At first it was hard to adapt to life in Bath and she found everything overwhelming. However, her grandfather told her to make the most of the experience, as they had been lucky to have got out of Ethiopia. He said that she and her sister Hirut should concentrate on their learning and education. The Princess says that, at least in front of her, the Emperor never wavered from believing that one day God would enable him to return home. He also thought that the British would help too. After all, it still was a major player then on the world stage with a large, albeit crumbling, empire.

The nursery room at Fairfield was upstairs towards the back of the house. It was out of the way, near the back stairs. The Princess says her grandfather did not come up to their room but he kept a strict eye on them nonetheless. He usually saw them once a day when he was not travelling, and would call them down to have some special talks. He would ask them what they had been doing, constructive or not, though it was clear to the Princess that his mind was focusing on many things. She says the Empress would provide a lot of support for him and all the children knew how to keep out of the way when things became particularly bad. On hearing some gloomy news from Ethiopia, the Emperor would pronounce gravely: 'God will send off these Italians.'

The Princess can recall being cold during the winters and hiding in her room. All the children were happy to hear the sound of coal being delivered. She realised that money was tight and often felt sorry for both her grandparents, who would try to shield them from the worst. However, her grandfather would give his grandchildren some regular pocket money and encourage them to keep within their spending limits. It was difficult for the royal exiles to pursue a diet they would have been used to at home. Injerra, the flat-bread spongy Ethiopian staple, was very hard to come by as were local spices such as berbere. However, Indian spices, including turmeric, were available and there were two Ethiopian cooks who tried to make life as normal as possible. Some English dishes also became part of the daily fare. Some of his grandchildren alive today can remember how dishes such as shepherd's pie were added to their array of meals while growing up in Ethiopia.

The Princess says her grandfather often talked wistfully about how much he missed riding his horses back in Ethiopia. He did occasionally go for a brief trot round the garden at Fairfield on a grey horse called Poppy, which belonged to a local tradesman. Dogs remained an important part of his life. While in Bath another dog in addition to Rosa became part of the Fairfield family. Even after Princess Seble was a fully-grown adult, the Emperor would often ask whether she had got herself a pet dog yet. The Princess believes her grandfather obtained his love of animals from his father.

Princess Seble (back row, second from the left) in Bath with some of her family and friends in the early 1940s. Kenah McConnell who provided this photograph is on the far left of the front row. Her mother taught the royal children to do cartwheels. The picture was taken at the house of Dr Marsh, a great friend of the family (centre)

Princess Seble can also remember the improvised church in the greenhouse. She referred to it as the Sedetennyaw Medhanialem, or the Saviour of Exiles. Clearly

CHAPTER 4

this was an important focus of community life in Fairfield. The services would be lengthy and on occasion the children were given permission to leave the greenhouse and play in the nearby conservatory. The Emperor would often say that whoever had recommended Bath to him had done him a favour and was a true friend. Bath was such a dignified place.

Surprisingly the Princess says that, although the Emperor could not afford to be seen openly laughing out loud in public, he did have a terrific sense of humour. She recalls one event when a diplomat attended a function at Fairfield and got a little carried away in some over-energetic dancing. Princess Seble's mother and aunt were laughing a lot. It was clear that the Emperor too had found the impromptu performance very amusing but kept his emotions to himself behind his best sphinx-like exterior.

CHAPTER FIVE
MURDER MOST FOUL

With the successful At Home reception under his belt, the Emperor may have justifiably been thinking that he had bought himself a little bit of breathing space. As 1937 got into its stride, it was now clear that he had been accepted into Bath society. Settling down at Fairfield was beginning to bring some stability for his family, despite the annoying financial problems. He had been frantically clinging on but had survived. And there were some small signs that life might be improving. However, the Emperor had always warned that sadness was usually mixed with joy. How right he was.

What the Emperor had no control over was the situation on the ground in his home country. By the end of January reports were circulating of Italians going uninvited into the houses of Ethiopian women, and abusing mothers and daughters. Italian doctors were also said to be conducting forcible internal examinations of Ethiopian women to check for any diseases. It was a move designed not to protect the women but the Italian men who were raping them. The Italian occupiers were also robbing Ethiopians of all the good houses. The local population were forbidden to walk on the same roads as Italians or eat in the same restaurants.

Towards the end of February 1937 the Emperor received two hammer blows from Ethiopia. First came the dreadful news of the massacre of thousands of Ethiopian civilians in Addis Ababa as a reprisal for the attempted assassination of the Italian Viceroy, Rodolfo Graziani. Just a few days later the Emperor heard that his son-in-law Ras Desta, one of his leading generals in the south, had been captured by the Italians and shot out of hand.

This litany of tragic news drove Haile Selassie into one of the darkest periods of his exile. His grief and sadness were heightened by a sense of impotence and exclusion. He had been receiving depressing reports for a while that his forces had

CHAPTER 5

been under pressure and were on the run. But there had been nothing like this so far while he had been in Bath.

THE MASSACRES OF ADDIS ABABA

On 19 February 1937 Graziani was holding a celebration to mark the birth date of the Prince of Naples. In the Ethiopian calendar this date is known as Yekatit 12, which still lives on in infamy. The ceremony was taking place at Haile Selassie's former palace, the Gennete Leul, which Graziani had requisitioned after taking over the leadership of all the Italian forces in Ethiopia. He had removed the troops stationed there by his predecessor Badoglio, and turned the compound into the nerve-centre of the Italian administration. Haile Selassie's palace had now become the Governo Generale.

The former Gennete Leul Palace, now the headquarters of the Institute of Ethiopian Studies

Graziani travelled to work in his office at the palace every day by mule from his house on the slopes of Entoto Mountain. Before becoming Viceroy of Italian East Africa and Governor-General of Addis Ababa and Shoa, Graziani had been commander of the Italian forces on the southern front in Ethiopia. As Viceroy, he was merciless and prickly. At the ceremony in February up to 3,000 Ethiopian beggars, disabled people, and destitute mothers gathered in the large space in front of the palace steps to receive alms from Graziani. Some Ethiopian clergy and young Ethiopian nobles were also in the crowd. Around midday the Viceroy was patiently waiting on the palace steps to distribute a pile of Maria Theresa thalers on a nearby table. Unknown to him, two Eritreans hidden in the crowd were starting to make their move, setting off an unimaginable and horrific chain of events.

The two plotters were Moges Asgadom and Abraha Deboch, both employed as translators by the ruling Italian civil administration. They were the enemy within. Like many other Ethiopians, their resentment against the occupying armies had been growing for some time. The author Ian Campbell has published a book suggesting there were at least four others directly implicated in the conspiracy. The plotters had been in the country in early May 1936 when the Italians shot many people accused of looting in Addis Ababa. They had endured the disappointment of late July when several groups of patriots tried unsuccessfully to recapture the city. They had witnessed the Italians removing the famous statute of Emperor Menelik from outside St George's Cathedral and the large crown from the top of Menelik's mausoleum. They had had to put up with the blatant racism shown to their fellow countrymen, including the despised order for audiences at local cinemas to be segregated. Their anger had reached boiling point and they could bear it no longer.

On that fateful morning of 19 February 1937 Abraha had already made his intentions perfectly clear. Before leaving home he had used a bayonet to pin an Italian flag to the ground at his residence just down the hill from the palace. He had also tied an Ethiopian flag to the handle of the bayonet, and on his door had put a note in Italian saying no entry to visitors. The assassination plan was simple. First, to kill Graziani by blowing him to bits in a grenade attack. The attackers then hoped that in the resulting chaos and confusion hundreds of Ethiopians would spontaneously rise up and overpower their Italian tormentors.

The Italian garrison had received a number of tip-offs that some sort of violent incident was going to be staged by rebel Ethiopians. As a result, the palace area was heavily-guarded with armed men at various strategic points, looking out for trouble. Many machine guns were trained on the crowd. Graziani's suspicions that something was afoot had been raised by a message from the Archbishop, Abuna Qerillos. He indicated that he could not attend the alms ceremony because he had fallen sick. The Viceroy was sceptical and sent a doctor to inspect the Archbishop. He was given the all-clear and the Italians became increasingly suspicious that the Archbishop had wanted to stay away because he had got wind of some sort of rebel strike. Waving away his reservations, Italian guards escorted the Archbishop to the ceremony. Graziani had been waiting for him before launching into what turned out to be a bombastic speech. Using a powerful microphone, he harangued the crowd, urging them to believe in and accept Italian rule.

With hearts pumping, the two Eritreans advanced through the crowd and managed to get near to the balcony above the dais where Graziani was standing. Shortly after the Viceroy began to distribute the alms money, the attackers threw up to ten Breda grenades, which had been earlier smuggled into the country. Shrapnel

CHAPTER 5

from the explosions wounded Graziani but he survived as he escaped a direct hit. The mission had failed. Nevertheless it still had dreadful consequences. A number of Italian troops in the vicinity were killed or injured. The head of the Italian air force lost one of his eyes and one of his legs. The Archbishop was also badly injured in the attack. His premonitions had been catastrophically accurate.

The two main plotters fled and managed to get completely away amid all the confusion. As he was being led away out of harm's way, Graziani is reported to have told his men to avenge him by killing everyone. The Italian commander of the fascist militia, Guido Cortese, ordered the troops to open fire on the helpless and terrified crowd. Cortese was reported to have fired the first shot himself. Hundreds of defenceless beggars, the blind, the deaf, the lame and other waifs and strays were mown down and killed in a three-hour shooting spree. All this slaughter took place on the spot where future generations of students would gather to kiss and cuddle. The massacre was to be the first of many hellish episodes in the city that day.

Graziani was bundled into a car and taken to hospital, bleeding profusely. He had multiple bomb splinters in his skin and muscle, with extensive lacerations to the back of his right knee. Altogether around 200 metal splinters were removed from his battered body. He had to spend nearly three months in hospital receiving treatment. He never forgot the injuries he received that day, lamenting that he had to live all his life with what he called his coat of blood.

Graziani also had many psychological scars. He was furious at the attack on his person and his authority. He was especially angry when it was later discovered the plotters had been working right under his nose. It made him look weak and he knew it. The Viceroy's demanding taskmaster, Mussolini, immediately blamed him for losing control of the occupation. The fascist leader learned of the attack while at a ski resort at Mount Terminillo in central Italy. Dressed in casual skiing gear, he inquired about the circumstances of the attack and then made some withering and critical comments about Graziani's performance as Viceroy. Before venturing out onto the slopes Il Duce made it clear that Graziani could no longer be allowed to be in charge because of what had happened. He would have to be replaced.

The Italian leadership in Ethiopia moved swiftly to prevent the assassination attempt spinning out of control. They suspended all communications to Europe to minimise adverse publicity. They also ordered that all cameras be confiscated. The fascist commanders were destabilised by the incident and were obviously keen to hunt down the perpetrators as soon as they could. Some Italian troops started ransacking the cathedral of St George in the northern part of the city and destroyed much of the interior. At one stage, an order was given to raze it to the ground but that was later rescinded. The cathedral was certainly hated by the Italians as it was a symbol of Ethiopia's victory at Adwa and, of course, the location of Haile Selassie's lavish coronation just seven years before.

Cortese, the fascist party apparatchik, was still not satisfied after his murderous work in the palace grounds. His blood was up and he wanted more revenge. Later in the day he issued a chilling proclamation, giving hundreds of Italian blackshirts carta bianca, or free licence, to destroy and kill Ethiopians in whatever way they wanted. He wanted no-one from what he called the cursed race to escape. The reprisals were planned from the party base in the Casa Littoria in the Piazza area. The building now plays host to a well-known Italian restaurant called Castelli's. It has an excellent reputation for fine Italian food and wine, with an abundant and delicious antipasti buffet – a scene far removed from the barbaric fare that emanated from the building on the day Graziani was attacked. Much blood had already been spilt but the massacre was only just beginning.

The former Casa Littoria building with Castelli's restaurant on the right

By 5pm there was a frenzy of activity. The Italian occupiers were in a panic that the local population would rise up against them. They also wanted to avenge the attack on their Viceroy. An array of weapons was handed out to blackshirts, fascist militia and civilian party members, even Italian labourers. They had all come running to answer the call, desperate to do their bit for king, duce and party. The mob was given a variety of weapons, including grenades, daggers, shovels, truncheons, hammers and guns.

Flamethrowers became the most widely-used weapon and hundreds of Ethiopian houses were set on fire. Many Ethiopians were burned to death as they were trapped inside. Some were even herded into the flames. Those who tried to escape the infernos were summarily shot dead or stabbed. The frenzied attackers wielding the daggers yelled out 'Duce, Duce, Duce!' Copious amounts of benzine and oil were poured

CHAPTER 5

onto the properties to make the fires burn more fiercely. People of all ages, men, women and children, were singled out at random for summary execution. Some victims had their throats cut and died slowly in terrible agony. Some babies were crushed to death by troops wearing big boots. Some local men were castrated and, as they lay dying, were forced to watch their wives being stripped naked and whipped to death.

After dark, things simply got worse and the killing became more systematic and organised. More than 4,000 houses were estimated to be burning. The innocent were butchered by any means available. A Hungarian doctor in the city, known as Dr Ladislav Sava, said that the streets literally ran red with blood. He expressed his disgust at Italian officers and their wives, who drove around the city in their fine cars looking for a better and closer view of the massacres.

Some of those unlucky to find themselves in the path of the marauding blackshirts died after they were dragged behind their vehicles. Others were shot, thrown off bridges, beaten or clubbed to death. A fire brigade captain said that he saw groups of blood-crazed Italians picking up bodies from the streets with pitchforks. They then threw the corpses into lorries. They took pictures of themselves jubilantly standing on the bodies. Some of the victims turned out to be still alive, writhing in pain. Many of the dead were buried in impromptu mass graves in the west of the city.

Eyewitnesses said that in the light of day next morning the city looked like the aftermath of a battlefield with dead bodies strewn in streets, gardens and under bridges. Vultures were hovering everywhere. The screaming of the dying and mutilated drifted through many quarters of the city. The blackened ruins of hundreds of houses were still smoking with the snapping of smouldering eucalyptus branches adding to the heartbreaking soundtrack of mass murder. Groups of bedraggled, traumatised residents wandered around looking for missing relatives. The stench of burned flesh added to their misery.

Part of the memorial in Addis Ababa to the victims of the massacres

Hundreds of Ethiopians were also rounded up and put in prison. Here they were still at grave risk from the savagery of the blackshirts. One group of prisoners was bayoneted to death as they tried to placate their raging thirst by gulping down water. The massacres continued for three days before a halt was finally called. It is not clear exactly how many people had been slaughtered. Many people simply disappeared and their bodies hidden. Estimates by some historians and observers put the death toll at between 3,000 to 6,000 but some say the figure is as high as 30,000. Italian historians dispute these figures, saying that a few hundred were killed. However, that is clearly a gross underestimation.

The English journalist George Steer, who had witnessed Haile Selassie's spirited defence of the town of Dessie, wrote a furious and graphic condemnation of the Italian killing spree. In a powerful piece in the *Spectator* magazine he said the army of murder had used its flashing romantic knives to carry out a frightful massacre which had left bodies in the smoking streets. He said the new flower had become a ruin, a butcher's shop where Italy hung Abyssinian flesh on hooks every day.

The streets of Addis Ababa were deserted for days afterwards. Several thousand residents had fled in terror, many hiding in the thick eucalyptus forests in the surrounding hills. The massacres became a great recruiting sergeant as hundreds joined the Ethiopian resistance forces, appalled at the wanton murder and savagery they had witnessed. The sadistic perpetrators of the killings showed no pity or remorse. They were more concerned with counting all the money they had stolen from their victims. Huge amounts of jewellery, rings and silver crosses had also been taken from the bodies of Ethiopian women before they had been mutilated or burned.

The repercussions of the failed grenade attack were to continue for months. The official line from Graziani was that young Ethiopian nobles were to blame, backed up by the British secret service. The Italians now had an excuse to move against some of Ethiopia's intelligent and independent-minded youthful elite. Many of them were members of the Black Lion organisation, which was loyal to the Emperor. On 26 February, 45 young men were shot without trial and another 26 were executed over the next few days. Graziani sneeringly referred to the nobles as creatures of the Emperor.

The Italians presented no evidence but simply declared that the young men were poisonous and dangerous. The nobles also had many valuable possessions in their houses, which the murderers grabbed and shared among themselves. Four execution points were designated in the city, including one near the stone steps of the palace where Graziani was attacked. Many of these nobles were known personally to Haile Selassie and he had arranged for some of them to be educated abroad. Among them were two sons of his Ethiopian representative in London, Dr Charles Martin. Losing such an amount of young talent was devastating, both in the short-term and in the

CHAPTER 5

longer-term. When Haile Selassie was restored to power in Ethiopia and wanted to build a more modern society, there were not enough educated experienced people to draw on. His estimate was that 75 per cent of all intellectuals were killed during the Italian occupation.

After the Graziani attack more than a thousand other young nobles were arrested and sent to Italy where they were put in prison. In his *Spectator* article George Steer condemned the Italian occupying forces for the murder of so many young nobles. He said they were dead because they spoke French, sometimes wore European clothes, behaved decently, loved their country and wanted to make it more efficient and more civilised. What went through the Emperor's mind when he heard about the massacres and the wave of official executions afterwards? He must have felt sick when he heard the news, either through the international press or his own sources in communications sent through Kenya or Sudan. Details were bound to have been sketchy and it was frustrating for the Emperor not to have been able to get more facts and interrogate the information. He was an outsider now, deprived to a large extent of the power of knowledge.

Sitting alone in his unheated chilly office in Fairfield House, he must have been in the depths of despair and grief. He had not been there in Addis Ababa to protect his people. He maybe also pondered how a so-called civilised and Christian country could stoop to such obscene tactics. Using poison gas against his military forces had been hard enough to take, but the random slaughter of innocent men, women and children was something that even in his darkest hours he could never have contemplated.

A glum Ethiopian contingent at a memorial service in London for the victims of the massacre in Addis Ababa. Left to right: Foreign Minister Heruy, Dr Charles Martin, Ras Kassa and the Emperor.

On 17 March 1937 the Emperor wrote to the League of Nations to protest about the massacres. He demanded that the Italians be investigated for war crimes in the light of both the murders and the earlier use of poison gas. The callous shootings in the grounds of the palace were referred to as a horrible hecatomb, a word from ancient Greece denoting extensive loss of life in sacrifices to the gods. The Emperor said the massacres were not a punishment but a collective vengeance. The next day he attended a special requiem mass at St George's Church in London's Bloomsbury Square to honour the victims. He also released a special Easter message and asked for compassion and help. He asked the people of Britain to imagine the terror of living in a town dominated by 30,000 troops who had behaved like this. Many refugees were in British colonies in Africa and he appealed for support of a fund to help them.

Ian Campbell, in his comprehensive book about the massacres, presents considerable evidence indicating that the Emperor knew in advance about the plot to assassinate Graziani. He even puts forward the theory that Haile Selassie himself ordered the attack from his base in the UK, though the evidence presented is circumstantial rather than definitive. Whatever the truth, the botched attempt on the Viceroy's life was a dark stain in Ethiopia's history and sparked off untold suffering on a massive scale.

THE HORRORS OF DEBRE LIBANOS

As if all the heartache over the Addis Ababa massacres was not enough, there was to be a massive sting in the tail in the months ahead. Italian investigators in pursuit of the two Eritrean plotters had discovered that one of them, Abraha, had taken his wife a few days before the attack to Debre Libanos monastery, one of the most important centres of the Ethiopian Orthodox Church. It was even suggested that he had gone back there to visit her as he made his way north after fleeing Addis Ababa. This information was seized upon by Graziani, still recovering from his painful wounds sustained in the grenade blasts. He had already been suspicious of Orthodox leaders following a previous visit to a church in Dire Dawa in the east of the country. There he had nearly fallen into a hole which he believed priests had deliberately tried to conceal by laying an ornate carpet over it. The paranoid Italian commander suspected the priests had been trying to kill or injure him.

Graziani also was aware of some hearsay evidence that monks at Debre Libanos had been talking about the grenade attacks. He needed no further proof and cooked up more evidence to show that the priests and monks there had been important conspirators in the plot to kill him. In May 1937 he took a staggering and cruel decision that is barely believable. He ordered that the entire community of priests, young deacons and church workers at Debre Libanos be murdered for their alleged crimes. The victims were duped into gathering in the main church building. They

CHAPTER 5

were then bundled into vehicles and taken to a number of remote sites. Some were driven to the edge of a nearby ravine and machine-gunned. The bodies were buried unceremoniously in mass graves.

Ian Campbell says that between 1,700 and 2,100 people were killed with another 1,000 taken away. Many never returned. Around 30 young boys were forcibly removed and sent to the notorious Danane concentration camp in Somaliland. The atrocity was described as the biggest cold-blooded massacre of clergy since the Muslim jihad of the 16th century. At the end of the operation Graziani received a terse message that no more trace remained of Debra Libanos monastery. Graziani's henchmen also hunted down and killed other Ethiopians they thought might be a security threat. Fortune-tellers, travelling singers and soothsayers were eliminated as it was believed they might be helping to spread information about the resistance.

The seeds of Graziani's callous methods of imposing control had been planted when he was commander of all the Italian forces in Libya in the 1920s. He had constructed austere detention camps there to subdue dissent. Hundreds of Libyans died in the appalling conditions from disease and starvation. Some were executed by hanging or were shot. His deeds earned him the nickname 'the Butcher of Fezzan' or 'Hyena of Libya,' though some of the Italian public lauded him for pacifying the country. After his cruel displays in Addis Ababa and Debre Libanos, details of Graziani's brutal past resurfaced and he was given the new nickname of the 'Butcher of Ethiopia'. He had always been in favour of carrying out mass executions in response to any civilian uprisings.

Graziani was never fully brought to account for his actions, despite clear indications that he had committed war crimes by systematically exterminating civilians. The Ethiopian authorities presented evidence to a United Nations commission on war crimes in 1948. However, the charges were dropped, partly due to the opposition of the British Foreign Office. For a variety of self-serving reasons the government in London did not want to link the Ethiopian/Italian conflict to the Second World War. In 1948 Graziani was convicted by an Italian inquiry and was given a long prison sentence. However, he only served a few months in jail and was released, following submissions by his lawyer that he had been only following orders, one of the oldest excuses in the book. In 2012 a decision to erect a monument to honour Graziani at his tomb in his home town of Affile created a wave of controversy and acrimony. Richard Pankhurst, a renowned scholar of Ethiopian history and the son of Sylvia Pankhurst, said that this was tantamount to honouring Mussolini himself. He and his wife Rita joined a protest outside the Italian Embassy in London.

The original commander of the Italian forces, Badoglio, also escaped any war-crime charges. The hundreds of Ethiopian soldiers killed by poison gas, the thousands of innocent civilians murdered in Addis Ababa, and the slaughtered priests and pilgrims of Debre Libanos, never received justice. The two Eritreans, who hurled the grenades that sparked off the reprisals, were executed by the Italians 18 months after their attack. They ran into trouble while hiding out in northern Ethiopia with some resistance forces.

THE KILLING OF RAS DESTA

Just a few days after the attempt on Graziani's life in February 1937, the situation was starting to unravel for the rump of the official Ethiopian forces still operating in the south of Ethiopia. The *Chronicle* reported on 22 February that a prominent commander, Gebre Mariam, had been run to ground and killed. He had had a price on his head. A spokesman at the Ethiopian legation in London said that the country had lost one of its bravest and most brilliant soldiers. He said the Emperor, in common with every other Ethiopian in England, was deeply grieved by the news as Gebre Mariam had been a popular and greatly beloved personality. For many months Gebre Mariam had been fighting a rearguard campaign against the Italians together with Ras Desta Damtew, the Emperor's son-in-law, who had temporarily managed to escape from the Italian military sweeps.

Soon afterwards came some more heartbreaking news for the Emperor. Ras Desta, the husband of his daughter Tenagneworq, had been captured and shot out of hand. As well as dealing with his own grief, the Emperor had to try to comfort his family. The Ras was the father of two sons and four daughters, including Princess Aida, Princess Hirut and Princess Seble. Once again the rooms of Fairfield House were filled with the wailing and crying of those in mourning. The full extent of the Emperor's grief was indicated by the *Gloucester Citizen*, which said the Emperor had locked himself away in his private suite when he heard the news by telephone. He postponed a planned visit to Gloucester because of his grief beyond words.

Ras Desta's luck had finally run out. Graziani, who was previously the commander of the southern forces, had been hunting him for months. He had not believed the Ras's apparent promises of submission and felt he had simply been playing for time. Four Italian columns numbering around 20,000 men eventually captured their quarry. The *Chronicle* attacked Graziani for his decision to summarily execute the Ras. It said that Rome, in the days of old, led its distinguished captives in chains, and recognised gallantry, in contrast to the current treatment of its prisoners. Ras Desta received a glowing obituary in the *Times* newspaper. It described him as a tall, handsome and princely figure, who was reserved in manner. The Ras had been an ally of the Emperor since his early days at court. Like Haile Selassie, Desta eschewed the fleshly pleasures of feasting, carousing and drinking. Ironically during his youth he had run away to become a monk at Debre Libanos monastery.

His death was a massive setback for the Emperor, who kept on losing friends and

CHAPTER 5

influential allies. It was also a terrible and destabilising blow for his widow Princess Tenagneworq. Within a few weeks she was admitted to the Forbes Fraser Hospital just down the road from Fairfield House. In the summer of 1937 she spent some time to regain her health, quietly studying English at Milton Mount College in Sussex. A short time after this devastating news, Romaneworq, Haile Selassie's daughter born before he met the Empress, was captured with her children and sent to Italy. Her husband Beyene Merid was also executed by Italian forces. Like many of her relatives, Romaneworq had to face an uncomfortable exile. She died from tuberculosis in a prison in Turin in 1941, heaping more misery on her father.

Coping with the shock of so many sudden and violent deaths must, of course, have been extremely tough and distressing. But everything was made harder as the Emperor's emotional reserves had already been weakened by the grinding pain of exile. In some ways the experience of separation from one's home is like a bereavement. In effect, everything familiar has died and been lost. Grief counsellors agree that everyone goes through similar emotional responses when dealing with loss. It is of course impossible to know exactly what the Emperor experienced when he was alone and out of public sight. But it is more than likely he suffered some or all of the emotions experienced in the cycles of grief.

The first reaction is often denial and a sense of isolation, as the brain puts up various defence mechanisms to absorb the shock. Other emotions come and go. Often there is great anger welling up from inside. In the Emperor's case, any rage would have been directed at Mussolini and the individuals actually responsible for the summary executions during the occupation. He is also likely to have been furious with himself for leaving his country to its fate. Another stage of grieving is that of bargaining, with an individual questioning himself whether the deaths could have been avoided if he or she had acted differently. Depression and despair are also very common. The Emperor may have hidden such feelings at this stage of his exile but certainly later on it would become clear that he was very depressed and demoralised. The final stage of grief is acceptance of the loss, though some people never reach that point. The Emperor was never fully resigned to his situation in exile, and he may have brought himself some peace by continually accepting that what had happened had somehow been the will of God.

The capture and execution of Ras Desta brought to an end the organised Ethiopian resistance to the Italian invasion. The attacks on Italian forces in some parts of the country continued but they were haphazard and not co-ordinated. The raids were carried out by the arbengoch or patriots, who refused to give up and were to be a thorn in the side of the Italian occupying forces for several years to come. Many of the patriots continued to regard Haile Selassie as a traitor for fleeing the country.

All of this piled even more pressure onto the Emperor, whose last dregs of influence over his forces in Ethiopia were now at an end. It was still less than a year since he had decided to abandon his troops and flee from Addis Ababa. He could never have believed then that everything would turn out so badly. Although not a warrior, he was left incredibly impotent, sitting helplessly at Fairfield and not being able to fight shoulder to shoulder with his military. The diplomatic appeal to the League of Nations had failed and now his army had disintegrated. Later the Emperor wrote that during his secluded life the constant news of the atrocities had increased the weight of his sadness and made him nervous. As a result, he endured many sleepless nights. He truly was suffering the 'mind of winter'.

CHAPTER 5

CHAPTER FIVE EYEWITNESS THE MYSTIC'S CAVE

In November 2013 I went by minibus from Addis Ababa to the monastery at Debre Libanos. The journey along a good Japanese-built road takes about two hours. The monastery is off a turning from the main road to the town of Bahir Dar, just before the highway descends into a huge gorge. Along the valley floor flows one of the main tributaries of the Abay or Blue Nile. Majestic birds of prey soar in circles up above the valley. The landscape is breathtaking, like a slightly smaller version of the Grand Canyon in America. Debre Libanos monastery may be in a beautiful setting but it has a dark secret. The depravity of Graziani in ordering the destruction of the religious community here seems all the more shocking because it took place in such a tranquil and inspiring location.

As in Bath, there has been a religious community at Debre Libanos for centuries. Haile Selassie knew the place when he was a young man when he served as the assistant governor of the nearby Selale region. He had then given Emperor Menelik a special Imperial ring, found while excavation work had been carried out at the monastery. Haile Selassie's presence is still clearly in evidence. His special chair can be seen in the modern church he had built in the early 1960s. The Empress had her own seat away from the section reserved for male worshippers. The modern church contains many stained glass windows. It is a welcome sign of beauty in a place associated with such a heinous crime. In the museum next door there are ecclesiastical relics and scriptures, interspersed with several photographs of the Emperor throughout his long reign.

I joined an official tour of the church compound given by a priest with a mischievous sense of humour. He made several jokes about the round leather cap he was wearing, saying he kept it on day and night. While paying for the trip, there were stern notices in the entrance hall. These warned that any menstruating woman or person who had had sexual relations in the last couple of days was deemed to be unclean and so could not enter the church. Cue embarrassed and wry looks between members of the tour group, wondering who was going to admit getting up to any risqué behaviour. During the tour the priest did not mention the massacres. When I asked him about them afterwards, he said that such had been the shock and confusion it had taken six months for services to be held again on the monastery site.

Up the hill from the church compound is the cave where the 13th century mystic Tekle Haimanot is said to have lived as a recluse in private contemplation and adoration of God. According to the legend, he spent 22 years standing in the cave in prayer. When one of his legs withered away, he stood on the other remaining leg for another seven years. The cave was a place that Haile Selassie would have visited. To get to it you have to walk on a steep and twisting path up a wooded hillside with huge boulders, tiny ravines and massive cliffs. It is certainly prime ankle-breaking territory.

The approach to the cave is draped in Ethiopian colours and looks like the entrance to a shrine. You have to take off your shoes and socks before going inside, then clamber gingerly over wet, mossy rocks and finally step over a dirty, tiny stream. Drips of water tumble down from the roof of the cave. This is regarded as holy water or sebel. The liquid comes down at the same rate each day whether it is the rainy or dry season. Some say the sebel waters are the tears of Tekle Haimanot. The water is lovingly collected in red plastic bowls and containers to distribute to the needy and infirm. A priest acting as the guardian to the sacred site told me that the Emperor would regularly come here before taking special trips abroad.

The wilful destruction of the entire community here on Graziani's orders would have shaken Haile Selassie to the core when he eventually discovered the full extent of what had happened. He would have regarded it as an attack on himself, his church and even his God.

CHAPTER 6

CHAPTER SIX
AIDING AND ABETTING

Although it was difficult to get to know the Emperor in any depth, he was not short of friends and well-wishers, who gave him invaluable support during his exile. On site at Fairfield House he had his family and trusted advisers, including the foreign minister Heruy, and Lorenzo Taezaz, his talented aide. Wolde Giorgis Wolde Yohannes, his private secretary, was a skilled political operator and fixer, and regularly commuted to Bath from the Ethiopian Legation in London. Another influential assistant to the Emperor was Abebe Retta, who had left Ethiopia before the Italian invasion to study at a bible college in Glasgow. He spent some time at Fairfield, studied at nearby Bristol University and had some dealings with the British press on behalf of the Emperor. Abebe Retta also had a relationship with Princess Tenagneworq, leading to the birth of a daughter in 1939. After the Second World War Abebe Retta became Ethiopia's first fully-fledged ambassador to the UK and held a number of other key government posts. The Emperor's closest adviser Ras Kassa also spent some of the exile period in Fairfield, though he lived for much of the time in Jerusalem. All of the Ethiopians in Bath were exiles themselves and struggling, like their Emperor, to deal with the emotions of estrangement, dislocation, bereavement and unfamiliarity.

Haile Selassie also had a large number of British supporters, ranging from merchants, neighbours and dignitaries in Bath to prominent political operators well-versed in the ways of UK society. Anthony Eden was a high-flying British government insider who had risen to the top job at the Foreign Office and had offered some support to the Ethiopian cause, though he was never fully trusted by the Emperor. Many well-wishers from Britain sent money in the post as stories spread about how the Emperor was struggling to make ends meet. The network of support for Haile Selassie spread across the world, including the United States and other parts of Africa. The man who regarded the Emperor as his own son, Father

Jarosseau, also continued to send him letters. He was taking refuge from the Italian invaders in a monastery in Toulouse in southern France.

Fairfield was nowhere near as busy as the Emperor's office had been in Addis Ababa but there were still many visitors. Various groups of freedom fighters, including members of the Polish and French resistance, would make their way to Bath to discuss international events. A private society to collect money in aid of Ethiopian refugees was started by an Englishman called Sir Norman Angell, a writer on international affairs who won the Nobel Peace Prize in 1933. Although the Emperor received no funds directly from this organisation, it did help him a great deal as it reduced his own obligations to his fellow exiles.

The Friends of Abyssinia Association was created in the summer of 1936 when Haile Selassie first came to Bath. On the first anniversary he sent the Association a message saying: 'It has been a year of deep sorrow and disappointment for us but I shall not lose hope. God give us strength and perseverance in your noble efforts.'

The founder of the Association Hazel Roper said that it had grown from two members to more than one thousand in just a year. She said that Ethiopia's tragic cry had echoed through the world. In his autobiography the Emperor said the British people had possessed goodwill and had helped him.

The Association was just one of several societies established to support the Ethiopian cause. Others included the Ethiopian Defence Fund and the Nile Society. Some of them even competed with each other. There were also a host of charity bazaars raising funds for the Emperor and rallying people of good will. Despite Foreign Office concerns over too much overt political campaigning, Haile Selassie continued regularly to make public appearances up and down the country to speak out against the Italian occupation. He gained warm support wherever he went.

On one occasion he gave a speech in French at Cambridge where he was made an honorary member of the University Society and received an honorary degree of Doctor of Law. The chamber was packed with members perched on window sills and sitting on the floor. As he entered the room, dressed in his traditional black cloak with gold clasps, all 600 students rose from their seats. They cheered, clapped, and stamped their feet for nearly five minutes. The union officers wore pink carnations in their lapels and arranged for the Ethiopian flag to be flown over the union building.

The Emperor was becoming something of a big national star and the Ethiopian question was becoming a very hot topic. He was not just popular because many British people sympathised with his political predicament. They also appreciated the courtesy and the respect he showed his hosts in return. They loved it when he raised his hat in polite response to a greeting. One example of his courtesy was in June 1937 when the Chief Constable of Bath, Nelson Ashton, was killed in a head-on crash with a lorry in Cheshire. In a cruel twist of fate he had been driving back from

CHAPTER 6

a conference of chief constables about road safety. The Emperor called on the Mayor of Bath shortly afterwards to offer his condolences. He certainly knew what the experience of dealing with sudden tragedy felt like.

Despite all the chaos swirling around him, the Emperor also carried out some other small acts of kindness. He meticulously kept some stamps for a local boy in Bath, whom he knew was interested in collecting them. Whenever the Emperor received envelopes from abroad, he would faithfully stockpile them. As well as the overall political support the Emperor received, many people in Bath offered friendship to his family. In her interview for this book the Emperor's granddaughter Princess Seble was at pains to praise the local people, who tried to make Haile Selassie's life a little easier. She said that if the British decided they were going to help you, then they really did. Even after all these years she was grateful to the King family for loaning their house on Caldey Island near Tenby in south Wales so the Emperor's family could take a short break.

The Kings, whose daughter Hilary appeared on the HTV documentary about the Bath exile, also arranged and paid for a delivery of coal to Fairfield as they knew the Emperor was struggling for cash. They owned the Little Theatre in Bath, a cinema which still exists to this day down a narrow street near the renovated spa baths. There the Emperor was given a private screening of newsreel footage about the Italian invasion of Ethiopia. It is also possible he later saw other international newsreel reports of the building tension in Europe. Princess Seble also mentioned other families who helped – the Batemans, the Nugents and the Tuckers, who owned a farm which the Emperor used to love visiting. Many of these families would open up their houses for the children at Fairfield.

The Little Theatre in Bath, still a thriving cinema today

Other local people who supported the Emperor included a young senior railway clerk at Bath Spa Station, Robina Maud Gray Hunt. She struck up a conversation with him on the frequent occasions he would be waiting for the train to London. According to Robina's son, Councillor Martin Veal, she would answer the Emperor's questions about market gardening and growing food. She found the royal passenger to be unassuming and grateful for the support he received locally.

Some of the characters who were especially close to the Emperor during his exile deserve a special mention.

THE BARTON FAMILY

One of the Emperor's longstanding English contacts was Sir Sidney Barton, the British government representative in Addis Ababa during the 1920s and 1930s. It was clear the Emperor valued Sir Sidney's wise counsel from an early stage. On one occasion a foreign diplomat had sought an audience with Haile Selassie and asked him to give him some advice on what to wear at an upcoming official function in Addis Ababa. The Emperor said that Sir Sidney would know. Sure enough the next day the diplomat turned up in the appropriate attire for the function – in morning suit, top hat and tails. Sir Sidney liked to do things properly and with style. He would regularly parade ceremonially in a white uniform on horseback as he made his way along the mule tracks to the Emperor's palace in Addis Ababa.

Haile Selassie with Lady Barton, the wife of Sir Sidney, at the Roseries garden party in Bath in July 1937. Behind them is Dr Marsh, the owner of Roseries

CHAPTER 6

Sir Sidney lived in the official residence in the sprawling, verdant British Embassy compound on land given by Emperor Menelik. The Embassy is still there to this day with its swish security gates, the Addis Arms social club, pet giant tortoises, a small golf course and horse-riding facilities. Sir Sidney was all too aware of the instability that would be caused in Addis by the entry of the occupying Italian forces. He astounded many people by arranging for a detachment of some crack troops from an Indian Army regiment to guard the legation. He also arranged for 2,000 refugees to camp out in the spacious Embassy grounds. For his services to Britain and Ethiopia he was knighted in 1937.

Shortly afterwards, Sir Sidney retired and went to work as head of the Abyssinian Refugees Fund, helping around 8,000 displaced Ethiopians and foreigners. Sir Sidney was appalled at the belligerent attitude of most in the Foreign Office and tried to use his contacts to push things the Emperor's way. But it was an uphill battle. Sir Sidney's wife Lady Barton had been a confidante of Empress Menen since Addis times. Both the Bartons were regular visitors at Fairfield.

In the late 1930s another prominent supporter of the Emperor, the journalist George Steer, became part of Sir Sidney's family when he married his daughter Esme. Steer had continued to be sympathetic to the Emperor ever since he had reported for the London *Times* and *New York Times* on his coronation, and on the horrors of the Italian invasion and occupation. Steer and Esme Barton had a refined society wedding in June 1939. They were married by the Bishop of London in the King's Chapel of St John the Baptist of the Savoy near the Strand in London. The Emperor, wearing a high-collared black cape, was in attendance as were Crown Prince Asfa-Wossen and Princess Tsehai, on release from her nursing duties. Before his marriage Steer had written in detail about his future father-in-law Sir Sidney Barton. He said Barton had a brisk manner and he would often become tired and cross as he suffered from low blood pressure. Presumably he later moderated his views after becoming a member of the family.

Barton spoke of the Emperor in terms of admiration but when he talked about things he disliked, such as Italian policy in Ethiopia, Haile Selassie 'simply twitched the long nose which jutted a little bonily from his thin intelligent face.' Like Barton, Steer greatly admired Haile Selassie. He said the Emperor's instincts were western, and his ruling instinct was for order and applied reason.

Steer had an ongoing rivalry with the satirist Evelyn Waugh, who it was said always accentuated the negative while Steer favoured the positive. It was also remarked that Waugh saw war as a comedy while Steer saw it as a tragedy. In a cutting reference to Steer's reporting of Ethiopia, Waugh said that only what he called a 'shit' could be good at this particular job. Sir Sidney Barton was exactly the sort of public figure that Waugh loved to parody. Sure enough it was not long before the former British ambassador made an unfavourable appearance in *Black Mischief*, Waugh's scathing satire of colonial life in Africa. When Esme Barton spotted Waugh some time afterwards, she threw a glass of champagne in his face.

Steer, who was born in South Africa, led an extraordinary life. As well as his exploits in Ethiopia, he also reported bravely on the Spanish civil war where he was the first to point out that German planes had taken part in the brutal bombing of Guernica in 1937. He also covered the invasion of the Soviet Red Army into Finland in 1939. Steer had married his first wife Margarita Herrero, a fellow journalist, while they were both in Addis Ababa in 1936, waiting with some trepidation for the encroaching Italian forces to arrive. Margarita worked for the French newspaper *Le Journal* and they spent their honeymoon cowering behind barbed wire on the compound of the British Legation where Steer's future father-in-law Sir Sidney had established his safe haven. Steer and three other journalists were soon expelled from Ethiopia for alleged anti-Italian espionage. The following year Steer suffered personal tragedy when Margarita died from complications in the later stages of pregnancy. Her unborn child also did not survive.

Steer was profoundly upset by what he witnessed during the Italian takeover of Ethiopia. In his book *Caesar in Abyssinia* he says he had seen a child nation almost beaten to death before it could breathe. All this had happened to a leader whom Steer greatly admired and respected, describing him as noble and intelligent. Steer believed that a journalist was not just a simple purveyor of the truth but should also be a historian of everyday events. As a historian, it was important to be filled with the most critical and most passionate attachment to the truth. Steer's barnstorming life was a testimony to his beliefs.

WILFRED THESIGER

The intrepid British explorer Wilfred Thesiger, famous for his treks in the Awash region of Ethiopia and several Arab lands, was born in Addis Ababa and remained a life-long friend of the Emperor. He came into the world in a tukul, or hut, near the British Legation building. His father had been one of the previous British representatives based there before Sir Sidney Barton arrived. While growing up in Ethiopia, the Thesiger family became known to the young Ras Teferi and he met Wilfred again during his Grand Tour of Europe in 1924. Thesiger was at Eton and expressed a wish to visit the land of his birth. The Emperor smiled and said that one day he would return as his guest. Sure enough Thesiger received a special invitation to the Emperor's coronation six years later.

Thesiger spoke out in favour of the Emperor's cause while he was in exile and the Emperor visited him a couple of times at Thesiger's family residence at Milebrook

CHAPTER 6

House near Knighton on the border between England and Wales. To this day there are locals in the area who have a fund of stories about the two men, handed down by previous generations. At the time of the Italian invasion Thesiger said bitterly that the country of his childhood was being raped yet England did nothing. As the Second World War approached, he complained to a friend that it did not look like any of his generation was going to have a future but that they didn't deserve it anyway after Abyssinia. The explorer also said that Haile Selassie was the only African leader who was not corrupt, though he was surrounded by corrupt people.

Thesiger had a private audience with Haile Selassie two days after he had arrived at Waterloo Station in those early days in exile. The explorer said that when the Emperor talked briefly about the suffering of his soldiers he became aware of what he called his unutterable sadness.

SYLVIA PANKHURST

Another extraordinary character to support Haile Selassie was the suffragette and campaigner for international justice Sylvia Pankhurst. She was hewn from hardy stock and so was a perfect candidate to become involved in the Emperor's cause. Sylvia's mother Emmeline was a resolute supporter of women's rights. Sylvia's sister Christabel was also active in campaigning for women. In the early 1920s one of Emmeline's colleagues, Emily Davison, threw herself under the King's horse in a race at Ascot to protest against the lack of the vote for women. She was crushed to death under the hooves. Such bravery and reckless dedication formed the backdrop against which Sylvia grew up. She herself was to be frequently arrested for civil disobedience and often staged hunger, thirst or sleep strikes.

Sylvia Pankhurst became interested in the Ethiopian cause after the Wal-Wal border incident, involving Italian and Ethiopian troops on the tense frontier between south-east Ethiopia and Italian Somaliland in 1934. Around 100 Ethiopian soldiers and a few Italians died in the skirmishes over what began as a minor dispute over the boundary line. It was just the pretext that Mussolini needed and he skilfully exploited the tension to claim justification for an invasion. Sylvia's campaigning blood was boiling. It was an obvious battle for her to join. She had spent the 1920s fighting against fascism in Italy, together with her long-term companion Silvio Corio, who was an Italian leftwing anarchist and an opponent of the fascisti. Sylvia also already had an international socialist conscience and was outraged by the bullying of Ethiopia by a much stronger European power. She loved sympathising with underdogs and scrapping on their behalf. As tension grew following the Wal-Wal incident, Sylvia wrote a series of letters to British newspapers, expressing her concern.

Well before the Italians reached Addis Ababa, Sylvia met the Ethiopian representative in London, Dr Charles Martin, and realised he was short of funds and staff. She was also impressed by his obvious integrity but, as her son Richard noted in his book about his mother, she believed that Dr Martin did not have the political guile needed to be very effective in England. She could also see that he was struggling to bring up his family in a different land. She gladly offered him her services and battle was joined.

Once Sylvia was roused, she was in for the fight for the long haul. She was brave, determined, energetic, independent-minded and unconventional. Although she lived for many years with Silvio Corio, she never married him. In her mid-forties she scandalised some of her own family and some conservative elements of English society by having her son Richard out of wedlock. His second name was Keir, in honour of Keir Hardie, one of the founders of the British Labour Party and a former intimate friend of Sylvia. Shortly before the Italians marched into Ethiopia on 5 May 1936, Sylvia founded her campaigning newspaper *New Times* and *Ethiopia News*. Because she wanted the paper to have as wide a forum as possible, she added the words New Times to give more of a popular appeal. She had based the phrase on the title of a popular film starring Charlie Chaplin called *Modern Times*. Such was Sylvia's chutzpah that she was prepared to use any legal means to fight for the Ethiopians. The first edition was actually published on the day the Italians entered Addis Ababa. It was also Sylvia's 54th birthday but she still had plenty of energy left to be the scourge of the British establishment for many years to come.

The *New Times* was published weekly from Sylvia's chaotic office at her home in Woodford in east London. Much of the team was made up of young girls who were in a constant struggle to keep the paper afloat, raising money at bazaars and garden fêtes. The paper though was distributed free to Members of Parliament. Many people were persuaded to write for it, including her companion Corio who wrote under the pen name of Crastinus, a heroic Roman centurion, or Luce, meaning light. The editorials were trenchant and Sylvia Pankhurst was a constant thorn in the side of the British government for what she regarded as its timid policy towards the Emperor. She was also a fierce critic of the right-wing forces in the Spanish civil war and of Italy's support for them. She said that the evils Mussolini had done in Ethiopia by getting mercenary black troops to fight for him to exterminate the local people were now being done in Europe.

It was only natural that Sylvia should be among the large crowd to greet the Emperor when he arrived at Waterloo in June 1936. She was smitten at first sight. Although she was no fan of any system of monarchy, this did not seem to matter as far as the Ethiopian King of Kings was concerned. In typical no-nonsense Pankhurst fashion, she told him straightaway that, as a republican, she supported him not because he was an emperor, but because she believed in his cause, the cause of Ethiopia. Despite herself, she immediately eulogised about him as a special man of destiny, elect of God, conquering lion of the tribe of Judah, King of Zion, King of Kings, Emperor of Ethiopia, chevalier sans peur et

CHAPTER 6

reproche (i.e. a knight without fear and reproach) and epitome of true nobility. Shortly after his arrival on British shores, Sylvia interviewed the Emperor for the *New Times* and *Ethiopia News*. They got along famously. She believed he was probably the most wonderful man she had ever met. Little wonder she described the Emperor as the soul of resistance to Mussolini, and wrote that in his irresistible eyes burned the quenchless fire of the hero who never failed his cause. Her eulogy continued like this: 'One sees in his build and bearing those features full of meaning, those fine and eager hands, the worker who toils unceasingly for the public weal, untouched by personal ambition or material desire for wealth or safety.'

Sylvia Pankhurst was also attracted to the Emperor's stated aims of modernising his country and sending young men to be educated in the west so they could help to build his country. Her son Richard reports that his mother spoke later in appreciation of the extent to which the Ethiopian war had assisted the breaking-down of parochialism in Africa and the emergence of wider pan-African thought. Over the months and years Sylvia was to visit Fairfield House several times and kept in constant touch with the Emperor. She had even come to see him on his first trip to Bath when he had stayed at the Bath Spa Hotel.

The circulation of the *New Times* in Britain was around 10,000. The paper created such a stir that Sylvia Pankhurst was even attacked by Mussolini, himself a journalist, who penned some scathing words about her. He confused her with her mother, and attacked her as an out-of-touch 80-year-old woman. He even claimed she liked being massaged by the strong agents of the British police. The *New Times* was translated into Amharic and was smuggled into Ethiopia. In later months, some of the staff crossed secretly into parts of Ethiopia where no Italian forces had penetrated. Sylvia's paper was also read in English-speaking Africa and in the West Indies.

Sylvia Pankhurst was indefatigable and drove British officials to distraction. She simply hated political bureaucrats and constantly did her best to puncture their egos. Since the 1920s the British secret service MI5 had kept a close eye on Sylvia, given her communist-supporting background and her foray into sensitive international relations. Around a decade ago the British government released her secret service file, which reveals how much many operatives and opponents hated her. Many of the reports contain a stream of venomous and offensive insults, several of them bordering on libel.

Roger Hollis, an MI5 officer who was later exposed as a spy, called Sylvia Pankhurst a crank on Abyssinian affairs. D.W. Lascelles wrote that he wholeheartedly agreed with the wish that this 'horrid old harridan should be choked to death with her own pamphlets.'

Other agents complained that the doughty campaigner had a 'bonnet full of bees,' 'ventilates her prejudices without discretion or discrimination' and 'made the most indiscreet and foolish speeches in public.' Another operative wondered how the 'tiresome Miss Pankhurst' could be muzzled and yet another accused her of being in the pay of the Emperor, receiving an alleged sum of £800 to finance her newspaper.

It is the case that Sylvia did not suffer fools gladly and was always convinced she was right. She was not an easy person to work with. For example, the author George Bernard Shaw often fell out with Sylvia Pankhurst. He accused her of living in a tempest of virtuous indignation. However, Haile Selassie was grateful for her qualities as a battering ram. It must have been some relief to have someone on his side pushing back against diffident British officials and timid European governments.

Several world leaders were contacted by Sylvia, who was a tireless letter-writer. One of them was the American President, Franklin Roosevelt, whose country, like the USSR, never recognised Italy's occupation of Ethiopia. Sylvia was loyal to Haile Selassie all the time he was in England. Here was someone she could admire and whose judgment she could respect. Above all, to her he was a living symbol of international justice.

LORENZO TAEZAZ

Lorenzo lived at Fairfield throughout the exile period and was an able diplomatic and administrative assistant to his Emperor. He was one of the new breed of intelligent young Ethiopians whom Haile Selassie wanted to train up as future Ethiopian leaders. Lorenzo's life had been changed irrevocably when as a young man he bumped into Haile Selassie by accident when he was in Aden. Lorenzo had escaped there after being frustrated by the prejudice he had experienced in the long-time Italian colony in Eritrea where he grew up. He was especially annoyed when he was hissed at by Italians in a cinema.

Clearly there was something special about Lorenzo, who, despite his talents, could not make ends meet as a young man. The future Emperor invited him to come to Addis Ababa and then arranged for him to go abroad to study. He was one of several promising and intelligent young men hand-picked by the Emperor to provide a loyal counterweight to the traditional independent-minded rases. Lorenzo went to Montpelier in southern France for eight years to study law. He was extremely smart, and could speak six languages. When he came back from France, his talents were quickly exploited and he served on the boundary commission which investigated the Wal-Wal border incident. He also ran Ethiopia's counter-espionage service to try to keep track of Italy's large network of spies and informers.

Lorenzo shared the Emperor's frustrations in trying to persuade the older and more conservative princes to adapt to the modern world. He also headed the new Emperor's press bureau from August 1935. George Steer described Lorenzo as suave and beady-eyed. The journalist was amused by Lorenzo's impersonations of other international correspondents. Lorenzo also saw active service on the front line as he was with the Emperor at the disastrous defeat at Maychew. He was also on hand when Haile Selassie and his family escaped from Addis on the train to Djibouti. Once in Europe he helped draft the famous speech at the League of Nations in Geneva and became an indispensable member of the Emperor's small team in Bath. One of Lorenzo's tasks was to keep in touch with various sources in Ethiopia to glean news about the progress of the Italian advance and the effectiveness of the guerrilla campaigns to resist them.

After the war Lorenzo served in the government but his talents were not given free rein as they had been in Bath. He served as Minister of Foreign Affairs and Minister for Post and Telecommunications. But he fell out with Wolde Giorgis, a minister in whom the Emperor then had complete trust, though he too later dropped out of favour. Lorenzo was marginalised, serving as the toothless president of the chamber of deputies and then as an ambassador to the Soviet Union. He died in his mid-forties after being taken ill while passing through Stockholm airport, once again away from his homeland. It was a sad and lonely end to a prolific life, one in which he seemed to thrive more in war and adversity than in the calmer waters of peacetime.

DR CHARLES MARTIN

The life of Dr Charles Martin, Ethiopia's London representative during the exile years, is perhaps the most extraordinary of all the extraordinary characters associated with Haile Selassie's time in Bath. At the age of three Dr Martin was found wandering alone on a battlefield in the Ethiopian highlands in 1868. He was taken to India, adopted by two British army officers, and trained as a medical doctor. He returned later to Ethiopia, discovered his true identity by chance, and served both Emperor Menelik and Haile Selassie.

As a tiny boy Dr Martin had been caught up in battle after he and his family were imprisoned by one of Haile Selassie's predecessors, the eccentric Teodros. He had fallen out with the British after he wrongly assumed Queen Victoria had snubbed him by refusing to answer some letters he had sent to London. In a fit of pique Teodros seized a group of hostages, some of them local inhabitants and some of them British workers. He holed up in the mountain region of Maqdala where he had installed a secret weapon. This was a huge cannon called Sebastopol which he believed would allow him to defeat any incursion by the British Army. He made a fateful miscalculation.

A British expeditionary force led by Charles Napier made short work of the Ethiopian forces. Sebastopol never got going. Teodros himself committed suicide by shooting himself. It was a move which brought him heroic status in some quarters as he had been seen to keep his integrity and had not surrendered. During the battle

Charles Martin had been looked after by his young aunt, but she lost contact with him amid the smoke and confusion. When he was discovered by British forces, it was assumed he was an orphan. He eventually ended up in India and was helped by two British army officers, one of whom had the Christian name Charles and the other who had the surname Martin. That is how he got his name. He later acquired the Ethiopian name of Hakim Workeneh Eshete. Hakim was his title, meaning doctor, and Workeneh means gold.

A replica of Sebastopol, now based on a roundabout in Addis Ababa

As a young adult, Dr Martin returned to Ethiopia to work as a medical doctor. He was spotted by accident by his grandmother, whose suspicions he was her missing relative were confirmed when she studied some scars on his arms and legs. She revealed to him the full story of his family and upbringing. After that revelation Dr Martin settled in Ethiopia for some time and eventually found himself treating the ageing Menelik after his stroke. He also made a smart move by marrying Ketsela, the attendant of Empress Zewditu. This meant he was accepted into the wider Imperial court with all its attendant privileges and influence. The young Ras Teferi came to value Dr Martin's judgement, and during the 1920s Dr Martin ran an elite school set up in Teferi's name. Dr Martin accompanied Ras Teferi and the young Ethiopian nobles on their Grand Tour of Europe in 1924. He also went on some unofficial diplomatic missions in London and America in 1927. While in the United States, he helped to negotiate a big contract for the building of a dam on the River Nile.

Dr Martin was sent to London in the summer of 1935 to boost Ethiopia's image and clout there. By now he was aged 70 and hard of hearing. As Sylvia Pankhurst had discovered, he was finding it difficult to adapt to the sophisticated workings of

CHAPTER 6

the British establishment. One issue that dogged him was having to deal with some tricky divorce proceedings following the breakup of his marriage with Ketsela. She had been accused of adultery and Dr Martin met with perhaps a surprising response by the Emperor when he confided in him. He said in his diary that the Emperor told him there was no shame about adultery in Ethiopia. Once, when Empress Zewditu had been caught in the act with her lover, nothing much had happened. The Emperor advised Dr Martin to handle the issue delicately and not make too much of a public fuss.

In London Dr Martin was given the brief of mobilising political support in Britain for the continuation of Ethiopia's independence. He also had some financial responsibilities and was asked to raise money through donations from the British public to buy weapons and provide humanitarian aid for his country. Dr Martin worked closely with the Foreign Secretary Anthony Eden though once Haile Selassie arrived in the UK he took charge of any high-level meetings.

Dr Martin often fell foul of those in the British government, who wanted to put the brake on any overt political and campaigning ambitions. His faith in the British establishment was severely tested by the foot-dragging he witnessed over Italian policy. At one stage he complained to Eden that Britain's attitude was like a giant going out of his way to 'kick a wounded pigmy.' In his diary Dr Martin says he made a distinction between the Establishment and the ordinary British people. He praised what he called the virtues and trustworthiness of lifelong friends, and also talked of their love of justice and fair play. Dr Martin also asked the British government to provide a loan, with western Ethiopia being provided as a guarantee. One British official replied haughtily that Haile Selassie was no longer in a position to offer any such guarantees, given he had fled his own country. Undeterred, Dr Martin also regularly acted as a spokesman for the Ethiopian cause and contributed articles to the *New Times* and *Ethiopia News*. One of his main lines of argument was that the Italians were simply robbers.

Dr Martin sharing a joke with the Emperor and some of his family

Overall, Dr Martin was deemed to have had more success in enhancing Ethiopia's reputation than he did in raising hard cash. But he continued to be plagued throughout his stay by personal difficulties. He was grieving for his two sons killed by Italian forces in the aftermath of the Graziani massacre. Several other family members, including his ex-wife, were taken to Italy and imprisoned there.

With this array of strong and inspirational characters on his side, the Emperor had a much better chance of surviving his exile. He had the wise consul of Heruy and Ras Kassa, the diplomatic nous of Sir Sidney Barton and the derring-do attitude of Barton's son-in-law George Steer, the thrusting energy of Wilfred Thesiger, the relentless campaigning energy of Sylvia Pankhurst, the cunning and versatility of Lorenzo Taezaz, and finally the support of a long-time ally at court, Charles Martin, although his influence was to wane later on in the exile period as he clashed with the Emperor over financial issues.

As 1937 wore on, the Emperor was going to need all of them as he slid further into a pit of despair.

CHAPTER 6

CHAPTER SIX EYEWITNESS COFFEE WITH THE PANKHURSTS

Finding the residence of Richard and Rita Pankhurst in the west of Addis Ababa was a lot easier than I had feared when I first arranged to call on them towards the end of 2013. On the phone I had gathered the house was by the ring road behind a military hospital and near a defence base known as Tor Hayloch or the forces of war. On arrival in the area I was not sure which of the narrow lanes I should venture down. But I needn't have worried. I simply mentioned the word Pankhurst to the first locals I saw and they immediately pointed me in the right direction. The Pankhursts are part of the furniture here. They have lived in the same place for around 60 years, apart from a ten year break they had in England during the repressive Derg rule in Ethiopia in the 1970s and 1980s.

The Pankhursts' house on the outskirts of Addis Ababa

IMPERIAL EXILE

Their bungalow is in a rambling compound with a pleasant lawned garden. It is comfortable but not lavish. The couple came here with Richard's mother Sylvia in 1956 on the invitation of the Emperor in gratitude for her support during the exile period. The military hospital was originally constructed in honour of the Emperor's vivacious daughter Tsehai after her death in pregnancy in 1942. Sylvia helped to raise funds abroad for the hospital and lived in the house until her death in 1960. At that time a large forest of eucalyptus trees, much loved by Sylvia, flanked much of the house. Now it is surrounded by houses and modern roads. I talked with Richard and Rita in the enclosed veranda at the front of the house, near a desk where Sylvia continued to work and study until she died. Richard was in poor health, though his mind was as sharp as ever.

Richard was a very young boy when he had his first sight of the Emperor. He was with his mother among the large crowd which greeted Haile Selassie when his train pulled into Waterloo Station in June 1936. Right at the outset of our conversation, Richard mentioned a photograph he had taken as a small boy of nine when he went with his parents to see the Emperor at Fairfield a few months later. Rita then took me inside into the living room where a tapestry copied from the original photograph is displayed proudly above the mantelpiece. The tapestry was made by a Swedish artist called Berit Sahlström, who was married to an Ethiopian/Eritrean.

The tapestry of the Emperor and Sylvia Pankhurst with probably Asfaw Kebede in close attendance

CHAPTER 6

The photograph was taken with a Brownie camera, at an angle looking upwards because Richard was so small at the time. His mother looks austere while the Emperor looks as neat and dapper as ever in one of his capes. The other man's identity has been much debated but it was probably Asfaw Kebede, who always watched the Emperor's back. It seems apt that the tapestry should have such pride of place. This meeting and other encounters led to the lives of the Pankhursts' and Emperor's family being closely intertwined for the next 80 years. Richard said he was never that interested in photography and did not take many pictures. So such a private and personal photograph is all the more precious because of its rarity. The Pankhursts had travelled to Bath from their home in Woodford in east London by train and taxi. They stayed at a bed and breakfast establishment run by an unusually named woman, Mrs Herring, who was anxious to reassure Richard that she was not a fish. Apart from these memories, Richard cannot remember much else about his trip to Bath.

As a young boy, Richard was constantly exposed to the Ethiopian cause. He would help his mother at fundraising events for the Emperor, often selling programmes and raffle tickets. He also played with some of the children of Dr Martin, the London representative. Dr Martin's medical skills also helped Richard to overcome the common complaints and minor ailments of childhood.

Looking back nearly 80 years, Richard thinks that Bath would have interested Haile Selassie because it was such a historic centre. He confirms the view that it was the Emperor's faith that kept him going, and also his confidence in the divine right of kings. Richard says the Emperor was always conscious of the need to preserve history, which is another reason why he could have written his autobiography while at Fairfield. Although the Ethiopian leader did not give much away about his emotions, Richard was sure his insides would have been quietly churning. Richard was to meet the Emperor several times after he came with his mother to Ethiopia. He helped to found the Institute of Ethiopian studies at Haile Selassie's Gennete Leul Palace and has made a significant contribution to Ethiopia's academic life. A library bearing his name is being built next to the palace. Richard also played an instrumental part in the successful campaign to push Italy to return an important obelisk to the holy city of Axum from where it had been looted by the occupying fascists.

The Pankhursts were married in Addis Ababa in a simple ceremony in September 1957. Princesses Hirut and Seble, who had played happily together as children in Fairfield House in Bath, came to help arrange flowers for the wedding. They were supplied free of charge from the Empress's farm. Rita Pankhurst was to form her own working relationship with Haile Selassie. A few months after she arrived in Ethiopia in October 1956 she was summoned out of the blue to the palace where the Emperor asked her to help organise a special exhibition. Rita said she thought of him as someone very different and very benign-looking. He was a reserved person, who

IMPERIAL EXILE

knew not to broadcast his opinions left and right. In her dealings with the Emperor, she says she had never known him to be angry.

The Pankhurst link to Ethiopia is as strong as ever. In 2010 a special service was held at Holy Trinity Cathedral to commemorate the 50th anniversary of Sylvia's death.

Rita and Richard Pankhurst (in the middle) on their wedding day. Richard's mother Sylvia is next to him. Princess Seble is next to Sylvia

CHAPTER SEVEN
HITTING ROCK BOTTOM

The first months of the Emperor's sojourn in Bath had been difficult but worse was to come. By the end of 1937 the Emperor would hit rock bottom and things would never really improve after that for a couple of years or so. As time wore on, the separation from home and the onerous challenges of a diminished day-to-day existence grew exponentially. Life was just hard work and extremely wearing, both physically and psychologically. As Haile Selassie struggled to deal with the aftermath of the massacres in Addis Ababa in early 1937, he tried to keep up a brave public face. He dutifully turned up in May 1937 to support the Bath Dog Show and Bath Horse Show, two causes close to his heart.

Arriving at the Bath Horse Show together with the Mayor of Bath

IMPERIAL EXILE

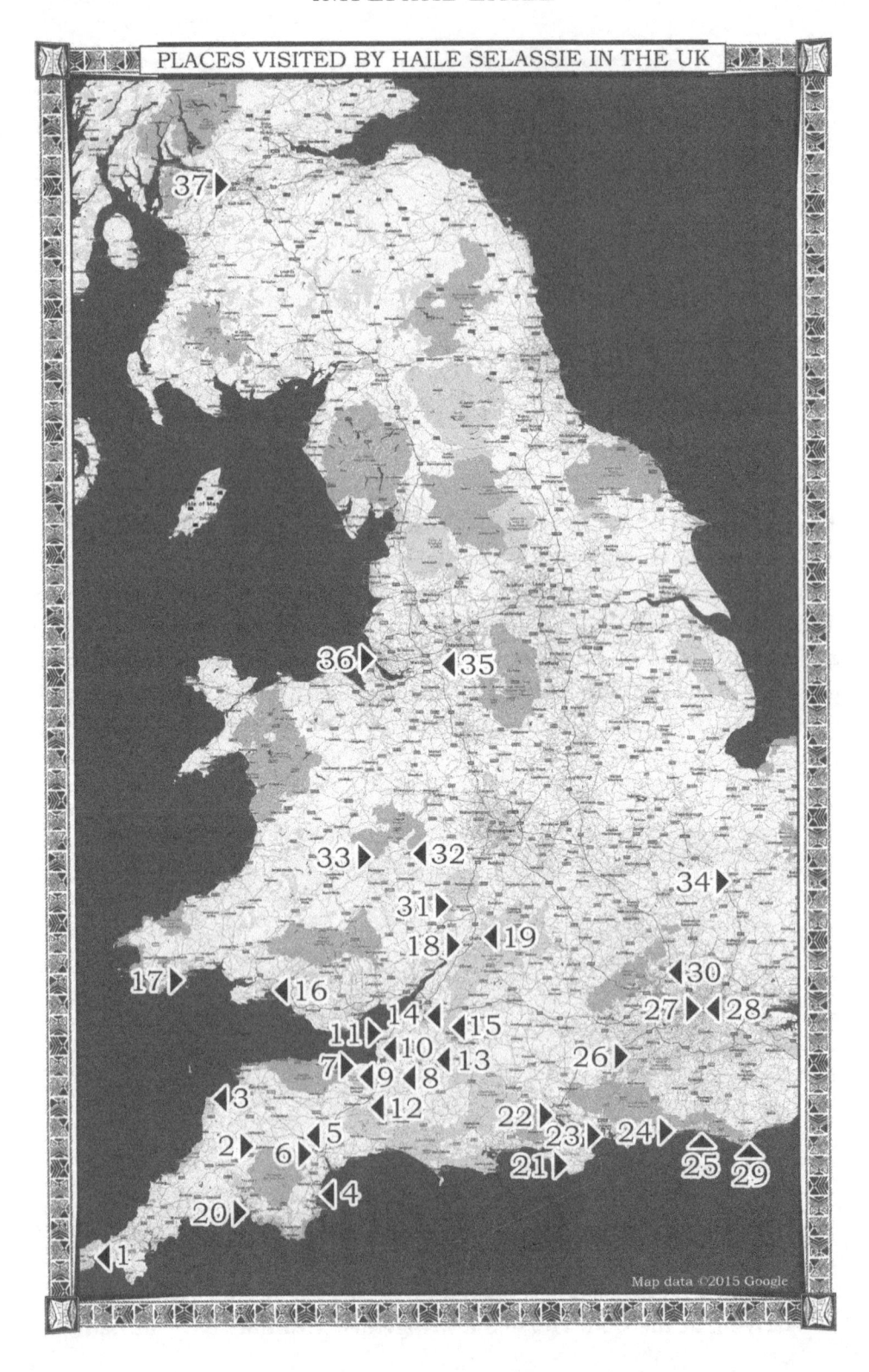

PLACES VISITED BY HAILE SELASSIE IN THE UK

CHAPTER 7

KEY

- 1 Penzance
- 2 Okehampton
- 3 Hartland
- 4 Torquay
- 5 Crediton
- 6 Exeter
- 7 Stogursey
- 8 Street
- 9 Bridgewater
- 10 Burnham-On-Sea
- 11 Weston-Super-Mare
- 12 Taunton
- 13 Wells
- 14 Bristol
- 15 Bath
- 16 Swansea
- 17 Tenby
- 18 Gloucester
- 19 Cheltenham
- 20 Plymouth
- 21 Isle of Wight
- 22 Southampton
- 23 Portsmouth
- 24 Worthing
- 25 Brighton
- 26 Aldershot
- 27 Wimbledon
- 28 London
- 29 Eastbourne
- 30 Abbots Langley
- 31 Malvern
- 32 Ludlow
- 33 Milebrook House
- 34 Cambridge
- 35 Dunham Massey
- 36 Liverpool
- 37 Glasgow

A few weeks later he attended a garden party at Fairfield with 80 guests to mark his 45th birthday. Beneath the refined atmosphere he must have felt nothing like celebrating a personal milestone. He was already in danger of losing his edge.

Fierce competition underway at the Bath Dog Show

In July the Emperor visited the nearby coastal resort of Weston-Super-Mare, a place he was to escape to several times during his time in Bath. He stayed with some of his family at the modest Severn Croft Hotel on the seafront.

The *Nottingham Evening Post* also contained a diary item in July, saying that the Emperor was now living a quiet life of a retired gentleman of modest means. It claimed one friend in Bath had tried to persuade him to take up trout fishing but he was no great fisherman. The paper also said he was an enthusiastic collector of beautiful pieces of porcelain and could often be seen visiting antique shops. However, over the coming months the financial, diplomatic and personal pressures of exile kept on mounting.

FINANCIAL WORRIES

The constant battle to make ends meet was debilitating and a blow to the pride of someone so regal. The Emperor's assumption had been that he would be able to return to Ethiopia soon after he had fled. That was not to materialise and now he somehow had to conjure up funds for the long-term. For one so reserved, he was surprisingly frank in public about the dire straits he found himself in. He told the *Chronicle* in the autumn of 1937 that he had only brought sufficient money for immediate needs. He also had to assist fellow refugees and to support litigation to recover money. The paper quoted him as saying that all he had brought with him was some silver, and no jewellery and no gold. He went on: 'It must be realised that we have absolutely no income. We must live on what little capital we have. When one has small capital and no income, when it is all outgoing and no incoming, anxiety is bound to happen.'

CHAPTER 7

Among the Bathonians reading these comments were bound to have been some who knew their Charles Dickens. The novelist had been a frequent visitor to Bath in the 19th century and loved drinking at the Saracens Head pub, the oldest one in the city. In the novel *David Copperfield* the author introduced the memorable character of William Micawber, who wrestled constantly with trying to keep afloat financially. Micawber uttered the immortal maxim: 'Annual income twenty pounds, annual expenditure nineteen pounds nineteen and six, result happiness. Annual income twenty pounds, annual expenditure twenty pounds nought and six, result misery.'

The thrust of Micawber's sentiments may have been in Haile Selassie's mind as he sat with his advisers poring over his accounts. The *Nottingham Evening Post* said that Haile Selassie must be the most pathetic figure in the whole world as he faced what it called the ogre of poverty. After all this publicity, a spokesman for the Emperor revealed that Fairfield House had been inundated with postal orders, food and even wine. However, the spokesman said that the Emperor did not want charity and suggested that any such help should be given to other Ethiopian exiles.

In the coming months, several rumours appeared in the *Chronicle* suggesting that the Emperor was contemplating moving elsewhere as Fairfield was becoming too expensive to maintain. The places mentioned included Bayswater, Weston-Super-Mare, Wimbledon, Kensington, and even the Firth of Clyde in Scotland. In November 1937 it was reported the Emperor was trying to sell the last of his three cars, and he said he was forced to take tramcars if he wanted to go into Bath. Money was so scarce that often he would travel by himself on the train to London. If any of his assistants accompanied him, they had to travel third-class.

As the winter months progressed it became a constant struggle to pay electricity and heating bills. The chairman of the regional electricity company became aware of Haile Selassie's plight. When he visited Fairfield on one occasion he discovered the Emperor sitting forlornly in an overcoat with a rug on his knees. The chairman promptly agreed to waive the bill. Food and money were sent to the house at Christmas by some in the local community. Years later, when the Emperor wrote the second part of his autobiography, it was clear this shortage of money still rankled. He concluded baldly that he had encountered grave financial difficulties and that these had been openly seen. He also talked about the political battles that had befallen him and the trials and tribulations that had occurred in his personal life. He said he had had to continue his struggle in solitude.

Despite his lack of funds, it seems that the Emperor did not forget his responsibility to give alms. One day a flag seller on behalf of the local hospital in Bath entered the grounds of Fairfield through the unlocked gates. She was gratified and surprised to have been given a pound note by none other than the Emperor himself. The *Chronicle* also proudly reported that there was one memento that he would never sell – a silver cup given to him by George V.

Ever since Haile Selassie arrived in Britain, the government had been monitoring his financial situation closely. They were all too well aware of the embarrassment that might ensure if the Emperor were to be formally declared bankrupt. Interminable discussions were held about whether a grant should be given to him from government funds. However, the talks quickly became bogged down in bureaucracy and petty inter-department squabbling. The tone was set by Lord Alexander Cadogan, the Under-Secretary at the Foreign Office. He recorded his doubts that what he called the luckless Emperor would ever be able to rid himself of leeches and other hangers-on. British officials were also continuing to be wary of being seen publicly to help Haile Selassie as that might upset the Italians, a perpetual fear of British mandarins. In February 1937 an ugly diplomatic row had broken out after the government officially invited the Emperor to the coronation of King George VI in May. The Italians protested and in the end the Emperor did not attend, though some of his representatives did.

One bold and imaginative proposal about the Emperor's finances came in November 1937 from the Foreign Secretary Anthony Eden. He inquired whether the now Chancellor of the Exchequer, Sir John Simon, should quietly release money to help the Emperor from, of all things, secret service funds. Sir John brusquely turned down this idea. He said this would be using monies for a purpose quite different to which they were intended and it would be embarrassing if such a plan leaked out.

Another sign of the mealy-mouthed and patronising approach of government supporters came in the form of a letter a few weeks later to Lord Cadogan from the MP for Bath, Loel Guinness. He said that he was coming under increasing pressure from the Emperor's sympathisers to raise the matter of a state grant to help Haile Selassie. However, Guinness swept the matter under the carpet, saying it would seem a pity to have a political controversy in his constituency over an individual emperor.

Mussolini with his well-informed network of Italian spies obviously got wind of the financial embarrassment of the Emperor. The Italian leader made several approaches to him, offering large financial inducements if he would announce his official abdication. Mussolini sent one emissary with a proposal that he would provide the Emperor with a palace in the country of his choosing and a one-off gift of one million guineas. Crown Prince Asfa-Wossen was also offered inducements to go back to Ethiopia and reign as a puppet leader. The Italians were obviously keen to subdue the population as much as possible. They also wanted to quickly end the Emperor's exile as they were well aware that many around the world were inspired by his stand against fascism and their doctrine was under threat as a result.

CHAPTER 7

Haile Selassie insisted that he would conduct any negotiations only through the League of Nations. He knew too that if he did abdicate then Britain would immediately change its de facto recognition of the Italian presence in Ethiopia into a de jure or legal recognition. The Emperor might end up returning to Ethiopia as part of an overall deal, but only as a nominal leader with his wings firmly clipped in charge of a tiny rump of the country. The Italian diplomatic overtures were rejected but only after some tense discussions within the Emperor's entourage in the UK. Debate raged about whether it was best now to accept Italy's offers, wait for help from other European countries or somehow return to Ethiopia and fight. As tension mounted, stories emerged of splits developing between the Fairfield House camp, the legation in London and the exiles in Jerusalem.

At one stage the foreign minister Heruy was reported to be in contact with the Jerusalem-based Kebede Tessema, the former court chamberlain, who had acted as that special bodyguard on the train to Djibouti. Kebede was urged to help keep the resistance alive. The tension between the two camps continued to simmer and in January 1939 the police had to be called in to quell rioting in Jerusalem between the different factions among the Ethiopian community. The Italians, for their part, were reported to be running into problems of their own on the ground in Ethiopia. Many of them were billeted in barbed wire enclosures and the train supply route from Addis to Djibouti was hazardous due to rebel attack. This was a rare piece of heartening news for the Emperor. Another boost for his battered morale was that the Butcher of Ethiopia, Graziani, had been moved on as Mussolini had indicated.

The replacement Viceroy was the Duke of Aosta, who came from privileged Italian royal stock and was a completely different character. Not only did he have a far less bombastic style but he had also been educated at those two pillars of British society, Eton College and Oxford University. He also enjoyed aristocratic pursuits such as fox hunting and playing polo. His approach as Viceroy would not be that of the overt iron fist. It is thought that his softer tactics stemmed from studying the mollifying colonial techniques used by the British in the running of their empire. The bureaucracy and corruption of the Italian administration set up to run Ethiopia did not impress the Duke. He was reported as saying that half his officials were inept, and a quarter were thieves. The Duke was not a pushover, as he had been an air force pilot during Italy's pacification of Libya in the early 1930s. Skirmishes between the Italian troops and Ethiopian rebels continued but the extreme brutality of the Graziani days did not resurface under the refined Duke. His appointment was certainly more acceptable to many in the British establishment.

In some ways the arrival of the Duke may not have been that positive for the Emperor. Many British politicians began to think that maybe the Italian operation in Ethiopia was not as bad as had been first thought. To them, the Duke was civilised, tolerant and even close to being 'one of us.' As arguments continued to rage about whether the Italian mission should be officially recognised by other European powers, the Duke's regal aura may well have been significant. He decided to set up his residence in the Gennete Leul Palace, yet another intrusion into the Emperor's privacy.

At Fairfield the constant battle to pay the electricity and coal bills was both embarrassing and a strain on a father trying to look after his family. The cold weather took a big toll on morale. Empress Menen especially found the winter hard. As the end of 1937 approached, the Fairfield community would have been filled with foreboding about having to soldier on through a second English winter. The temperature in Addis Ababa can fall to around 7 degrees centigrade at night in parts of the year because of the city's elevation, around 2,500 metres above sea level. But the royal residents at Fairfield would not have previously had to endure snow, frost and ice with very cold daytime temperatures as well as at night. The Bath stone would have made the unheated and draughty rooms feel even colder in the British winter. Many years later the Emperor baldly recalled that Fairfield had many rooms and was chilly. His view of the climate was vastly different to that of the denizens of Georgian high society who had flocked to the city in its 18th century heyday. They believed that Bath was unbearably hot in the summer and so kept well away at that time. For them the time to be in Bath was during the cooler months from around October to May.

The Imperial family, probably at Bath in late 1937 or 1938
Back row: Makonnen, Crown Prince Asfa-Wossen, Empress Menen, Emperor Haile Selassie, Princess Tsehai, Princess Tenagneworq
Front row: Hirut, Amaha, Sahle Selassie, Aida, Iskender holding Rosa the dog, Seble

CHAPTER 7

Back in Ethiopia in happier times a bevy of Imperial servants would have kept fires lit in the evening. Supplies of firewood would have been plentiful. At Fairfield the number of servants was limited and fuel was scarce and expensive. There may also have been some psychological factors which added to the perception that the UK was like a giant icebox. Everything was so unfamiliar and uncertain. In such circumstances any disruption of basic creature comforts can be magnified. The royal family were living in a city of exquisite Georgian architecture but the beauty of Bath could not answer some of their fundamental human needs to keep warm and to feel secure.

The financial crisis engulfing the Emperor led to rising tension with his long-time friend and minister in London, Dr Martin. The Emperor believed that Dr Martin was not doing enough to raise money and had repeatedly asked questions about his spending and accounting of Ethiopian funds. The two men clashed fiercely over a complicated row about the property used by the Ethiopian Legation in Princes Gate in west London. This had apparently been bought by Dr Martin through his personal funds along with another property in Princes Gate. Dr Martin decided to sell both properties as he was under increasing financial pressures of his own. He believed the profits should be his. But the Emperor's view was that the money should go to keeping the Ethiopian cause alive and challenged Dr Martin's claim to full ownership of the properties. Relations between the two men worsened and soon they were barely talking to each other. In October 1937 Dr Martin wanted to go to India, the land of his upbringing, to take care of pressing family issues, but he said the Emperor manipulated the housing dispute to prevent him from leaving. A furious Dr Martin wrote in his diary that the Emperor had brought up the matter with the view to keeping him in the UK. For Dr Martin it was what he called the usual underhand trick. The two men also argued over various subscription funds and relations worsened. However, before his death in 1952, Dr Martin returned to Ethiopia where he and the Emperor had a reconciliation of sorts and patched up their differences.

Haile Selassie had no luck with various court cases he had been pursuing in an attempt to claim funds he asserted were due to him as Ethiopian leader. One case was brought before a court in Paris where the Emperor was trying to realise his half share in the Djibouti to Addis Ababa railway company. The shares were valued at around £30,000 and, if cashed in, would have solved many of his financial headaches at a stroke. The deal originated from Emperor Menelik's decision to grant a French company a concession to build the line through Ethiopian territory. Haile Selassie said the agreement was registered in the name of the government of Abyssinia and was therefore part of his estate. The claim was contested but the Italians said they were now the sovereign power in Ethiopia. The referee court said it was not competent to deal with the issue and it would have to be heard by a civil tribunal. This legal process reportedly came to nothing in the end.

The attempt to retrieve assets from the Bank of Egypt, which had been holding substantial funds from the Bank of Ethiopia, now dissolved by the Italians, ended in failure. In the final stages of the case in London in May 1937, Justice Clauson airily referred to Haile Selassie as the fugitive Emperor and dismissed his claim. The ruling in effect recognised Italian sovereignty in Ethiopia. Supporters of the Emperor said he had been wantonly robbed. The *New Times* and *Ethiopia News*, in its edition of 12 June, carried an angry statement by Colonel Maurice Spencer. He said: 'We have recognised the burglar and view with equanimity his clearing off with the swag.'

The Emperor was successful in two libel cases against the *Evening Standard*, which printed allegations that he had given orders to torture a rebel prisoner in Ethiopia by breaking his legs. Haile Selassie said he had to correct the report to preserve his reputation in Britain. He said he was deeply conscious of hospitality afforded him by the people of the UK and felt incumbent to make it clear there was not a word of truth of any kind in the allegations. After the libel was repeated in 1938, he was awarded a tidy sum of around £6,000 in damages.

One legal action was actually brought against Haile Selassie by an American businessman Leo Chertok. He was claiming funds spent as part of an attempt to gain oil and mineral concessions in Ethiopia while the Emperor was still in power. The damages claim was for £23,000. Chertok's legal representatives tried to serve the writ at Fairfield House but the Emperor referred the matter to his London solicitors. They argued that the writ be set aside because sovereigns, like diplomats, were exempt from proceedings.

The most intense and damaging legal case the Emperor was involved in was the claim against the expanding telecommunications company Cable and Wireless. The case rumbled on for two years from early January 1937 with many twists and turns along the way. Cable and Wireless throughout accepted that it owed more than £10,000 in connection with royalties for the introduction of a radio telegraph service between London and Addis Ababa. This is around £620,000 in today's money. The issue was to whom should they pay it, now that there was doubt over who was the sovereign power in Ethiopia – the Emperor or the Italian state. The arguments went back and forward in various courts, each time racking up crippling charges for a monarch who could not even pay his coal and electricity bills regularly. In another humiliation it was announced in Ethiopia that new postage stamps were to be issued by the Italian authorities, replacing the face of Haile Selassie with that of King Emmanuel.

Despite all his worries the Emperor still strove throughout 1937 to maintain a dignified face and continued to attend society events. He travelled to other towns in south-west England, including Torquay and Street. In September the Emperor and some of the royal family went on a tour of the Queen Mary liner docked in Southampton. It was about a year since the ship had broken the record for the fastest transatlantic crossing between the UK and the United States. The *Chronicle* reported

CHAPTER 7

that the royal party was escorted by someone described as a giant Ethiopian, who acted as a bodyguard. They all took tea in the ship's private dining saloon. The royal party also toured Admiral Nelson's flagship *HMS Victory* along the south coast in Portsmouth. The Emperor was seen smiling when he was told that Nelson, while he lay dying, knew he had achieved a great victory. On the surface it seemed the Emperor was leading a normal life and taking full advantage of British social life. He was behaving in some ways like a perfect English gentleman. But in reality just about everything was going wrong.

DESPERATE DAYS

By the end of 1937 the pressures on the Emperor were building up to a crescendo. An incident at Christmas summed up the low ebb of his fortunes. While he was on his way by taxi from Paddington Station to record a seasonal radio message to thank his supporters in America, the vehicle was involved in a serious accident. The Emperor broke a collar bone and also injured his knee in the collision. In typical stoical fashion he gritted his teeth and delivered the radio address as planned. His talk was carried by about 100 stations in the United States. The Emperor then tried to seek help from a doctor in Harley Street and from Sir Sidney Barton, but could not get hold of either of them on the phone. Despite the pain he was enduring, the Emperor also fulfilled a more personal engagement. He attended a Christmas party at Great Ormond Street Children's Hospital where Princess Tsehai was still working. It was not until he reached home in Bath that his injury was properly seen to.

A few weeks later Empress Menen departed for the warmer climes of Jerusalem. She had finally had enough of the Bath winter and a legation spokesman admitted she had been ill. Several British newspapers reported tearful scenes at Victoria Station in London as the Empress left. Among her fellow travellers were her son Sahle Selassie and Ras Kassa, whose absence was to be a further blow to the Emperor. A large number of well-wishers gathered on the station platform and the Empress broke down in tears, covering her face with a handkerchief.

Ras Kassa went to Jerusalem for at least two reasons. He wanted to support his wife and family, still grieving over the loss of three of his sons. In addition, he took on the role of giving some leadership to the wider Ethiopian community in the city. Tension had been erupting between those who had already been living in Jerusalem before the Italian invasion, and the new exiles from Ethiopia. Now it was Ras Kassa's job to bring peace. He was to keep in regular touch by letter with the Emperor back in Bath.

Haile Selassie tried to carry on as normal. He let it be known that his shoulder was improving, and that he liked nothing better than seeing fresh scenes in England

and meeting new friends. However, it all sounded a little threadbare. The Emperor was giving the appearance of a man going through the motions. Meanwhile, news from Ethiopia was worsening. The population was facing a growing threat of famine with talk of serious shortages of meat and milk supplies. Some local chiefs had been imprisoned, and Italian troops had forced some peasants to leave their farms and work for the occupiers for next to nothing. Some Ethiopians left their homes to cross the border into Kenya where they stayed in basic camps run by the British. The dangers involved in the journey was highlighted by a gruesome despatch carried by the *New Times* and *Ethiopia News*. Four people at the rear of a small band of refugees were attacked, killed and eaten by three lions.

With the Empress away, Haile Selassie went on a mini tour of England to try to keep himself busy. Such restlessness and an inability to feel settled are typical symptoms of exile. At times it seemed the Emperor simply had to escape what may have on occasion appeared to be the cage of Fairfield House and get on the road to somewhere else. He managed somehow to find access to some ready cash for this latest trip. He spent several days towards the end of January 1938 at the resplendent country home of Walcot Hall in remote countryside near the village of Lydbury North in Shropshire. He was staying with Ronald and Noel Stevens, and arrived with a large number of trunks and several staff. The grounds of the handsome Georgian house contained a mile-long lake, a private zoo and bird sanctuary. The Emperor was the first African many people in the area had ever seen. Many locals were curious to catch a glimpse of him and even touch him. Police were on duty throughout the visit but the Emperor was cheered wherever he went. One resident remembers him being driven around in a yellow Rolls Royce. The royal visitor also received a civic reception at the nearby village of Bishop's Castle near the border with Wales.

The mini tour of England continued in early February when the Emperor took up residence for a few days at the Castle Towers hotel facing Wimbledon Common in south London. He was guarded by private detectives. The *Chronicle* in Bath reported that the Emperor's party arrived in four cars, and that he wanted to be based in Wimbledon to be close to any political developments in central London. The Emperor was to be jolted out of his malaise and diversionary travels by a diplomatic crisis of huge proportions. For months the British government had been softening its resistance to recognising the Italian occupation in Ethiopia. Later in February 1938 the Emperor was dealt a serious blow when his ally, the Foreign Secretary Anthony Eden, resigned because of growing tensions over British policy towards Italy. He had disagreed with Prime Minister Neville Chamberlain about opening formal talks with Rome over the de jure issue.

Eden received a lot of public support for his stance but that was no comfort to him or Haile Selassie. The Italians were delighted and Eden's resignation was

CHAPTER 7

seen as a great victory for Il Duce. One of the most prominent scourges of fascism was now gone from the scene. Mussolini had once contemptuously derided Eden as the 'best dressed fool in Europe.' Haile Selassie, already nearing the end of his tether, was plunged further into more gloom by the loss of an influential ally but the resignation also roused him to enter back into the political fray. Eden's successor Lord Halifax was much less sympathetic to the Ethiopian cause and took a hard-headed approach. He believed that it was sheer folly to continue annoying the Italians with Hitler increasingly on the prowl. In any case he argued that no-one could deny that Mussolini was the winner of the war in Abyssinia. Lord Halifax also was not impressed by pressure put on him by the Abyssinian Association to release government funds to help the Emperor.

The Association had already become more aggressive in its campaigning. It announced it was planning to organise a worldwide appeal to help the Emperor. This was despite the opposition of some of the supporters, who were concerned that, despite his apparent consent to the plan, Haile Selassie would be humiliated by being made the object of public charity. The debate rumbled on throughout the summer of 1938. Lord Halifax was swayed by arguments from among his own supporters. They argued that the Association's high-profile campaigning was a breach of the Emperor's promise given when he first came to the UK that he would not engage openly in political action. Halifax's public support of Italy greatly irritated and alarmed Haile Selassie. He wanted to make public a letter he sent to the Prime Minister complaining about Halifax's pro-Italian statements in parliament.

After a diplomatic kerfuffle, the Emperor agreed to keep his criticisms out of the public eye. Intriguingly, Halifax gave a briefing to cabinet colleagues in which he revealed some sensitive discussions he had held with the Emperor. According to Halifax's version of events, Haile Selassie had said he was warmly with the British government in its desire to introduce appeasement into the world. As his contribution to that policy, the Emperor would be willing to consider a compromise with the Italian government under which he would accept sovereignty over only a part of his former dominion. Such a potential climb down was at odds with the Emperor's stated public position. It is true we only have Halifax's account of this conversation and the Emperor may in any case only have been saying these soothing words to give the impression of being conciliatory. However, it may also reveal why there was so much tension among the Ethiopian camp about how to deal with the various Italian inducements to sue for peace.

Given his worsening diplomatic hand, the Emperor may just have flirted with the thought that to have access to some cake rather than none at all might just about be the best realistic option left. Indeed, his American adviser John Spencer stated that on occasion it was Haile Selassie's camp that opened up negotiations with the Italian side, including one attempt through the good offices of the Vatican. In the end the Emperor did not close any deal with Italy, but he could painfully see which way the wind was blowing over the de jure recognition issue. In the last two weeks of March he succumbed to what was described as a severe bout of flu. It was a lonely and dispiriting time as he was emotionally and physically exhausted. He must have wondered whether he would ever see his homeland again.

One great burden would have been the pressure of facing up to an unknown future and feeling the pain of losing the opportunities he assumed he would have had. This assumptive loss is a hidden factor in experiencing the bitter pill of exile or indeed in coping with any unexpected loss that arises from traumatic events such as compulsory redundancy or a life-changing accident. After his coronation the Emperor would have figured that he would be in power for years and that he would validate his rule by a series of actions and reforms. Now he faced the prospect not only of never going back to Ethiopia but of a life just stretching out ahead of him into nothingness and oblivion. Like many other exiles, he had suffered economic hardship, a conflicted identity and the shock of trying to survive in a culture alien to his own. He had gone through a searing loss. Now he had the uncomfortable pressures of relating to the present and was trying to fathom how to deal with an uncertain and unappealing future. The song of exile by Paul Tabori says that 'exile is the ego that shrinks, for how can you prove what you are and what you did?'

These sentiments would appear to be an accurate description of the turmoil the Emperor was now undergoing. It is no wonder that many exiles through the ages have suffered from alcoholism, mental breakdown and suicidal tendencies. Like many other exiles, Haile Selassie was in danger of being worn down by being obsessively on the alert for any sign of weakness in his enemy, which could open the door to get back home. He was even more of a prisoner than someone actually serving a sentence in jail. There was no escape. Prince Beede Mariam says that his grandfather used to tell him that the darkest hours in his life had been while he was in Bath. Prince Beede says the Emperor had always faced challenges. He had had no youth as he had been thrust into testing government duties from early teenage years. However, nothing compared to the dire and tough days of exile, made worse by the unprecedented decision to flee his country, which would undoubtedly have played on his mind. The Prince believes the generosity of the British people helped to keep his grandfather going. But the most important support mechanism was his trust in God.

The Emperor's faith had always been a bedrock in his life and it is possible that the Emperor found some comfort by recalling some specific incidents in the Holy Scriptures. As a good student of the Bible, he would have been aware of the story of the Old Testament prophet Job. His faith was severely tested when, from a position of prosperity and security, he suddenly lost his home, health, status and members of

CHAPTER 7

his family. However, the prophet never abandoned his faith in God. In the end Job underwent a powerful redemptive experience and his fortunes were restored.

The Old Testament also contains the story of the Israelites struggling in exile in Egypt and then eventually escaping to their homeland. The Emperor could certainly identify with the lament in the book of Psalms about how can you sing the Lord's song in a strange land. Did any of these biblical stories give the Emperor hope? What really helped him to cling on through those dark, desolate days in his bedroom at Fairfield in the early part of 1938? Of course, it should not be forgotten that the Emperor all his life had been resilient and, if necessary, could be a street fighter with a very tough streak. But now he was on the verge of being totally overwhelmed.

The iconic photograph of a downcast Emperor on the West Pier in Brighton

Stories about the Emperor were still regularly appearing in the British press. The Emperor cancelled a trip he was to have made to Trondheim in Norway to give a lecture. Because of the political uncertainty he instead delivered the lecture in English by telephone. On another occasion he opened a church bazaar by telephone in the northern town of Bradford. In April 1938 a waxwork model of the Emperor was added to the collection at Madame Tussauds, along with a number of famous sportsmen, including the cricketer Wally Hammond. A bizarre diary item appeared in the *Dundee Courier and Advertiser*, talking about the Emperor's diet. It said that he was now often eating kippers for breakfast after finding them delicious when urged to try them. His health improved a little as he started to go for walks again and he also visited Great Malvern to present the prizes at Clarendon School attended by his granddaughters, Hirut and Seble. He stayed at the Abbey Hotel, a former Benedictine monastery with extensive landscaped grounds. He was a guest there several times during his exile.

In April the Emperor was photographed in a simple wooden deck chair on the West Pier at the resort of Brighton on the south coast, well wrapped up in an overcoat to ward off the early spring chill. In Addis Ababa he had been used to sitting on a throne. Now he was reduced to sitting in the most basic of chairs, used by thousands of families in Britain while on holiday.

While at Brighton he visited St Paul's Church, following his familiar pattern of getting to know some of the local places of worship.

Outside the Royal Pavilion in Brighton with Crown Prince Asfa-Wossen and Princess Tenagneworq

The south coast of England seemed to appeal to the Emperor a great deal. On his earlier visit to Worthing along the coast from Brighton, he had stayed in great secrecy in a specially decorated and refurbished suite at the Warnes Hotel. The hotel later installed the emblem of a crown to mark the Imperial visit. This had to be rescued by a conservationist when the Warnes burned down in a disastrous fire in 1987. In another intriguing coincidence it is rumoured locally that Churchill planned the D-Day landings from a suite in the hotel.

CHAPTER 7

During the early summer of 1938 the harsh political realities were relentlessly closing in. In May the Emperor made a desperate trip to Geneva as the League of Nations gathered to discuss Halifax's motion suggesting that each nation could do as it pleased about the Italian occupation. The Emperor confirmed he had been seriously ill in the previous few weeks and his health was still in a critical condition. During the whole trip to and from Geneva he was attended by a special physician every morning and evening. On the way the ailing ruler had a rare moment of solace when he was able to spend two hours at Paris railway station with Empress Menen, who, by chance, was passing through while returning to Bath after her winter break in Jerusalem. Because of the Emperor's ill-health there was to be no repeat of his electrifying appearance in 1936 at the League of Nations. He walked up to the same podium from where he had done all he could to prick the consciences of the League members two years previously. But this time exhaustion got the better of him. He knew that many in the audience were now apathetic or even actively against him.

The Emperor began with a few sentences in French but found the effort and occasion too overwhelming. His assistant Lorenzo Taezaz had to step in and read the full script. The words reflected the weak and difficult diplomatic position Haile Selassie was in, especially as he was about to publicly challenge the British, who had granted him asylum: 'I deeply regret that I must enter into conflict with the Government for which I feel the sincerest respect and which is according me hospitality.'

While Taezaz was reading the speech, the Emperor was said to have remained immobile with downcast eyes. The League took no notice of the Emperor's words and passed Halifax's motion. Some nations had already given de jure recognition and others expressed their intention to do so, including Britain. An agreement was signed soon afterwards between London and Rome to that effect, though it was to be several months before it came into force. The Emperor could not have imagined anything worse. He undoubtedly felt completely betrayed and deflated. Even the *Chronicle*, until now a faithful supporter of the Emperor, stabbed him in the back in an editorial. It said:

> *'The sympathy that is felt for Haile Selassie is natural and proper – and in Bath where he has become a citizen, it is especially warm – but it would be unnatural and improper to uphold his cause at the cost, as Lord Halifax pointed out, of probably greater consequent trouble in Europe. The cause of general peace is of far greater omen than the fate of Abyssinia, a fact which the League Council with only a few dissenters have recognised.'*

Perhaps the *Chronicle* should not be blamed too much for its volte face, as it may only have been reflecting a shift in British public opinion. The truth was that the novelty of the Emperor was simply wearing off. The British were becoming very nervous and alarmed at events much closer to home than a faraway place in the Horn of Africa. However, newspapers in France took a very different view of the way the Emperor had been treated. *Le Journal* said the League had him leave without a word and with no gesture of courtesy. A sizeable crowd also gathered in support as the Emperor left by train.

The Emperor was at a very low ebb when he returned from Geneva and the will to fight on was draining away. He cancelled an important meeting at Central Hall in Westminster and the reason given was that he was too sick in mind and body. The *Chronicle* was a little more sympathetic in its report of the Emperor's homecoming to Bath. It said that, although virtually deprived of his empire by league delegates, he had maintained his characteristic dignified bearing. As usual, the paper was obsessed with the Emperor's outfit. On this occasion he wore a black trilby hat, black cloak and light brown brogue shoes. The reporter recorded a touching scene as the Negus removed his hat and kissed each of his two sons who were at the station to greet him. He then made his way to Fairfield where he was reunited with the Empress. She had brought with her the last of the crown jewels they had taken from the country in an attempt to keep the fight going. Together they were refusing to give up, despite the League's diplomatic bombshell.

Churchill was also in Bath at this time making a speech about peace and freedom. Like every other British politician, he was alarmed by Hitler's increasingly aggressive stance. In February 1938 the German leader's forces had entered Austria in the Anschluss and there was mounting concern that Czechoslovakia might be next. By this time the Ethiopian Legation at 5 Princes Gate in London was officially closed. It had been struggling along for months, funded only by the various public appeals by Charles Martin. Although the Legation now had no official credentials, it continued to operate from a smaller rented house at 43 Gloucester Square in London. The Emperor occasionally spent the night there and also received visitors.

At the end of May in 1938 Haile Selassie went to the Isle of Wight for a rest and to lick his wounds after the latest setback in Geneva. He was turning into a man of leisure, finding gentle ways of filling his time. Naturally the local paper in the area, the *Isle of Wight Mercury*, was fascinated by its royal visitor. It said it understood the Emperor was coming for a rest and to recover his health in the sea air, as he had recently been adversely affected by stress.

CHAPTER 7

Boat trip on the Isle of Wight

The Emperor and his assistant stayed in the island town of Ventnor where the Emperor was spotted strolling along the promenade, wearing a cloth cap favoured by the working classes, not his usual bowler. A local boat owner took him out for a trip by sea to Puckaster Cove. The weather was warm with temperatures recorded of more than 20 degrees Celsius. The Emperor stayed at the Beach Hotel on the esplanade where he was given exclusive use of a private sitting room on the ground floor. He spent most of the time walking, though he attended the cinema on two evenings. The Emperor also took tea with the Irish author Henry de Vere Stacpoole in the nearby village of Bonchurch. He was most famous for his romantic novel *Blue Lagoon*, which has been turned into a feature film on several occasions. In nearby Portsmouth there was also the opportunity for the Emperor to indulge one of his passions by inspecting an array of aeroplanes, including Hawker Hurricanes.

In June the Emperor was invited to stay with the Earl of Stamford, Roger Grey, whose family seat was at the spectacular Georgian property of Dunham Massey in Altrincham near Manchester. The Earl, who came from a long distinguished line of English nobility, had contacted the Emperor after being moved by his speech at the League of Nations in 1936. Dunham Massey had opened its doors to several hundred wounded British soldiers during World War 1. The Earl arranged for the Ethiopian flag to fly over the house on the Emperor's birthday on July 23, a tradition which was reinstated in 2012 by the National Trust, the current owners of Dunham Massey.

The public debate over the Emperor's future continued unabated throughout the summer. Surprisingly, some backing for returning on Italian terms came from the Archbishop of Canterbury. He wondered whether Haile Selassie should end the threat of perpetual exile, and make a sacrifice by giving up his full title and returning to his land to make it peaceful. In parliament, one Member of Parliament suggested that Britain should offer Haile Selassie the opportunity to rule over part of the British colony of Tanganyika in East Africa. Among his new subjects would be some of the 6,000 refugees from Ethiopia, currently living a precarious existence in Kenya. Amid the gloom came a glimmer of good news in the wrangling over funds for the Emperor. It was announced that a private and unidentified benefactor had agreed to provide him with an overall sum of £10,000. The government reckoned that £2,000 a year would be enough for the Emperor to live on. It therefore arranged for a sum of £500 to be paid every three months. Under the terms of the gift, which the desperate Emperor eventually gratefully accepted after some prevarication, the benefactor was to remain strictly anonymous.

The intervention by the private donor had got the Foreign Office off the hook. It had still been pushing Eden's suggestion about obtaining money from secret service funds but had continued to face opposition from other government departments. Above all, the government as a whole was relieved that the murky and shabby political wrangles over the finances had not been exposed to the public. Even Halifax wrote that the position would have become extremely awkward had the government not been saved from embarrassment by the anonymous philanthropist.

Official papers held at the National Archives in Kew reveal the mysterious benefactor as a Lieutenant-Colonel Sir William Cox. He was a former Royal Artillery officer who had served during World War I and had been awarded the DSO. He had been wounded twice and received a serious spinal injury which ended his military career. He had made his money as managing director of the vastly wealthy Ellerman Property Trust Limited. The internecine warfare between government departments over the Emperor's money re-emerged when the tax authorities indicated that Cox's gift was subject to income tax, cutting the total amount to be given to the Emperor by around £3,000. The issue meandered along inconclusively before being submerged in far more pressing diplomatic matters as war approached.

The Emperor continued to limp along during the summer of 1938. In July he was again photographed reading a newspaper in a deckchair, this time in the southern coastal resort of Eastbourne. At the end of the month there was another betrayal in Bath. It was a further chink in the previously solid front that had been put forward by the civic authorities. The Guildhall opened its doors to some distinguished visitors from France, Belgium and, horror of horrors, Italy. Toasts were made to all the royal families of the countries represented, including to the Italian king and Il Duce. The Italian anthem was also played. It was a good job Fairfield was far enough away from

CHAPTER 7

the centre of Bath so that the Emperor was spared having to hear the strains of *Marcia Reale d'Ordinanza* ringing round.

A couple of months later the Emperor's steadfast companion, the foreign minister Heruy Wolde-Selassie, died at the age of 60. He had been ill for some time and had already drawn up a will while in Bath. Heruy had the highly appropriate title of Blattengeta, which means the 'chief business manager of the king.' He was an intellectual giant, who had done much to serve his country. Financial records show that he made two payments of £1,000 to boost the Emperor's income, around £120,000 in today's money. In his autobiography the Emperor described Heruy as brilliant and iron-willed, and as his confidant and helper. He had put Ethiopia on the map from a diplomatic point of view and was part of the delegation when Ethiopia joined the League of Nations in 1923.

Heruy, a thoughtful figure with a grey goatee beard, was on Haile Selassie's Grand Tour of Europe in 1924. He also made a ground-breaking trip to Japan as foreign secretary – a country which was seen as the model for how to modernise after being isolated for centuries. Heruy's output as an author was impressive and he wrote more than 20 books in all, including a short novel about the conflict between modernisers and traditionalists in Ethiopia. His last great work, on the history of Ethiopia, was in the hands of the printers when war with Italy broke out. One of Heruy's sons, Fekade Selassie, known as George, was educated at Cambridge University. He was killed by the Italians in Addis Ababa after the attempt to kill Graziani. Heruy's other son Sirak attended Brasenose College at Oxford University and translated Samuel Johnson's 18th century poetic novel *Rasselas* into Amharic. The story is about an Abyssinian prince who is bored with his rural life at home, and travels abroad in search of happiness. However, he realises he has made a mistake and quickly returns to be enveloped in the warm embrace of his homeland. The murder of Heruy's son George and the lengthy enforced separation from other family members, including his wife who was held as a captive in Italy, took its toll. Heruy never had a robust constitution and the *Times* obituary said that, as the world crumbled around him, the strain became too great.

Heruy's funeral took place at Locksbrook Cemetery in Bath after private rites were observed at the makeshift chapel at Fairfield. It was attended by the Emperor and family members, and was probably one of the most distinctive funerals ever held in Bath. The ceremony was a true Ethiopian experience. The Emperor delivered the oration at the graveside and his voice broke on several occasions. According to the Ethiopian historian Bahru Zewde, it was only the second time since his coronation that the Emperor abandoned the royal 'we' in his speech and reverted to a much more personal 'I' form. The only other such occasion had been in his moving speech at the League of Nations in 1936. During the funeral oration the Emperor said:

'Although the storm generated by wicked people destabilised the world and buffeted you, it did not defeat you. Yet you had to obey the rule of the Great and Kind Lord. We are all subject to this eventually… We bid you goodbye from this hospitable land where we came as guests.'

Many mourners were in tears as they gazed at the coffin draped in Ethiopian colours. Orthodox priests wore black robes and stoles of scarlet, gold and blue. Tapers were lit in best Ethiopian tradition and handed round to the grieving crowd. After the body was laid to rest mourners filed past and threw handfuls of earth onto the coffin. The exile in Bath had claimed its first life.

The Emperor was now even more alone. He had lost Heruy, and Ras Kassa was away in Jerusalem. Many of the Emperor's support mechanisms were being kicked away from under his feet. Like many exiles, he was now caught in no man's land – unable to return home and yet unable to settle into a new life in his new base. Deep down Haile Selassie must have been incredibly restless and starting to question his role in life. However, he would have been well aware that the threat of war in Europe was growing and maybe that did create some limited grounds for optimism. He could well have surmised that the convulsions of war might somehow lead to him returning to Ethiopia. All other possible avenues seem to have been closed off. Now the impending Armageddon could be the final throw of the dice.

However, in the autumn of 1938 an opportunity arose for the Emperor to take some action and escape his passivity. His trusted ally George Steer helped to broker a deal in Paris with anti-fascist campaigners to undertake a couple of reconnaissance missions to Ethiopia. The purpose was to test the strength of the rebel forces and the level of political support for the Emperor. Lorenzo Taezaz was released from his administrative duties in Bath to travel undercover in Ethiopia. He showed his versatility by donning various disguises to acquire information. It was a tentative attempt by the Emperor to take the initiative. Monsignor Jarosseau, the Emperor's former teacher from his birthplace of Harar, had also sensed that an opportunity might be presenting itself. In a letter in the summer of 1938 he had encouraged his former pupil to make an appearance around Khartoum near the border of Ethiopia. He said he hoped that England might grasp the importance of such a move and that the Italians might then be forced to remove their forces from the civil war in Spain.

Any such hopes had to be temporarily suspended in October 1938 when Prime Minister Neville Chamberlain came back from a conference in Berlin with Hitler and Mussolini about Czechoslovakia. Waving his now infamous piece of paper, Chamberlain claimed he had reached a peace agreement with Hitler. War had been averted but at a cost. The area in dispute in Czechoslovakia was Sudetenland where

CHAPTER 7

many ethnic Germans lived. This had now been sacrificed to Nazi Germany. Haile Selassie would have been appalled. He was for the most part against appeasement in principle and on pragmatic grounds knew that his last chance for ending his wretched exile could be slipping away. Many in Britain were ecstatic that hostilities had been avoided. However, despite the hoopla over the accord, it was reported that 14 trenches were being built in Bath. Each of them could hold 100 people during air raids. The *Chronicle's* front page was certain that a catastrophe had been avoided. It carried a reproduction of a beautiful picture by a Bath artist, who had forwarded it to Chamberlain. The paper said it was a small token of the immense gratitude towards a great statesman.

The newsreel of Chamberlain arriving back in London after his so-called breakthrough talks would possibly have been seen by the Emperor at the Little Theatre in Bath. Now he could only wait and ponder. A more realistic assessment of the state of security in Europe was given at a meeting of the West of England branch of the Abyssinian Society attended by the Emperor. The president of the society drew what he called an instructive parallel between the tragic experiences of Ethiopia and more recent events in Czechoslovakia. He warned against indulging in a spirit of false confidence. By December the resistance of the Ethiopian rebels had much reduced, according to details given by Lord Halifax to the British cabinet. He said the only area where the Italians were not in full control was around one of Ethiopia's former capitals, Ankober, a mountainous settlement just over 100 miles north east of the capital. Little seemed to be going the Emperor's way. One of his increasingly rare public appearances came in a visit to the Fry's chocolate factory, a few miles from Bath. It was probably a pleasant enough diversion but as far removed from the political fray as could be imagined.

The royal family watching a worker at Fry's chocolate factory near Bristol

A major rebuff for the Emperor came at the beginning of December 1938. Chamberlain told the House of Commons that the government was now intending to implement the agreement giving de jure recognition of the Italian government occupying Ethiopia. It capped a totally dreadful year for the Emperor. What made this announcement even more catastrophic was that it came the day before a much delayed hearing on his legal claim against Cable and Wireless. This diplomatic news totally scuppered any chance he might have had of winning. It meant the Italians would receive the money from Cable and Wireless while the Emperor was left to settle his large legal bills. It was a total defeat.

Thereafter newspaper reports increasingly referred to him as the ex-Emperor, as did many in official circles in the British government. His whole identity and purpose in life had been ripped to shreds. All his talents had been neutered. Other refugees and victims of political conflict are known to experience a profound loss of hope and a sense of futility. It would have been difficult for Haile Selassie to have avoided such moments of darkness. In his essay on separation and dislocation, Professor Said said that exile was like death but without death's ultimate mercy. This was certainly the state that Haile Selassie now found himself in.

CHAPTER 7

CHAPTER SEVEN EYEWITNESS OPEN DAY AT FAIRFIELD HOUSE

I have been to Fairfield House a number of times as my current home is in Bath. By bicycle the journey takes about 25 minutes. One route is via the scenic cycle path alongside the River Avon. The other way by road is along the route Haile Selassie would have taken by car, on foot or by tramcar. This way involves taking the upper Bristol Road from the centre of town, which runs along the bottom of the Royal Victoria Park with its splendid botanical gardens and green open spaces. After about a mile the road splits and you have to take the right turn up Newbridge Hill for about another mile before reaching the discreet entrance to Fairfield House. All this area was developed in Victorian times and, while attractive and quiet, does not reach the architectural heights of the Georgian parts of Bath. If you continue on past Fairfield House, you quickly emerge into green fields as the boundaries of Bath are left behind on the road to the picturesque village of Kelston.

Fairfield House today

The main drive of Fairfield House is now padlocked so any flag sellers, like everyone else, have to go round the back, up alongside Partis College and then along a narrow road, one of the original entrances to the house. A number of bungalows for the elderly are situated next to this road which is in the original grounds. The housing development reflects its local heritage, bearing the name of Empress Menen Gardens. These bungalows stand on the site of the cottage in the grounds where Ras Kassa and foreign minister Heruy lived. About 100 yards away from the main house is a small house, the home of the caretaker at Fairfield. Much of the original stone wall remains and the garden had obviously been quite extensive in Haile Selassie's day. Nearer to the main house, nothing is left of the greenhouse, which served as the makeshift Orthodox chapel and was such a source of comfort to the royal family. However, it is possible to see where it was situated as the grass and earth are a different colour.

From the garden you can look back up towards the top of Lansdown Hill and see a structure known as Beckford's Tower. This was built in the 19th century by a rich eccentric William Beckford to house his fine books and manuscripts. Perhaps this structure attracted the Royal family's attention as they may have been curious about their surroundings. Beckford himself said that the tower was a useful landmark for drunken farmers returning home, not that Haile Selassie would ever have found himself in that state.

Standing guard at Fairfield House

To the left of the back entrance is a carved tribute to the Emperor. A couple of years ago the figure of the lion was shaped out of the remnants of a tree trunk. The view to

CHAPTER 7

the opposite side of the valley is now mainly blocked by tall trees so it would have been hard today for the Emperor to have been reminded of his beloved Harar hills.

Inside, the downstairs rooms appear to be in the same layout as in the Emperor's time, though the furnishings are now more austere. I closed my eyes immediately and tried to imagine the slight figure of the Emperor walking slowly in the hallway with servants bowing to him, or the sound of the various children running up and down the stairs.

I was there on one occasion in mid January when the weather was biting, windy and wet. It was the sort of day that left the Empress in despair. I tried to imagine the cold seeping inside the house and had to ignore the effects of a central heating boiler installed after the royal family left. The occasion of one of my visits was to join some members of the Ethiopian community from Bristol and surrounding areas to celebrate Ethiopian Christmas, which falls in early January. No doubt the royal family would have celebrated the feast too in the best way they could while they were here.

One of the invited guests was Ezra Tsegaye, an Ethiopian living in Bath, but he could not come due to illness. Ezra is connected to the Emperor in a couple of ways. His father built for the Emperor a modern version of St Stephen's Church near Meskel Square in Addis Ababa. His sister-in-law Lydia was a childhood friend of Princesses Seble and Hirut. They used to play together in the nursery at Fairfield.

The first floor at the house is a labyrinth. There are two or three big rooms at the front but towards the back are a variety of cubby holes and small rooms. No-one is totally sure which one was the Emperor's bedroom. However, a small museum has been established in the most likely candidate where the windows directly face the front. On the wall are some evocative photographs of the Royal Family at Fairfield when they lived there. Even on the day I visited in mid-January, it felt a bit cool and draughty upstairs. One can only imagine what it would have been like when the only heat circulating would have been from two or three fireplaces. It would definitely have been time to bring out an overcoat.

CHAPTER EIGHT
THE GREAT ESCAPE

At the start of 1939 all the Emperor could do was to bide his time and see how international events would unfold. The Emperor's position was so weak that there was not a lot he could do himself to influence his destiny. Britain's de jure recognition of Italy's position had left him powerless. He had lost too many battles and was struggling not to be totally crushed. His official activities were fewer than they had been at the start of the exile. The autobiography was finished, and his relationship with the League of Nations, once his cherished hope, had effectively come to an end. However, the Emperor still made several visits to London to brief himself on the activities of the legation and to try to discern the British government's general war strategy.

He also tried to keep himself in the public eye and granted full access into his life at Fairfield to a writer from the popular *Sunday Post* newspaper. The paper was based in Scotland but had many readers in England too. It promoted respectable family and religious values with a blend of escapism and charm, a highly appropriate public relations vehicle for the Emperor. The full-page spread said that he must run the strangest community in Britain and gave a lot more details than the public knew at that time. It is unclear how accurate the lyrical article was but it did throw up an intriguing picture of the royal exile.

The article said there were a bewildering number of clocks in the house, every one of them chiming the hour. The reporter described an old leather-bound book of psalms and prayers which Haile Selassie read regularly to his loyal band of followers. He quoted a favourite saying of the Emperor as 'a wise man rolls his tongue seven times round his mouth before speaking his thoughts.' According to the article, the death of his son-in-law Ras Desta in early 1937 was the only time the Emperor had broken down in front of his supporters. The writer described much of the furniture

CHAPTER 8

and furnishings at Fairfield – quaint ebony carvings, black and white monkey skin rugs, old carpets worth £100 a yard and Abyssinian watercolour paintings. While researching the article, the writer spotted the Emperor's faithful dog snoring at his master's feet while he went through his accounts.

Haile Selassie's love of gadgets was also mentioned in the report, which said he was fascinated by watches, clocks, binoculars, and engines. He talked about a ciné camera he owned, and especially enjoyed operating a makeshift switchboard connecting him with other parts of the Fairfield property. One superficial dilemma admitted by the Emperor, according to the article, was how to choose which shoes he should wear each day from his large collection. Over the years the Emperor greatly prized his shoes, some of them made by John Lobb in London, which had provided Queen Victoria with her footwear. Haile Selassie also obtained suits from the exclusive firm of Gieves and Hawkes, based at the prestigious address of 1 Savile Row in London. In subsequent years he was to be credited with helping to make double-breasted suits fashionable and he was named a few years ago by one fashion guru as being one of the ten best-dressed men of all time.

Another insider account of life at Fairfield around this time was published by a young friend of the family called Mary Lishman, the daughter of the vicar of Shadwell of Leeds. She said she spent several months staying at the house in the run-up to the war and often partnered the Emperor in doubles matches of tennis in the garden. She said that Makonnen was very witty and loved careering around the grounds of Fairfield on his sports bike. His brother the Crown Prince loved swimming, dancing and going to watch films.

Mary and the Emperor discussed a wide range of topics including riding, English sport and the theatre. She said he had by now assimilated some European ideas and customs. Mary described how during services at the chapel in the grounds the Empress would sit hidden from view beneath a canopy, with the others sitting behind her. The Emperor would usually remain standing, even in long services.

By now the Emperor had massively reduced his public engagements and was mainly seen in public on his way to private visits. The *Nottingham Evening Post* reported him as saying his intentions were to make England his permanent home. If this quote is accurate, it revealed how much the Emperor had sunk into melancholia and was at least preparing himself for the prospect of never returning to his homeland. In February the Emperor went behind the scenes of a film being shot at Denham studios near London. The film was an espionage drama called *Peace in Our Time*. Press reports quoted the Emperor saying that he was enthusiastic about films and attended the cinema twice a week, preferring stories about dramatic and real life adventures. A few weeks later the Emperor went by car with several members of his family to

Gloucester to watch a film at the Plaza cinema. He was said to be tired looking and frail and was described as one of the world's most tragic kings.

Like everyone else in Britain, Haile Selassie was watching closely the moves of Hitler and was able to plot and scheme with his advisers about the disturbing turn of events. He continued to keep his trust in God and, despite his deepening pessimism at times, tried to cling on to his belief that he would return home one day. But on earth, the fury and chaos of an all-out war with fascism seemed to be the main thing that could help him now. One other factor was still in play. During these early months of 1939 his resourceful lieutenant Lorenzo Taezaz was still operating in secret in Ethiopia. The Emperor was presumably hoping against hope that something positive would emerge. However, in some ways maybe the torment of faint hope was even harder to bear than the finality of definitively knowing that his previous life and persona had come to an end.

Naturally Haile Selassie continued his routine daily schedule at Fairfield House and kept himself busy somehow. His trips to cultured towns in Britain also continued. However, his appearances in the Bath *Chronicle* became increasingly rare as the year progressed. The Emperor now seemed to be too marginal and inconsequential a figure. The Ethiopian issue was becoming old hat and was dwarfed by the looming prospect of war in Europe.

Already the *Chronicle's* rapture over the Munich agreement was being reassessed. The British people soon realised that Chamberlain's famous piece of paper outlining a peace deal with Hitler was worthless. In February Czechoslovakia was invaded in defiance of the agreement. War between the great powers of Europe seemed inevitable.

Bathonians had started 1939 in great spirits with a glittering New Year's ball at the newly restored Upper Assembly Rooms. They were thrilled that their famous social venue had been revived from its slumber, and danced like there was no tomorrow. As part of the festivities to celebrate the opening, a leading member of the British royal family, Mary the Princess Royal, paid several visits to Bath. Haile Selassie was certainly a figure of fascination but there was nothing like home-grown royalty to really fire the imagination of Bath's citizens. Princess Mary was lionised as the fairy princess, who had helped to bring Bath back to life. Balls, society fashion and royal court gossip did not form part of Haile Selassie's agenda but that was what Bathonians wanted in these uncertain times. It was an era to be inward-looking rather than having time and energy for the problems of others, especially those who lived a long way away in an unknown and often misunderstood continent.

Bath was booming despite the concerns over international security. The city was waking up from its sleep of a hundred years. In February 1939 the Mayor proudly announced that Bath was now one of the richest cities in the United Kingdom with

CHAPTER 8

more than 200 surtax payers living there. The residents had already been told several months previously that Bath would become a goldmine. Experts had discovered more about the healing properties of the mineral waters and the possibilities for mud as well as water treatments were enormous. The spa waters were deemed to be especially good for treating kidney diseases, insomnia and shell-shock. Haile Selassie, shivering in his eyrie at Fairfield, must have wished that some of this optimism, health and wealth could have filtered down to him.

TAXING ISSUES

Although Sir William Cox had secretly stepped in as a benefactor, the Emperor's financial humiliations were far from over. In February 1939 he lost his tax-free status as a head of state. This had been granted to him in 1937 when he was still recognised as Emperor but after the UK's official blessing of the Italian occupation this agreement had now expired. During his early days in Bath the Emperor had had some initial contacts with the tax authorities. Now he was forced to complete a tax return and be transparent about all his financial affairs. The authorities were content to give him something of a tax break and not totally reclaim their full pound of flesh. His new status was as a person resident but not domiciled nor ordinarily resident in Britain. Tax was therefore payable on income arising on monies or securities remitted to Britain instead of the usual basis of on all amounts and income arising abroad.

The local tax office in Bath had quietly been keeping an eye on its unusual guest. A large file of its contacts with the Emperor and his staff is stored at the National Archives in Kew. Most of the liaison was carried out by Mr T.H. Hore, who visited Fairfield officially on a number of occasions. But his private home was also in the area and that meant he could also gather all the local gossip about the royal visitors. In one letter to his bosses Mr Hore said that the family's style of living suggested no sign of affluence and the previous large number of retainers had been considerably reduced in number. He said Fairfield was now shabby, not well-equipped, and the gardens were ordinary. The Emperor was now running a German car called a Horch and one of his sons had an 8 horse power Morris. According to Mr Hore, the ladies normally travelled around in hired taxis but the men used buses or trams.

Later in the spring of 1939 Mr Hore had a delicate phone conversation about tax affairs after he was called by Sirak Heruy, one of the Emperor's staff and son of the late foreign minister. According to the tax inspector, the caller became chatty during the interview and confirmed that the Emperor was having great difficulty in making ends meet. Mr Hore said the caller told him everyone living and working at Fairfield thought themselves lucky to get food and clothing. None of them had a salary, although they did receive a little pocket money from time to time.

In some later reports Mr Hore started to make some cutting political observations about the Emperor, confirming how low his fortunes had slumped. Mr Hore referred to Haile Selassie as the ex-Emperor and even the late Emperor. He said that none of the family took part in any activities in Bath and the local people seemed to have lost all interest in them. According to Mr Hore, the Emperor was increasingly withdrawing from the public gaze and had given up his Ethiopian form of dress. In the file at the National Archives there are several of the Emperor's tax records. A list of his investments in June 1939 was provided by a Mr Walgate from the National Provincial Bank in London where a deposit account was held. Mr Walgate said the Emperor's future intention was to give all his savings and investments to his family. His object in life was to see his children provided for, and to hold himself immediately available to throw in his lot in favour of any nation which might take steps to force the Italians out of Ethiopia.

The assets listed confirm that the Emperor was reasonably well-off in terms of savings for his family but he constantly struggled to find cash for everyday purposes. The amount he eventually declared meant he was not subject to significant levels of tax in the UK. The holdings in the bank included shares in a number of engineering and transport companies. Among these were 750 shares in Hawker Siddeley Aircraft, and 550 shares in John Brown and Co engineering. By 1941 the dividend income from these shares was 490 pounds no shillings and four pence with a tax liability of 118 pounds seven shillings and six pence.

Mr Walgate also reported that the Emperor held some other holdings, including £4,500 in Canadian Pacific Railway, £2,500 in Huddersfield Building Society, and £4,000 in Leeds Building Society. As a way of comparison, it is worth recalling that the amount paid for Fairfield was £3,500 in 1936. The list of assets confirmed that the Emperor owned a property in Switzerland, though the rental income was low. The Empress is listed as owning a property in Jerusalem with a rental income of £90 a year. She and the children had war loans and shares made out in their names. The family also received child allowance for seven children and grandchildren altogether.

As well as having to suffer the indignities of being scrutinised by the taxman, the run of bad luck over the Emperor's finances continued. In February 1939 it was reported that his new benefactor Sir William Cox had collapsed and died while travelling on a train. His quarterly income payments continued but Sir William's death sparked off another unseemly round of government wrangling over income tax and death duties. The overall lump sum originally promised to the hapless Ethiopian monarch would now be reduced.

TURNING THE TABLES

Bath was changing fast outside the cloistered and troubled world of Haile Selassie. In

CHAPTER 8

May the city said goodbye to its trams with thousands turning out in the evening to see the Mayor drive the last tramcar from the Guildhall back to the depot. The trams were replaced by a fleet of modern buses but there are no reports about whether the Emperor ever boarded one of them. Unemployment in Bath fell to the lowest on record amid a mini-boom with the construction of buildings, public works and hotels.

During all this activity Haile Selassie was taking a quiet holiday in the nearby resort of Burnham-on-Sea. He said he liked the place and might be interested in living there one day, but he had no current plans to leave Bath. As a keen reader of the national and international press, he would have been following the news that Britain was now playing host to another royal exile fleeing from Mussolini's invading armies. The unfortunate monarch in question was King Zog of Albania, who first settled with his entourage in the Ritz, one of London's most expensive and exclusive hotels. The King had had some warning that the Italians were going to take over his country so he had managed to stockpile some gold from Albania's banks to pay the bills while in exile. However, soon he was to follow the example of Haile Selassie and went to live in two private residences, in Berkshire and Buckinghamshire on the fringes of greater London. King Zog shared one unfortunate honour with Haile Selassie. Both of them had been made Knights of the Supreme Order of the Most Holy Annunciation in Italy when relations with Mussolini had been less bellicose.

Another item of international news may also have caught the Emperor's attention. In April 1939 Reuters reported that the people of Ceylon had offered to provide a home for the beleaguered exile. They said that living in Colombo would be warmer. A report from India also picked up the theme and even claimed that the Emperor would be going to Ceylon to learn yoga.

The Emperor's fourth summer in Britain suddenly brought some good news. Lorenzo Taezaz returned from his secret mission in Ethiopia and was in a positive frame of mind. He reported that the majority of the population still supported their exiled leader and that the situation was ripe for rebellion. What the Emperor needed now was an external spark to ignite this volatile support. For the first time in a long while he could perhaps allow himself a modicum of optimism.

In Bath there were more reminders of approaching Armageddon with the first official air raid exercise under war time conditions being held at midnight. In August the Italians made another move to try to get Haile Selassie to officially renounce his throne. Mussolini even publicly challenged the Ethiopian leader to return home to help restore calm and order. The call was turned down, with his spokesman saying the Italians were in trouble because of continuing rebel activity. Foodstuffs for their forces were in short supply and some Italian troops were under siege. Whatever else it meant, Italy's latest overture was perhaps an indication that the Emperor was not completely irrelevant on the international stage after all, even though he had largely been forgotten in Bath.

As war remorselessly approached, the Emperor seized the diplomatic initiative and tried to turn international events to his advantage. On 29 August he sent a neat handwritten note in the graceful Amharic script to King George VI. The Imperial Seal was prominent at the top of the letter. The accompanying English translation reveals that the Emperor was offering his services to Britain and wanted the two countries to march side by side in what he called this hour of trial. The letter led to a bout of head scratching in government circles about how the King should respond and various draft replies were exchanged. One school of thought was that the Emperor should not be encouraged to think that in the event of war with Italy that he could be returned to his throne on British and French bayonets.

Despite some appearances in the public arena, the Emperor spent most of the final few days of peace in a surprising and secluded activity. He joined a camp near Swansea together with staff and boys from the secondary school at the Bible College of Wales. Two of his extended family circle were now studying there – Ras Kassa's only remaining son Asserate and his friend Abiye Abebe, who was later to marry Princess Tsehai back in Ethiopia.

The college followed the principles of an intense form of protestant evangelicalism, a brand of Christianity very different from the approach of the Ethiopian Orthodox Church. The founder of the school was a devout former Welsh miner called Rees Howell. He became friends with the Emperor and they regularly stayed in touch. One of Howell's big projects at the time was to help Jewish children who had become refugees from fascism in Europe. Haile Selassie said he heartily approved of this endeavour, declaring that he was a refugee himself.

With the campers at Penllergaer School. The college founder Rees Howells is seated next to his wife Lizzie to the left of the Emperor

CHAPTER 8

During the summer camp at Penllergaer School the Emperor stayed in a tent which bore a printed notice, His Majesty Emperor of Abyssinia. He was quoted as saying that the last time he had been under canvas was near Maychew in northern Ethiopia when he had been under immediate peril of bombardment from Italian war planes. During the two week camp the royal visitor played tennis and rounders, and joined in songs at the camp fire. He also shared the same food as the students, apart from eating a fig sent to him every day in the post from Fairfield House. After attending the camp the Emperor sent a note to Rees Howell. He said: 'It is an inspiration to have seen all the wonderful things that the Lord is doing among those of your people and those who have found a refuge in your country.'

On September 3 war officially came to Britain with Chamberlain's sombre announcement about the onset of hostilities. One wonders whether Haile Selassie and his advisers were listening to the broadcast at Fairfield and, if so, what they made of it. The *Chronicle* makes no mention of the Emperor's views, perhaps a further sign of how irrelevant he had become in the city. By contrast, Sylvia Pankhurst's paper *New Times* and *Ethiopia News* welcomed the outbreak of war with Germany. She also continued to denounce Mussolini, criticisms the British government did not want to hear at this sensitive stage. It therefore tried to prevent the export of the paper to neutral countries.

The entry of Britain into the war meant that everything on the international stage was now unpredictable. But a chain of events had been set in play that would jolt the Emperor from his sleepy isolation at Fairfield. On the day war was declared the Mayor of Bath welcomed evacuated children from London, the latest refugees to arrive in the city. It was not long before the horrors of war came home to local residents. Just three weeks later six men from Bath lost their lives when a submarine they were serving on was sunk in the Atlantic.

Shortly after war broke out the former Foreign Secretary Anthony Eden was brought back into government as Secretary of State for Dominion Affairs. His recall offered some encouragement for the Emperor who now had another conduit for his lobbying efforts. On one occasion Princess Tenagneworq, the Emperor's daughter, was entrusted with carrying a secret letter from her father to Eden. She hid it in a chocolate box well away from any unwelcome prying eyes. Haile Selassie largely disappeared from view during the 'phoney war' period in the first few months after Chamberlain's sombre announcement. However, his active mind was undoubtedly scheming and going through the permutation of several scenarios.

The winter of early 1940 was the coldest on record and seven inches of ice formed on the lake at Royal Victoria Park, just down the road from Fairfield. To make matters worse, food rationing was introduced across Britain because of the privations of the war. No exception was made for the residents of Fairfield House and the lodge in the grounds. Although the Empress normally ran the finances and domestic arrangements of the house, the Emperor had some involvement in dividing up the spoils of butter, sugar, eggs, tea and other commodities. In January 1940 the Emperor was spotted in the distinguished spa town of Cheltenham where he went to see a collection of paintings by his friend Sir William Rothenstein.

Despite the distractions of the war effort, the tax inspector Mr Hore was continuing to keep a close eye on the Emperor. He reported in February 1940 that the Ethiopian leader had again been trying to sell Fairfield. The *Chronicle* did find space in March to print a photograph of Haile Selassie, who had just taken possession of a new car, a Morris 10. It was delivered by Bath Garages, which had already supplied the royal exiles with another Morris car a few years earlier.

Special delivery from Bath Garages

In an echo of the words of the Bath tax inspector, the *Nottingham Evening Post* noted that Haile Selassie was wearing western clothing. It said he had discarded his picturesque black cloak in favour of a Melton overcoat and Homburg hat. At Easter the Abyssinian Association sent a greeting to the Emperor, noting sadly that what it called the anarchic soul of man was imprisoned by fears, oppressions and wars.

In early May the Emperor received more tragic news when he heard of the early death of Dr Melaku Bayen. The doctor had been with him at the battle of Maychew and had expressed concern about Princess Tsehai's dancing partner at the Bath Spa Hotel back in 1936. The doctor died in America from pneumonia. He was only 40. Once again Fairfield House was a place of mourning as the Emperor remembered in sadness the life of his faithful doctor.

CHAPTER 8

The really significant breakthrough for the Emperor came when Chamberlain resigned as Prime Minister on May 10 in 1940. He had paid the price for the discredited policy of appeasement which Haile Selassie had spoken out against so eloquently four years previously in Geneva. The Emperor was obviously thrilled that his replacement was Winston Churchill whom he thought would be an effective supporter of his cause. Eden was also given a more prominent position as Minister for War. Virtually straightaway the Emperor fired off a letter of congratulation to Churchill. He said the appointment had given him great pleasure and renewed hope, not only because his gifts and energy would secure victory for the allies, but because he had always been a loyal supporter and advocate of the League of Nations. In an attempt to spur the new Prime Minister into action, the Emperor referred back to the letter he had sent to the King in the summer of 1939, fully offering his services.

FLIGHT TO SUDAN

The month of June began quietly enough after this flurry of diplomatic activity. On the 8th the Emperor was in London again for the christening of the son of the redoubtable George Steer and his wife Esme. Her father Sir Sidney Barton also attended the event, held amid the ceremonial splendour of St Paul's Cathedral. During the service the Emperor placed a gold cross round the neck of the baby, now his new godson. Steer said he patted his son on the head with the friendliness that 'dictators would do well to study between fits of dynamism and bad temper.' It must have been some encouragement for the Ethiopian leader to be back among some of his biggest supporters.

Two days later external events suddenly swung in the Emperor's favour and his personal fortunes were about to completely change around. After months of posturing, Mussolini declared war on the allied powers. In response, Churchill called him a jackal of an Emperor. For Haile Selassie there was now a good chance of ending his long and lonely exile at Fairfield. Little did he know that he would not see the house again for another 14 years nor that he would be separated from his wife and family for more than a year.

The Foreign Office now began to take notice of the Emperor's lobbying as they definitively shared a common enemy. Foreign Office records show that British ministers, after considerable debate, had begun to convince themselves that the Emperor was the best option for uniting Ethiopia against the Italians. They knew that his reputation had taken a terrible beating because he had run away but they were aware that he had been keeping in touch with some rebel groups. There was no strong alternative. After a series of discussions with his supporters in London on the 10th and 11th of June, Haile Selassie informed the Foreign Office that he was prepared to go back to Ethiopia right away and lead an operation to remove the Italians.

Sylvia Pankhurst heard Mussolini's war declaration on BBC Radio as she was at home eating macaroni with some Italian anti-fascist refugees. The announcement of his bellicose intentions caused a wave of energy in the room. The diners were all filled with great hope that it would lead to his eventual downfall and would also boost the chances of Haile Selassie returning home. The Emperor's spokesman gave little away, saying he was merely keeping in close touch with developments. Like a skilled poker player, the Ethiopian Solomonic King knew he was back in the game and recognised a potentially strong hand when he saw one. After years of trying to persuade Britain to take on Mussolini head-on, he saw that this could now happen. And with Churchill in charge he was bound to have felt considerable confidence. Everything had changed in the twinkle of an eye.

The Emperor was now back in the news. A photograph of him at his London hotel appeared in the papers. The Ethiopian flag was also seen flying in the areas of Jerusalem populated by Ethiopian exiles. At a cabinet meeting on 16 June British ministers discussed an action plan drawn up by the Foreign Office. They affirmed that Britain was ready to co-operate with the Emperor and said all possible steps should be taken to foment anti-Italian sentiment in Ethiopia. Secrecy was vital both to protect the Emperor and also to avoid tipping off the Italians. The Foreign Office paper also confirmed that in the past it had been deliberately lukewarm towards the Emperor, though that had been something of an open secret. It admitted that its position had been to provide as little help as possible to ensure Mussolini did not take offence. Steer later mocked their stance as a gentlemen's agreement giving recognition to the biggest cad of modern times.

Mussolini's announcement fired the Emperor into action and he wrote a feisty press communiqué about the decision of the 'tyrant.' He said he had been pleading for five years that the suffering of his people be heard: 'Now the time has come to say: Enough.' He said Ethiopia had been free for 2,000 years and soon would be free again. The *New Times* and *Ethiopia News* carried banner headlines about Mussolini's declaration, claiming that both axis powers would now perish together. Charles Martin wrote of his satisfaction at the news, saying that it was an ill wind that brought no-one any good. However, events progressed too slowly in London for the Emperor and his supporters. His letter to Churchill was greeted initially by what the Ethiopian diplomat Emmanuel Abraham described as a non-committal reply. Sylvia Pankhurst described how she found the Emperor crestfallen waiting for news at the Great Western Hotel in Paddington. 'Why won't they send me back?' he asked her in desperation.

Fortunately for the Emperor, he did not have to suffer his doubts and frustration for long. He contacted Churchill again, making a more forceful request for help. This time Churchill relented. Soon afterwards the Emperor heard that he and a small team

CHAPTER 8

of supporters had been given the go-ahead to leave for Sudan as soon as possible on the first step of the plan to drive out the Italians from Ethiopia. The Emperor's departure was set for 24 June 1940. His plotters-in-chief not surprisingly included the resourceful journalist George Steer.

Steer was involved in elaborate moves to keep secret the departure of the Emperor from London and wrote entertainingly about his experiences in his book *Sealed and Delivered*. He often described the Emperor rather affectionately but cheekily as 'the little man.' On the day of departure Haile Selassie's assistants removed only small parcels of luggage from their hotel so as not to alert nosey staff and any observant Italian spies that they might be checking out for good. The group had a boisterous lunch at George Steer's house in Chelsea. They raided the larder where they had secreted a variety of goodies from the upmarket store of Fortnum & Mason – champagne, lobster, caviar and foie gras. Joyful toasts were made.

The conviviality was certainly a major change from the silent, downbeat meal times in the draughty rooms of Fairfield House. However, given the Emperor's fastidious ways, it is unlikely that he tucked into this sumptuous fare as enthusiastically as his British companions. During the meal Steer just about managed to avoid a major faux pas. He suddenly spotted his maid May approaching the guests with dessert plates, which had been looted from the palace in Addis Ababa in 1936. The plates had been given to Steer and his wife Esme as a wedding present. Fortunately Steer was able to usher her out of sight before the Emperor noticed.

Among the Emperor's group was his second son, Makonnen. He was still in his teens and, from a modern day perspective, seemed a little young for such an ambitious mission. However, in Ethiopia it was still commonplace for people to assume great responsibility at an early age. Life could be brutal and short with disease and war taking their toll. Haile Selassie himself of course had been made a dejezmach at just 13 so he would not have been fazed by Makonnen's inexperience. Makonnen had already shown a confident, outgoing spirit of adventure and would have added energy and enterprise to the group.

After their indulgent lunch the party then drove off in two Daimler cars. The first car contained Haile Selassie, Makonnen and a British major. Steer was in the second car with two of the Emperor's most trusted aides, Lorenzo Taezaz and Wolde Giorgis. Steer said his job for the next eight hours as they drove around was to keep his eyes peeled to ensure the vehicles were not followed. In a bizarre moment the small convoy got lost a couple of times as all signposts in London had been removed to befuddle any German parachutists.

The group was making its way to the south coast to catch a flying boat. On the Wiltshire Downs they made a brief stop during which another bottle of champagne was downed as a country lad passed by whistling. By 10pm they had reached Plymouth and boarded a Sunderland flying boat piloted by a squadron leader from Australia. The trip was so secret that even the pilot did not know who was going to be on board. The Emperor was travelling under the name of Mr Strong. It took two attempts to rise above the sea but soon they were on their way to Bordeaux and heading further south over the unsafe and risky skies of Vichy France.

The journey was perilous, icy and uncomfortable. A fierce electrical storm erupted, which Steer said ripped the velvet of the night sky and danced the plane like a pea on a drum. The Emperor slept on a forward bunk dressed in a greatcoat to ward off the cold night air. Despite the privations the Emperor's mind would have been working furiously. He had escaped dramatically from the clutches of his exile. He was free and soaring in the air like an eagle over the Simien Mountains in northern Ethiopia. But many vital questions were still waiting to be answered. How nervous was he about the task ahead? How worried was he about how his people would respond to him, given that he had left Ethiopia with his tail between his legs? How would he deal with any desire to exact revenge on the Italians? But overall there was great hope. At long last the chains of exile had been ripped off.

The plane made a detour over Tunisia as reports circulated that Italian planes were out hunting for the Emperor. The aircraft eventually touched down in the waters off Alexandria in northern Egypt late that afternoon after a precarious fuel stop on the besieged island of Malta. Maintaining secrecy was still important, especially as there were many Italians in Alexandria who might have seized the chance to attack the Emperor. Some British officials and diplomats in the region were also known to be very sceptical about backing Haile Selassie and could have compromised the mission. It was therefore deemed safer to keep news of his presence to a limited select group of supporters.

George Steer was well aware that the Emperor still had his enemies and detractors among many pockets of the British establishment, especially among the colonial service in north-east Africa. They thought he would be of no use in dislodging Italian forces. Steer said the Emperor's habits also made many of them 'see red over their pink gins.' As a result, the Emperor and his son stayed onboard the flying boat until it was dark. Then his supporters provoked an artificial commotion on the quayside to distract inquisitive bystanders. Out of the line of sight the Emperor, muffled in a cloak, was smuggled past the immigration authorities into the local yacht club, previously run by some Italians.

Here the 'Boys Own' caper continued and a party was soon in full swing. Portraits of Mussolini in a fascist steel helmet were taken down and banished to the toilet. Nothing could dampen the euphoric mood. The Emperor had his first square meal for some time and clearly enjoyed what he later described as good hospitality. This included some Italian Chianti which was brought up from the club's cellars. The

CHAPTER 8

Emperor gave a gold watch to the pilot of the seaplane and breezily announced that the next time they met he would be wearing a crown. To get in the regal mood the Emperor changed out of his civilian clothes into a brand new smart generalissimo uniform, complete with medals and other military decorations. Then he was again smuggled out to the seaplane with his face muffled.

Despite the cloak and dagger tactics, news of the Emperor's presence in the region began to spread. As a result, the Sudanese capital Khartoum was deemed to be too much of a security risk. His plane had to land instead at Wadi Halfa where the conditions were extremely torrid and sultry. However, it must have been a tremendous feeling for the Emperor to be back in Africa again where he was more used to the light and the landscape. The remains of an ancient Coptic church were in the area and Steer says the Emperor gazed in long fascination at these first traces of his people's religion.

His spirits were to be further uplifted when he went for a walk by the Nile with Edwin Chapman-Andrews, a British diplomat who had served in Harar at the time of the Italian invasion and had been influential in persuading Haile Selassie not to change his mind about escaping by train to Djibouti. The two men were downstream of Khartoum where the mighty Nile river assumes its full grandeur with the meeting of its two main tributaries. The White Nile comes up from Lake Victoria in Uganda and the Blue Nile rushes down from the Ethiopian highlands, starting its journey at Lake Tana. When the Emperor saw the Nile, he exclaimed joyfully that it was the water of his country. He scooped up some of the water and sipped some of it. Later he admitted that he had been moved by feelings of deep nostalgia.

At the end of July the *New Times* and *Ethiopia News* carried a statement from the Emperor, saying that it should be remembered that he had not abdicated and had never renounced his title to his ancient throne. In an editorial the paper teased those who thought that supporting the Emperor had previously been flogging a dead horse. Now everyone had been forced to acknowledge that the horse had risen from the mire.

However, soon the euphoria was to cool as the perennial fissures in his relationship with the British government resurfaced. The Emperor became becalmed in Sudan as disagreements emerged with the British military command over policy, strategy and tactics. Initially the Emperor's party had to stay in seclusion at Jebel Aulia, around 30 miles from Khartoum. This had been one of the bases of General Gordon, the legendary British officer who met his death at the hands of the ebullient Mahdi forces.

The Emperor found it difficult to be away from the centre of the action. For once, his placid calm evaporated and he boiled over with rage and frustration. In one incident, described by George Steer, he was totally exasperated when he heard that the British had not come up with supplies of any modern artillery or planes. They were just offering a few thousand old and rusty guns. The Emperor recalled bitterly that he had been promised full air support in London. But virtually nothing had materialised and he blurted out testily: 'It would have been better had I never left England.'

Steer also described how the Emperor had been deeply distressed and had struck the side of his head several times with his delicate hand. He still felt marginalised even after his entourage moved closer to Khartoum and stayed incognito at the Pink Palace, a small country house owned by Sharif Yusuf el Hindi. The days of waiting turned into weeks and then months.

The irrepressible Steer though was loving every minute of it. He was put in charge of protecting the Emperor in Sudan and was given a personal weapon. His skills as a wordsmith were also put to good use as he was placed at the head of a propaganda unit to further the Emperor's cause. Steer acted as a kind of aide de camp, driving the Emperor to carry out various errands at Indian tailors and Armenian boot makers. They lunched together every day at their remote palace and Steer said the Emperor had become:

> 'a strange co-mingling of sweetness and bitterness, of far sight and obstinacy, a sponge as it were for all the emotions of exile, a person enamelled always by his lovely manners and solidified by a patience which prepared him to wait till Doomsday for what he wanted, without showing that he was waiting for anything at all.'

Having made a break for freedom from his confinement at Bath, the Emperor was in danger of slipping back into a kind of no-man's land. His exile was not quite over after all, and he still did not have control over his own actions and destiny. He was within tantalising distance of home, yet was without most of his family. There was no chance to enjoy the sounds and sight of young children running around. The Empress and the rest of the royal group were carrying on living at Fairfield while the Emperor patiently waited for his next move. In her interview for this book Princess Seble said they did not have the chance to say goodbye to their grandfather. He went to London often and they thought he had just left from Fairfield House on one of his normal trips. She said her family gradually came to terms with the fact he had gone for good. They understood why his departure had had to be kept secret and they knew he was doing the right thing for his life.

Charles Martin was kept completely in the dark about the Emperor's departure – a sign of how far his relationship with the Emperor had deteriorated. The press in London were also left clueless and continually pestered Emmanuel Abraham at the Ethiopian Legation for any news of the Emperor's whereabouts. He stalled them by saying simply that the Emperor had gone on holiday.

Haile Selassie was usually skilled in masking his inner feelings but a telegram to his British supporter, Sir Sidney Barton, showed how much his concern for his family

CHAPTER 8

gnawed away at him. The telegram stated sadly that there had been no letters from the family, not even from his beloved daughter Tsehai. He said five letters remained unanswered and he was very worried.

The *Chronicle* in Bath had continued to take an interest in the Emperor, now he was becoming an influential force again. It gave prominence to a discussion in the House of Commons in London in which Rab Butler, the Under Secretary for Foreign Affairs, was asked a series of questions: whether there had been contact between the government and the Emperor; whether England recognised as lawful the government of Ethiopia; whether it would be admitted to the status of an ally; and would he give assurances that Ethiopian independence would be assured once the war was won? A forthright and unequivocal 'Yes, sir' was the reply. A reporter from the *Chronicle*, unaware of the secret deal under which Haile Selassie had been spirited away to Sudan, rushed round to Fairfield House to inform the household of the Commons exchange. He claimed to be the first person to convey the news to the Emperor's entourage that the British government, after all those years of posturing, now recognised the Negus as the lawful ruler of Ethiopia.

While the Emperor was kicking his heels near Khartoum, did he think much about his exile in Bath? How much did he reflect on what he had learned from the experience? His mind is likely to have wandered at times to think of his family in Bath and in Jerusalem too. But the task at hand was very consuming of his time and energy. He kept his steely focus on the future and was concentrating on formulating a strategy for how he would resume his reign. At least he was back in the game now and there was some sort of stage on which to parade his gifts for political cunning.

In November 1940 the people of Bath were reminded of their famous exile when special newsreel footage was shown at the cinema of the Emperor with his troops in Sudan. The Empress attended with some of her family. Many of the British public were pleased that the mills of God were starting to grind Mussolini down. One of the Emperor's major concerns was how much he could trust the British government, which continued to show its ambivalence towards him. Some of his own supporters believed that the British intended to sideline him and claim Ethiopia as occupiers rather than liberators. The Emperor did receive some support from Colonel Daniel Sandford with whom he had started a farming and milling business in Ethiopia back in the 1920s.

Sandford had been tasked with going on a series of reconnaissance missions to prepare and train various groups of Ethiopian rebels. His operation was known as Mission 101, apparently named after fuse 101, which was widely used in many calibres of British guns at the time. The idea was that this operation would be the fuse to ignite rebellion inside Ethiopia. Sandford continually insisted that only the presence of the Emperor inside the country would unite the rebels and lead to eventual victory.

IMPERIAL EXILE

ENTRY INTO ETHIOPIA

After months of delay and indecision in defining the mission and collecting the resources to carry it out, some energy and steel was eventually injected into the Sudan operation. The breakthrough came when Eden, now into his stride as the Minister of War, came to a top level conference in Khartoum to discuss the next military steps. Eden pushed for the operation to be seen as a war of liberation and negotiated the means to implement it. The British then appointed a charismatic and gifted soldier, Major General Orde Wingate, to lead a small army into Ethiopia with the Emperor by his side. Steer described him as lank and sallow with the stoop of a hyena. He was a genuine eccentric and would sometimes receive visitors while naked.

Wingate's collection of men was called Gideon Force, a biblical reference to warm the heart of any religious person, especially the Elect of God, now thrilled that the end seemed to be in sight. Ethiopians were also greatly heartened by the news that the hated Butcher of Ethiopia, Graziani, now in charge of the Italian forces in Egypt, had been heavily defeated by the British army at Sidi Barrani. The tide was turning and the Emperor's nightmarish exclusion from his country was nearly over.

In Sudan waiting to strike

In January 1941 Haile Selassie told the reporter Leonard Mosley that he was breathing the air from his country, carried on the winds from his homeland. He was often wearing khaki shorts and the jacket of the British army. He was guarded night and day by a special detachment of Sudanese soldiers who had pledged their lives to

CHAPTER 8

defend him. Every night 44 royal war drums of all sizes made from hollowed-out tree trunks could be heard across the border. They were drummed in a special royal beat announcing that the Emperor was present nearby. Many Ethiopian chiefs were arriving in the camp to show their support for their country's cause. Back home the *Gloucestershire Echo* mused that it was less than a year ago that the Emperor had been in Cheltenham to view some paintings and few then would have thought he would now be about to enter his country in triumph. He was on the verge of an astonishing comeback.

The Emperor finally set foot on Ethiopian territory in mid January 1941, though his appearance was more of an elaborate public relations exercise rather than a vital part of the military campaign. He was flown to a remote border crossing on the Dinder River near the village of Um Iddla to join a small detachment of the Gideon Force, which by now was fully geared up for action.

The Emperor's aircraft had an escort of fighter planes and shaved the treetops as it came into land on an improvised strip hacked out of the surrounding jungle. A symbolic welcoming ceremony was held on the dried-out river bed with some crocodiles in the distance, insouciantly resting in some rock pools. The Emperor was dressed in khaki with a sunhat to protect himself from the fierce midday sun. He only had to make a short walk across the river bed before he was once again on Ethiopian soil. The red, green and gold flag of Ethiopia with a Lion of Judah inset was raised on a makeshift flag pole with a bugle blaring out in celebration. The small gathering included British army advisers, Ethiopian soldiers, and an Orthodox priest specially flown out from Jerusalem.

In Sudan returning from a flight, possibly after setting foot on Ethiopian soil

What an indescribable moment for Haile Selassie to set foot again on home soil. What range of emotions would have burned behind that impassive mask – relief, joy, gratitude or trepidation about the days ahead? His constant belief that he would get back home one day had been vindicated. Now he could look forward to being back in his palace and resuming his rule. He would also have been forgiven for feeling some unease over the reaction he would receive from some of his own people. He must have feared finding out the extent of the physical and psychological damage inflicted on his nation after nearly five years of Italian occupation. During the brief ceremony the Emperor said that death was better than captivity and that to be exiled was better than surrendering one's own country. He said that anyone who persevered in his faith would see his hope fulfilled.

Crown Prince Asfa-Wossen and Makonnen, the Emperor's two elder sons, were also both with him at his moment of triumph. So too was his faithful companion from Bath, his cousin Ras Kassa. Now they could take a stroll round the earth of their homeland rather than have to pass the time walking around the gardens of Fairfield. The Emperor's exploits received widespread coverage back in the UK. The *Western Daily Press* said it was like Napoleon returning from his exile in Elba. It said there were many romantic aspects to the story, including the moment a tribesman turned up on a white donkey with a scrap of paper saying that Italian forces were in flight.

A few days later the death was announced in France of Haile Selassie's mentor, Father Jarosseau. He had given nearly sixty years of his life serving in Harar in eastern Ethiopia and it seemed fitting that he died at the time of his protégé's return in triumph.

The British cabinet was still showing its ambivalence towards the Emperor, even though he was back on home territory. Given the uncertainties over what lay ahead, the cabinet decided in early February that it was 'still premature to recognise Abyssinia as an ally of this country.' That meant that the Ethiopian anthem could still not be played on the BBC in its compendium of the anthems of other allied nations. This stance further infuriated Sylvia Pankhurst, who went on the warpath against the British establishment once again.

Gideon Force was made up of only 1,700 men and was heavily outnumbered by the Italian forces it was seeking to topple. However, the force was well supplied with a train of 15,000 camels loaded with equipment. It could also count on the support of groups of patriots in the Gojam region inside Ethiopia and they quickly joined forces. Sandford's preparations had done the trick. The explorer Wilfred Thesiger also continued to show his loyalty to the Emperor and was involved in some of the fighting in Ethiopia. He was awarded the DSO after he captured around 8,000 Italian soldiers at the town of Mekane Selam, following a march of 50 miles in a day with his men. British and other forces including South African troops had also been entering

CHAPTER 8

Ethiopia from the north and from the south-east. The weary and homesick Italian forces began to crumble.

The British public were able to follow the joint British and patriot advance into Ethiopia as a variety of despatches were published in an array of newspapers. In an interview with the Emperor at an undisclosed location, he said in good but slow English that he could already smell the scents of trees and aromas in the air that he had missed during the tribulation of exile. Inside his camouflaged army tent there was just a table, chair, camp bed and a radio set with a couple of Persian carpets to provide a hint of comfort.

Back in the UK, Princess Tsehai announced she was about to make her own contribution to the campaign in Ethiopia. In a radio interview she said she would soon be giving up her nursing duties in England and would be returning to her own country with an ambulance unit. She said that while living in what she called smoky London she had loved the children she nursed at Great Ormond Street. The Princess had also worked at several other London hospitals and had helped to treat victims of the blitz. In her broadcast the Princess also recalled how she had originally left Ethiopia on the *Enterprise* naval ship. She said the kind officers had done everything possible to turn a warship of steel into a home for the royal family.

In February 1941 Empress Menen issued a rare public statement, saying she was hoping to return home soon, though confessed she was feeling nervous about the presence of her husband and two of their sons in the fighting. Amid the seriousness of war it was reported in the UK that Pat, one of the lions presented by Haile Selassie to King George V during his European tour of 1924, had died in his zoo enclosure.

The Emperor was soon within striking distance of the Ethiopian capital. He did make time to stop and pray at Debre Libanos monastery, the scene of the terrible massacre a few years before. He could have experienced very few poignant moments like this in his entire life. He later admitted that seeing the monastery had made him extremely sad and had left him deeply moved. Soon the allied forces had reached the outskirts of Addis Ababa without too much resistance. However, yet again the British adopted their now accustomed curmudgeonly role of party-poopers. Orders were handed down urging that the Emperor hold his position and not enter Addis Ababa for the time being. The reason given was that some in the British military command believed that a hasty appearance might cause instability and disorder. The Ethiopian camp thought this was merely an excuse. They suspected the British wanted to soak up the credit for liberating Addis Ababa, and also take the chance to establish some grip over the city.

News that Addis Ababa had fallen was understandably greeted with great joy at Fairfield House. The *Chronicle* reported that the Empress had been at prayer in the makeshift chapel in the grounds but was interrupted by one of her staff with information that could not wait. When the news was confirmed, the Empress had an impromptu celebration in the drawing room and the Lenten fast was temporarily abandoned. The children were allowed to stay up later than normal and there was excited talk round the fire of an early return to Addis Ababa.

Back in Ethiopia, Haile Selassie grew tired of waiting outside Addis Ababa and announced he was going to his capital come what may. All that remained was to plan the victorious entrance. On his way into the city the Emperor stopped in the hills of Entoto, Menelik's former capital. As the triumphant group reached the gates of the city, the Emperor was greatly shocked by the actions of some of the British soldiers. Only around 50 camels out of the original 15,000 had survived the arduous journey. However, the ones who had survived were promptly killed by the British, presumably guided by military regulations. The Emperor later revealed that he had been simply horrified to witness what he described as this incredible cruelty.

Wingate chose to ride into Addis Ababa on a white horse, emulating the actions of the Italian commander Badoglio when he entered and captured the city. Some time after all the fuss had died down, the mercurial Wingate tried to slit his own throat, probably because he felt he had not been given enough recognition for his part in chasing the Italians away. Haile Selassie made his appearance in the victory parade in a commandeered car, which was escorted by Ethiopian police carrying carbines on horseback. Steer was in the vanguard in a vehicle flying the Ethiopian flag with loudspeakers blaring.

The Emperor on his triumphant return to Addis Ababa

This was one of the first major victories for Allied forces in the Second World War and was to have considerable impact on their morale and future strategy. For Haile Selassie it was a chance to rid himself of the cheap British jokes involving the corruption of his

CHAPTER 8

name. He had moved on from Evelyn Waugh's 'Highly Salacious' to a new respectful British nickname of 'Highly Satisfactory.' For Mussolini it was the disintegration of a colonial obsession, which in the end had cost him and his country dearly.

However, the day mainly belonged to the Emperor, who received a rapturous welcome from a crowd of around 100,000 lining the streets. As the victory procession passed by, many fell prostrate to the ground in his honour. Five years to the day since the Italians captured Addis Ababa the King of Kings was back home in triumph. He had lived up to his reputation of moving like a mouse and striking like a lion. His exile was finally well and truly over.

CHAPTER EIGHT EYEWITNESS THE VIEW FROM ENTOTO

A trip to Menelik's former capital on the Entoto hills is one of the treats for a modern visitor to Addis Ababa. The vertiginous road winds its way through dense clumps of eucalyptus trees, planted by Menelik to ensure a supply of firewood for the residents of the city. On the way you can sometimes bump into some elite Ethiopian long-distance runners training at altitude. By contrast, you can also see many women bent double carrying huge bundles of eucalyptus branches to sell for fuel. Nearby is a sanctuary for many HIV sufferers, who come to the mountainside to bathe in the local stream waters, believed to be holy and curative. Entoto was a special place for Haile Selassie as it had been so important for Menelik, who had given him so much care after his father had died. The church of St Mary established nearby is regarded as a very holy religious centre. Menelik's former palace, in a hollow beneath the church, can still be seen today. There is a bell tower, royal bedrooms and an aderash hall, which also acted as a mini parliament.

A few years ago I came to watch a performance of Shakespeare's tragic play *Macbeth* with the backdrop of the palace as a stage. The play seemed very appropriate for such an Imperial setting as it deals with courtly intrigue, superstition, murder, jealousy and a desperate lust to extend regal power. The first half of the play, which is more calm, took place in daylight just before the sun was setting. But the second half was performed by candlelight in the gathering gloom, capturing the dark and ugly events unleashed as *Macbeth* comes to its tragic climax.

Entoto is also important because it was the place where Addis Ababa was conceived as the new capital. The story goes that Emperor Menelik's wife Taitu, looking out from the mountain top, spotted some steam rising in the valley below. This aroused her curiosity and on further inspection the steam turned out to be the source of several hot springs. Eventually Menelik decided to move his capital there at the end

CHAPTER 8

of the 19th century so the royal couple could take full advantage of the soothing waters. He also established his palace, the old gebbi, just above the springs. Today the Hilton Hotel, with its large shaded gardens, occupies the site of one of the springs. Swimming in the popular pool can be like taking a hot sauna, especially when the water has just been changed.

The view from the top of Entoto is breathtaking as one can see all the seven large hills which surround Addis Ababa. If Taitu or indeed Haile Selassie stood on the mountain today and looked down they would be astonished. The modern day city is spreading into all available spaces in the valley below. Here there are many visible high-rise business buildings around Bole Road, Megananya and the area near many government ministries in the centre of the city. Everywhere are imposing blocks of condominiums as many residents move from their traditional houses in compounds to communal living in modern flats. Towards the south of the city is the distinctive tall building that serves as the headquarters of the African Union, donated by the Chinese at a cost of 200 million US dollars. In the distance you can see planes landing and taking off at Bole Airport, now one of the busiest in Africa. By 2020 the airport plans to handle 20 million passengers a year and in the next thirty years there are plans to build a new airport, which can handle up to 70 million passengers, about the number that London's frenetic Heathrow airport caters for now.

Back in May 1941 the Emperor's mood must have been ecstatic, gulping down the fresh mountain air of Entoto and treading once again in the domain of one of his forebears. When he arrived at the summit around midday, he went straight into the church of the Virgin Mary and was seen in tears as he prostrated himself on the carpet. He said later that he had been deeply moved by the affection the people had shown towards him but had also been saddened by their abject condition. As he left the dim sanctuary for the light of day, a correspondent for the *Times* described how tears welled in the Emperor's eyes. His son Makonnen also put an affectionate arm around his father. The *Times* correspondent said that on this mountaintop Haile Selassie had again become the head of his people and a fount of inspiration.

On this occasion the Emperor was not ashamed to display his emotions in public. His homecoming was in complete contrast to the return to Iran of the exiled Islamic revolutionary spiritual leader Ayatollah Khomeini in 1979. When asked by a foreign correspondent what his emotions were just before arriving back home by plane, he tersely replied with one word in Farsi, 'hichi,' which means 'nothing.' For the Lion of Judah his return was everything. His identity and purpose in life had been fully restored and he could become whole once again. His faith had kept him going at times of extreme despair and now he was ensuring that he showed his gratitude to God.

Menelik is the only person whom the Emperor was said to have regarded as his equal. Paying homage to his memory must have given him extra strength for the challenging task ahead of rebuilding his shattered nation. Around Entoto a spectacular procession of excitable warriors, children and vehicles began to form. People dressed in the blue, crimson and mauve costumes of a peacock were singing, waving palm fronds and carrying umbrellas fringed with silk. Soon the returning King of Kings pressed on, down the winding road through the eucalyptus trees before he finally reached home.

CHAPTER 9

CHAPTER NINE
COUNTING THE COST

Amid the chaos of war it was obviously going to take some time before Haile Selassie was completely back in charge, and recovering the poise and authority he had displayed after his coronation. His capital was nursing many psychological and physical wounds. The Emperor would have been shocked to see the number of changes that had taken place while he had been away. During their stay the Italians had looted valuable artworks, manuscripts and important documents from the Imperial archives. They had removed the iconic statue of Menelik on his horse which had stood outside St George's Cathedral and the massive crown from the top of the dome at the Ba'ata Mausoleum where Emperor Menelik was buried. They had both been hidden away but had not been destroyed and were soon to be restored to their rightful places. However, the Lion of Judah statue, which had stood outside the train station in Addis Ababa, had been spirited away to Rome. It was erected near the Italian capital's own railway terminus as a visual symbol that the Italian government had tamed the Ethiopian lion. It was not returned until many years later. In Addis Ababa the town market or merkato had been moved further away from the centre to its present site. The Italians wanted to segregate the local population from the occupying forces. The Emperor would also have discovered that an Ethiopian-built plane named after his daughter Tsehai had also been dismantled and shipped to Italy. Even the alga, the historic bed-throne belonging to the Emperor, had disappeared and everyone assumed it had been sent to Italy.

New Times and *Ethiopia News*, the paper began by Sylvia Pankhurst, ran a series of disturbing articles in 1940 and 1941, exposing how violent and corrupt the Italian occupation had been. They were written by a Hungarian doctor under the pseudonym of Ladislav Sava. Part of his disturbing eyewitness account of the aftermath of the Graziani massacres has already been mentioned in Chapter Five. However, the real name of the doctor was Saska Laszlo. He was now free to speak because he had moved to Tanganyika. Laszlo and his wife took many surreptitious photographs of the devastated streets of Addis, despite a ban on foreigners owning cameras. He said the Italian soldiers had been obsessed with pornographic images of Ethiopian women and had forced many of them into prostitution to give sexual favours to the troops. Laszlo described how many of the Italian units were made up of violent criminals, released from Italian jails on condition they would go to Ethiopia. He confirmed that many Ethiopians had been killed by firing squad. In an especially callous tactic some young notables had died after being deliberately placed on medical wards for patients suffering from dangerous infectious diseases.

Despite all of the horrors inflicted on the city dwellers, the Emperor insisted firmly that there should be no reprisals against the Italians stationed in Ethiopia. Revenge was far from his mind. It would have perhaps been easy to have resorted to the eye for an eye mentality that existed widely in Ethiopia in his youth. The massacres following the attempt on Graziani's life, and the subsequent slaughtering of the religious innocents at Debre Libanos monastery provided ample reasons to punish the Italian forces in kind. Instead, the returning leader plumped for a laudable statesmanlike response when he addressed the ecstatic masses:

> 'Do not return evil for evil. Do not indulge in the atrocities which the enemy has been practicing in his usual way, even to the last. Take care not to spoil the good name of Ethiopia by acts which are worthy of the enemy.'

Given his grief and suffering in exile, the Emperor was perhaps sick of violence and bloodshed. It was also important to control any lust for revenge in the interests of establishing a new order. Despite the widespread misery caused by the occupying Italian forces, there had been some positive changes in the infrastructure. Mussolini had sent in thousands of workers to construct roads and buildings for the Italian military, many of which survive to this day. The Emperor always described the Italians as builders rather than soldiers. The British view was that virtually all the Italians soldiers and civilian workers should be sent home. The Emperor demurred. He could see that the engineers and road builders could be useful in getting the country back on its feet. He even ordered that some Italians, slated for repatriation, be hidden in official buildings so they could remain. The Italians left an indelible mark on Addis Ababa. Today macchiato is drunk in hundreds of cafes across Addis Ababa. The area of Piazza is still known by its Italian name. So too in a droll way is the neighbourhood of Cazanchis beneath Menelik's gebbi. The word is a corruption of Casa INCIS or Casa Institute Nazionale per Case Deli Impiegati Cello Stato to give the full title in Italian. In other words, the National Institution for Housing Employees of the State.

CHAPTER 9

Although he was anxious to curb any bloodletting instinct, Haile Selassie was keen to celebrate fully his triumph. Maybe he had dreamed many times of these sweet moments during his fitful nights of sleep at Fairfield. One of his first acts in entering Addis Ababa was to attend a service of thanksgiving at St George's Cathedral where he had been crowned as Emperor eleven long years before. He could never have envisaged then how his life would have progressed. It would have given him great satisfaction to witness the Italian flag being hauled down and the Ethiopian flag raised at several places in the capital. The Emperor could not contain his delight. He fired off a number of messages, including a telegram to Rees Howell at the Bible School of Wales where he had been camping two years previously. The Emperor said he was sure that Mr Howell would share in his joy at re-entering his capital, and said he was sending the telegram in remembrance of past sympathy and help.

The Emperor with his trusty friend and aide George Steer shortly after returning to Addis Ababa

IMPERIAL EXILE

Six hundred rases came to pay homage to Haile Selassie. There was just one woman among them – an extraordinary 50 year old white haired patriot fighter called Weyzero Shoaregued. The English press dubbed her the Abyssinian Boadicea, a queen of the Iceni tribe in Britain who led a rebellion again the Roman forces 2,000 years ago. Shoaregued's hatred for the Italians had been stirred when she had been captured in the mountains by Italian forces, tied to a tree and a golden cross snatched from around her neck.

The Emperor was in a triumphalist mood and later gave a televised interview in English, sitting nonchalantly in a chair in the grounds of his beloved Gennete Leul Palace. With birds tweeting in the background, he was clearly relishing his victory, despite being an underdog. Dressed in a military uniform complete with a row of medals, he said

> 'People who see this throughout the world will realise that, even in the 20th century with courage and a just cause, David will still beat Goliath.'

The Emperor would have seen to his disgust some winding stone steps leading nowhere, built by the Italian occupiers in front of his palace. Each step marked a year since Mussolini came to power in 1922. It was a cynical violation of the Emperor's seat of power. However, he was to have the last laugh as a stone lion was to be built on top of the final step. The Lion of Judah had returned in earnest and was letting out a huge roar.

The winding steps at the Palace

REACTION IN BATH

Back at Fairfield House in Bath the Empress was also in a celebratory mood. She hosted a garden party in the grounds of the house just ten days after the recapture of Addis Ababa. It was a fine spring day and the visitors were treated to champagne.

CHAPTER 9

They could all share in some good news at last. Among the guests were a number of Bath mayors, who had spoken up for the Emperor during his stay. The Empress was to leave Fairfield later in 1941 and return home with her daughter Tsehai. Because of the heavy wartime fighting in Egypt it was not possible to pass through the Suez Canal. They therefore had to travel via South Africa before rejoining the Emperor in Addis Ababa.

The Emperor had been back home for nearly a year when in April 1942 Bath suffered one of its darkest days. More than 400 people were killed during the so-called Baedeker raids by German bombers in retaliation for the RAF bombing of the tourist areas of Lubeck. Around 19,000 buildings were damaged. Part of the Royal Crescent was hit and the Upper Assembly Rooms, so lavishly and recently restored, were totally devastated. The people of Bath, like their adopted Emperor, had now also suffered at first hand from fascist bombs.

Princess Tenagneworq carried on living in Bath with some of the children for a couple of years after her mother left. Fairfield must have seemed strangely empty without so many of the original exiles. Living in war time conditions in Bath as the only responsible adult in the family cannot have been easy, and the Princess partly kept up her spirits by regularly meeting Sylvia Pankhurst for lunch in London. In 1943 she returned to Ethiopia and took with her the Emperor's son Sahle Selassie, and her sons Iskender and Amaha, who by this time had been suffering from tuberculosis for some years. He was to die a short while afterwards in Harar.

Some of the Emperor's grandchildren continued their education for several years afterwards at English schools and colleges. As adults, some of them were also to make their homes in the UK, and across the Atlantic in the United States.

PRIORITIES IN ETHIOPIA

One of the Emperor's first priorities back in Addis Ababa was completing Holy Trinity Cathedral, which he had started to build before the Italian invasion. A burial space was created to honour those who had fought against the invaders. The Cathedral was officially opened in January 1944 and became a symbol of Haile Selassie's victory over the Italians, just as his predecessor Menelik had built St George's Cathedral to commemorate his defeat of the Italians at Adwa. Near the dome there is a painting of the Emperor's appearance at the League of Nations in 1936 when the rabble-rousing Italian journalists were given short shrift by a Romanian delegate.

The Cathedral is home to many sacred parchments, crowns and crosses. Some of them date back to the 15th century. A throne-style chair was installed for the Emperor with two ornate wood lions carved in the arms. The feet of the chair rest on figures of lions. When the Emperor worshipped here, did his mind ever wander back to the simple religious services they had conducted in the greenhouse at Fairfield? He now had the comfort of establishing his own church. Perhaps it helped to repair some of the sorrow he had felt when hearing of the slaying of the Debre Libanos clergy.

The Greek-designed Holy Trinity Cathedral

Another church was also built in Addis Ababa to mark Ethiopia's victory. This was constructed near the site of the Gennete Leul Palace. It was given two names: Sedetennya Medhanialem (The Saviour of Exiles), and Meske Yuzne (The Sanctuary of people who are sad). The consecrated stone or tabot from the makeshift chapel at Fairfield House now resides here.

The Saviour of Exiles, the current resting place of the tabot from Fairfield House

CHAPTER 9

While Ethiopians tried to recover from the occupation, the Emperor had to deal with his own emotions. We shall never know how long it took him to get over the traumatic experiences of his exile. With his steely focus and capacity for hard work, he may well have kept at bay the majority of psychological repercussions from his bruising time away. What is clear is that throughout the next decades the Emperor was keen to extend his powers and centralise the activities of his government. The Ethiopian historian Bahru Zewde described this post-exile period as a drive to absolutism. The Emperor had been given a second chance to rule and he was not going to waste it. All those maddening and humiliating days of powerlessness at Fairfield could now be purged. The author John Markakis described the Emperor as a coldly rational manipulator of men and that talent could now be expressed ruthlessly.

Over the years the returning exile showed how desperate he was not only to increase his power but to ensure none of it was eroded. The number of spies in the secret service was greatly expanded to keep an eye on potential troublemakers. Networks of unofficial informants were also set in place so the Emperor would hear of the first whiff of any rebellion and be able to snuff it out. Hans Wilhelm Lockot, the Imperial librarian, revealed how the Emperor would spend hours at the weekends observing his people. He would look through a telescope at unsuspecting groups in a busy marketplace or watch pedestrians in the road leading to the palace.

Such behaviour would appear to border on paranoia, some of it likely to have been incubated in the chilly rooms of Fairfield. Many foreigners were also monitored to see what they were up to in Addis Ababa and whether they posed any threat. For the vast majority of us who are not monarchs, it is extremely difficult to comprehend what it must feel like to have lost a crown in such turbulent circumstances, lived as a largely irrelevant commoner, and then regained a kingdom. The Emperor tried to ensure that no-one was going to be allowed to take power away from him again.

The fear of being permanently branded a coward must also have gnawed away at the Emperor on those long winter nights in Bath. His willingness to take a risk by returning to Ethiopia in a dangerous and unpredictable mission could have gone some way to reducing that concern, though his American adviser John Spencer said that the charge of cowardice was to haunt him for decades after his return. In 1941 the Emperor must have been pleased that so many of his people had welcomed him back so quickly. However, some of the staunchest patriots could not conceal their resentment at his return. They were frustrated that the Emperor and other exiles had been rewarded with positions of power and privilege. Even collaborators went unpunished. Among their ranks was Ras Hailu of Gojam, who had been turfed off the train when the Emperor fled to Djibouti. All that was required of the treacherous Ras was that he stay in Addis Ababa where he could easily be monitored.

Several patriots were to show their anger by organising revolts and assassination attempts. One of the prime movers was Takele Walde-Hawaryat, who had argued so vehemently at the council meeting in 1936 against the Emperor fleeing to Europe. Before the Italian occupation he had been a loyal supporter of the Imperial government. Perhaps in recognition of this, attempts were made to buy him off with a range of tempting positions of influence. However, Takele could not rid himself of his bitterness and outrage. When his latest attempt to murder the Emperor failed in 1969, he was surrounded by police at his house. Takele shot himself when he realised his position was hopeless. He had never been one for tamely surrendering.

The tension between the returning exiles, patriots and collaborators was to be a powerful dynamic in Ethiopian politics for years to come. It provided the Emperor with an opportunity to play off various interest groups against each other to consolidate his own power. His reasoning was likely to have been that it was better for these influential factions to be busy feuding with one another rather than any of them having time to challenge him.

In domestic policy one of the Emperor's first measures was to end slavery once and for all in Ethiopia, and to impose binding measures to make sure the legislation worked. Before his exile he had tried on a number of occasions to free slaves, partly in response to growing international pressure. However, his attempts had been resisted by regional princes and dukes, who relied on unpaid labour to run their fiefdoms. The measures to ban slavery, introduced in 1942, were not only modernising and humanising but also helped the Emperor to establish some authority over those troublesome princes. Critics of the Emperor believed that little changed because of these measures and Ethiopia was still a heartless, feudal society with the masses condemned to wretched lives of poverty and despair.

FAMILY MATTERS

The Emperor never forgot his commitment to educating young people. At Fairfield he had constantly reminded his granddaughter Princess Seble of the importance of working hard at her studies and doing something for her country. Now he quickly turned his mind to how to improve the education system in his country. One of the few advantages of his exile was that he had seen firsthand a variety of schools and colleges in Britain. His attempts to modernise though were sorely hampered by the absence of many of the talented young generation mercilessly cut down by Graziani.

Despite the pressures of governing, the Emperor continued to make time for his children and grandchildren, just as he had done in Bath. Princess Mary, one of the daughters of Crown Prince Asfa-Wossen, can clearly recall today playing with her grandfather, then in his sixties, on a family holiday at the seaside resort of Massawa in Eritrea. The coastal region was then in federation with Ethiopia – a move which

CHAPTER 9

at last satisfied Ethiopia's quest to possess a sea port. The Princess and other members of her family threw sand on the Emperor while he was resting on the beach and buried him up to his neck. The great Lion of Judah, who had sworn a solemn vow before God at his glittering coronation in 1930, merely laughed and giggled at his discomfiture. It seems he never totally lost his sense of playfulness and enjoyment of the younger generation.

Another grandson, Prince Beede Mariam, says that when he was growing up his grandfather always had time for him. He was encouraged to approach the Emperor at any time, apart from when he was doing his daily gymnastics. That period was sacrosanct. All the grandchildren were welcome to ask questions, which the Emperor would always take time to answer. The Prince said his grandfather believed that no-one was too young to understand.

EXPRESSING THANKS

One consequence of Haile Selassie's exile was that it increased his sense of gratitude for favours received. Just three months after arriving back home, he sent a letter of thanks to Pop Smith, the leather trader whose advice he had come to rely on in Bath. Pop was also among those from the city who were invited to Ethiopia for the Emperor's silver jubilee in 1955 as a special way of saying thank you. The Emperor kept the memory of Fairfield alive by giving its name to one of his weekend retreats at Debre Zeit to the south of Addis. Several roads in Addis Ababa were named after a number of British stalwarts who helped the Emperor at crucial stages of the exile period. Churchill Road is now a busy thoroughfare running up from the new business district to Piazza. Sylvia Pankhurst also has a street named after her and there is still a school in the city bearing the name of Wingate.

Churchill Road today

IMPERIAL EXILE

In the winter of 1947 Britain was subjected to severe flooding, causing widespread misery and suffering. After a special fund was set up to relieve the plight of the victims, the Emperor sent a cheque for £1,000 to help offset the harshness of the weather in what he referred to as a great and pleasant land.

Philippa Langdon, the daughter of Colonel Sandford who helped rouse the Ethiopian resistance before the Emperor's return, also believes he never forgot anyone who had done him a favour. She tells the story of how after the war he would come to the family farm north of Addis Ababa for breakfast where he would sit around the kitchen table and chat in English and Amharic. The Emperor was out of the country on the way back from a state visit to Nigeria when Philippa's father died. On hearing the news he arranged for a radio message to be sent to the Sandford family, saying he wanted to be at the funeral and could they please wait for him. The family willingly delayed the interment and it became almost like a state event, with a full church service and a burial at the war graves site. Philippa can also remember a volley of shots being fired. She said the Emperor spoke in person to each member of the family and said to her in English: 'Be brave.'

During his reign the Emperor walked behind many funeral cortèges as he believed it was important to be seen paying his final respects, especially to those who had helped him. When Sylvia Pankhurst died in Addis Ababa in 1960, she was granted a full state funeral, a sign of the Emperor's gratitude for her campaigning zeal for Ethiopia. At the service she was described as 'welete cristos,' a daughter of Christ. Her body was buried at Holy Trinity Cathedral in a plot reserved to honour those who had done the most to oppose Italian aggression.

Sylvia Pankhurst's grave outside the entrance to Holy Trinity Cathedral

CHAPTER 9

Another veteran of the Gideon Force also died before the Emperor did. The journalist George Steer's star burned very brightly while it lasted, but tragically he was killed in a humdrum traffic accident in Burma in 1944. Steer died when driving an overloaded army jeep and his skull was shattered in the impact. Haile Selassie had lost yet another friend in terrible circumstances.

The Emperor continued to keep in touch with other foreign supporters who had been so influential during his exile. The explorer Wilfred Thesiger recalled how he went on a private trip to Addis Ababa in 1959, only to be summoned to attend a private audience with the Emperor, a rare honour for an unofficial guest. The Emperor provided Thesiger with letters of permission to help smooth the way for an expedition he was planning to Lalibela, the site of the rock-hewn churches where Haile Selassie had sought spiritual guidance during the Italian invasion. When Thesiger told the Ethiopian ruler he had been honoured to have served under him in the battle to free Abyssinia, he said in reply that he owed much to the British during that campaign.

Despite some positive consequences of his time in England, it is clear that the Emperor continued to grapple with at least two issues which had troubled him during his exile: the frustration of dealing with the British government, and coping with the chastening experience of living like a relative pauper for so many years.

DEALING WITH THE BRITISH

The tensions between the Emperor and the British government, which had been smouldering for years, did not evaporate once the Lion of Judah had been reinstalled.

Indeed, a power struggle quickly ensued between him and the British authorities who believed they should strongly influence the destiny of Ethiopia as they had been instrumental in its liberation. There was still a war to be won and Ethiopia's strategic position in the Horn of Africa was seen by the British government as too important to relinquish. British officials talked of their role in the country as merely occupying enemy territory recovered from the Italians and not restoring Ethiopia's independence. They only cared about the broader military picture in North Africa. After all, the UK already ruled a lot of the territories in the region. The Emperor just wanted to go back to the status quo ante and be left alone to run the country as he saw fit.

After they entered Addis Ababa, the British set up an administration to help run Ethiopia from its diplomatic base in Nairobi in neighbouring Kenya. It was operating in parallel to the state ministries the Emperor was trying to revive. Once again the Emperor was in a head to head with the British establishment. British officials in Nairobi toyed with all kinds of plans to carve up parts of Ethiopia. One was to add the British occupied Ogaden in the south east to a Greater Somalian project. In the north, a proposal was considered to merge Tigray with the neighbouring area of Eritrea, now reclaimed from the Italians, who had established a colony there in 1890. The British government also was unwilling or unable to provide the minimum assistance in men and materials needed to get the government back on its feet. It did not respond positively to the Emperor's repeated request for help in building roads and communications.

However, this time the Emperor held the advantage. He was playing at home, on territory he knew far better than his British diplomatic adversaries. Equally, British administrators had to grapple with the culture and practices of a country very alien to them. Biding his time as usual, Haile Selassie slowly managed to assert his independence and authority. This power struggle ignited the campaigning flames of Sylvia Pankhurst, who went on the warpath again, saying she had now to rescue the Emperor from his liberators. Ethiopia was officially under British administration until the end of 1942. It was only then that Britain began to recognise the independence of Ethiopia, though the British maintained considerable influence and control for some time after that. By 1944 Haile Selassie managed to negotiate a formal agreement with the British, which reduced London's powers to more marginal levels. The Emperor admitted to these struggles with Britain in the second volume of his autobiography. He said he had become involved in an intricate political imbroglio with British officials in East Africa. The Emperor also accused the British military leaders of trying to divide Ethiopia along ethnic lines.

As the years passed, the Emperor turned his diplomatic focus away from interfering British diplomats. He would have recognised that Britain's once mighty empire was ebbing away and London was losing a lot of its global influence. Instead, the Emperor became increasingly interested in strengthening ties with the United States, which was gaining greater influence in the world. Haile Selassie never forgot that an American president, Franklin Roosevelt, had steadfastly refused to recognise Italy's occupation of Ethiopia. He also would have remembered Britain's opposition to Ethiopia joining the League of Nations in 1923.

The Emperor had long harboured a desire to develop a deeper relationship with Washington. In 1927 he had sent Charles Martin to the United States to negotiate a deal over building a dam in Ethiopia. His famous speech to the League of Nations had been co-authored by his American advisor John Spencer. While in exile in Bath, the Emperor had kept a channel open to the American public. When he had broken his collar bone it was on the day he had been broadcasting a special Christmas greeting to the United States. In 1942, while he was feuding with British bureaucrats, Haile Selassie sent a letter to President Roosevelt. The American president replied in warm terms. The Emperor used this diplomatic opening to grow closer to the United States and within a year the two nations had signed a mutual aid agreement. The Lion of Judah was weaning himself away from British and European support, and increasingly

CHAPTER 9

turned his gaze further west across the Atlantic. In 1943 John Spencer was made a principal adviser to the Ethiopian Foreign Ministry. Spencer was appalled by what he saw as British attempts to partition Ethiopia and he played a large role in formulating a pro-American approach.

Two years later the Emperor pulled off a great diplomatic coup. Somehow he managed to wangle an invitation to meet Roosevelt in person. The ailing and exhausted American President was only two months away from death. He was on his way back from the Yalta Conference where he had met Churchill and Stalin to discuss a post war settlement. The meeting was set up on the American battle cruiser Quincy at Great Bitter Lake in Egypt. The Emperor was flown in great secrecy to Egypt from Addis Ababa on an American air force DC-3 plane. When British diplomats got wind of the meeting they were alarmed that they might be losing even more influence in the Horn of Africa. In a trice arrangements were made for Churchill to travel to Egypt to get in on the act. His face to face talks with Haile Selassie were reported to be irritable and tense. In contrast, the Ethiopian leader's meeting with Roosevelt was very positive and laid the groundwork for further decades of co-operation between Washington and Addis Ababa.

In all, Haile Selassie met five American Presidents and made numerous visits to the United States. He received a tumultuous ticker tape reception on his first trip to New York in 1954 when hundreds of thousands of Americans lined the streets to cheer him on. The Emperor made the mile long journey along Broadway in an open top car. It was vastly different to his subdued exile in Bath when he had travelled into town on a humble tramcar.

Many African Americans, along with millions in Africa and the Caribbean, had always supported Haile Selassie since his country was invaded. He had become an early symbol of the growing independence movements, anxious to create their own separate identity on the African continent. As trade and diplomatic links strengthened, the United States entered into many constructive partnerships with Ethiopians. American aviation experts provided the know-how to create the national carrier Ethiopian Airlines, which today is regarded as one of the best and fastest growing airlines in Africa. The United States also helped to develop a modern military, telecommunications industry and better highways.

Haile Selassie, increasingly disillusioned with the former great European powers, became an enthusiast of the non-aligned movement and began to turn his attention to the rest of the African continent. In 1963 he was one of the driving forces behind the formation of the Organisation of African Unity and actively encouraged the anti-colonial spirit that was sweeping through Africa. Despite opposition from countries like Nigeria, he fought for the organisation to have its headquarters in Addis Ababa. The successor to the OAU, the African Union, is still based in the Ethiopian capital today. The Emperor's struggle against the Italians had given him considerable authority and respect among other Africans.

Nelson Mandela, who was 17 at the time of Mussolini's invasion, said that it had created in him a widespread hatred of all forms of fascism. Mandela was to visit Ethiopia for talks with Haile Selassie in February 1962. He stayed in a room at the Ras Hotel in the capital, at the bottom of Churchill Road. Today there is a plaque at the hotel marking Mandela's visit and a large photograph of him on the approach to the third floor. You can even stay in the suite of rooms he inhabited. But it will cost you at least 100 dollars a night for the privilege, about three times the normal rate.

After the Emperor returned to Ethiopia he visited many other countries and is one of the best travelled world leaders of all time. One local saying is that he slept in as many beds as Queen Elizabeth of England. The glamorous milieu of international affairs may well have been much more palatable than coping with the resentment towards what a growing number considered to be his autocratic and privileged rule at home. The respect he was accorded as head of state would also have been a chance to purge his exile experience when ignored by so many governments.

In Bath the world had been closing in on the Emperor, driving him further into the recesses of his own mind. He had been well and truly trapped. He had had neither the resources nor the opportunity to travel that much, an extremely frustrating and constraining position to be in. Now he was free to go where he wanted, when he wanted. Richard Pankhurst believes that the exile experience gave the Emperor a ringside seat to view the intricacies of European diplomatic manoeuvring. This unique access gave him great insight and knowledge, which he put to constructive use when carrying out his energetic international diplomacy in later years.

Haile Selassie also remained loyal to the principle of collective security. He sent a contingent of Ethiopian troops to fight in the Korean War and also contributed to the UN peacekeeping force in Congo in 1960. On one of his travels the Emperor went to Jamaica in 1966. Hundreds of thousands of Rastafari turned up at the airport to greet him. The idea that the Emperor was divine had been circulating since the 1930s. Now many Jamaican admirers had the chance to see him in person. In 1948 the Emperor had given the Rastafarians some land near the busy crossroads town of Shashamane in southern Ethiopia. Rastafarian communities still live there to this day.

THE QUESTION OF MONEY

The lack of money during the Emperor's exile was one of the most debilitating and embarrassing aspects of his exclusion from a life of power and privilege. In his eyes he had been living a wretched, insolvent life. He obviously returned to Ethiopia determined not to be placed in that position again and became very obsessive in controlling the country's finances. He never again wanted to be faced with the embarrassment of not

CHAPTER 9

being able to pay a bill. One unflattering criticism was that the Emperor became a miser with a cash box. He insisted on personally approving virtually all items of public expenditure, even those involving tiny amounts. His American adviser John Spencer also described what he called his avarice during the post-liberation period. However, according to Edward Ullendorff, the Emperor paid back the money proffered by the British government soon after his return to Addis Ababa. It is also the case that the Emperor set up a number of charities to help disadvantaged people.

Developing business interests also became a preoccupation for the once impecunious Emperor. He was accused of amassing a large financial empire without distinguishing too carefully between state and private funds. The Emperor became what was described as Ethiopia's first beer baron as he owned two major breweries. He also bought shares in a number of concerns, including the Anbessa bus company, and was also the country's biggest landowner. Incredibly it appears that the Emperor never had a bank account after returning from the UK. This was revealed many years later in the 1970s by the then Governor of the Bank of Ethiopia Taffara Deguefé. He said that the Emperor had been bruised by the court case he had lost while in exile when he tried to reclaim money from the Bank of Egypt. He simply never wanted to trust any bank again.

The Emperor also modernised his palace after reclaiming it from the Italians. It must have been a great relief to have been back in familiar surroundings and to lack for nothing. Modern bathrooms and bedrooms were installed. These private quarters are still preserved to this day as part of the palace museum, though the green bath and wash basins now seem rather gaudy and dated. At the time they would have been considered state-of-the-art, and probably a considerable improvement on the facilities at Fairfield.

In the palace museum an old-fashioned white telephone can also still be seen by the Emperor's bedside. This was the hotline used to bring urgent news of government business and appointments. After his exile the Emperor continued to use the administrative practice known as shumshir to promote and demote government officials. Patronage belonged to him. In Bath he had had virtually no staff, let alone having the opportunity to organise a big civil service apparatus. Everything had been done on a very small scale. Once back at the head of a huge bureaucracy, the Emperor could once again indulge his fondness and talent for rewarding favours and settling scores. The hotline would inevitably be busy.

Amid all these cosmetic changes was the Emperor ever able to wipe from his mind that the hated Italian oppressors once roamed round his home? Was he also able to keep away the memories of the awful events following the attempt on Graziani's life on the palace steps?

ILL WINDS

Although the Emperor successfully tightened his grip on power in the 1950s, his joys inevitably continued to be mixed with sadnesses. One of the worst moments came in 1957 when his beloved and flamboyant son Makonnen was killed in a car crash near Debra Zeit. His father could not contain his emotions of grief as he walked behind the coffin to the church. Rita Pankhurst was among the large crowd of mourners and she said the Emperor looked so frail and the Empress so pale.

The year before, the Emperor's faithful companion Ras Kassa had died of a heart attack while visiting a monastery in a remote region in northern Ethiopia. Ras Kassa had been by the Emperor's side at all the vital moments of his life. The Ras was there when Haile Selassie became Crown Prince in 1916; on the Grand Tour of Europe in 1924; at the coronation in 1930; on the frontline against Italy in 1935-6; in exile at Fairfield in Bath and on the triumphant return to Addis Ababa in 1941. Although Ras Kassa had held no official post since then, he had had a regular weekly advisory meeting with the Emperor when they discussed the biggest thorny questions facing the country. The deaths of these two favourites left Haile Selassie in despair and took its toll on his emotional life.

The Emperor with Ras Kassa in the 1950s at the outside arena of Jan Meda for an annual event raising money for the Red Cross

In 1960 his equilibrium was again completely thrown off balance. While the Emperor was away on a tour of Brazil, the Commander of the Imperial Guard and his brother burst into the Gennete Leul Palace as part of an attempted coup. They were frustrated

CHAPTER 9

by the lack of social and economic progress and accused the Emperor of becoming too authoritarian and remote from his people. The plotters took some hostages, including senior government figures. In the turmoil that followed 15 of the captives were mercilessly gunned down in cold blood by the plotters as they fled the scene. This time the Emperor and Empress could no longer bear to live with the memories of murder within the royal residence. They moved out, and the palace was turned into a new university, which at that time bore the name of Haile Selassie I. One of the first people to run the fledgling university was Lij Kassa Welde-Maryam, the husband of Princess Seble Desta, who had played ping pong with her grandfather at Fairfield House.

The cataclysmic events of the attempted coup in 1960 were still some way off when Haile Selassie had his final encounter with the people of Bath.

CHAPTER NINE EYEWITNESS THE WEEKEND RETREAT

In Haile Selassie's day the journey from Addis Ababa to the weekend retreat he named after Bath's Fairfield House would have been vastly different from the journey I took in 2014. The Ethiopian Fairfield is based in the volcanic lake region of Debre Zeit. Although it is only 30 miles south of the capital, the town is much warmer due to its lower altitude down in the Rift Valley. The main road to Debre Zeit was chaotic with hundreds of trucks, minibuses and private cars jostling for space. In the Emperor's time traffic levels were much lighter, though of course fewer roads would have been paved. The modern route is especially dangerous and busy. After Debre Zeit the road winds its way to the port of Djibouti, Ethiopia's main trading link to the rest of the world. However, the traffic flow has recently improved due to the opening of a spanking new three lane highway built with the help of Chinese loans and know-how.

On my way south I could see remnants of the French built railway line along which the royal family had fled way back in 1936. China is also helping to build a modern railway line along this route. On the way into Debre Zeit there is a huge Chinese-sponsored industrial zone where hundreds of local workers are employed in a range of industries, including shoemaking. It is an economic powerhouse that would have amazed the Emperor, whose country struggled to emerge from its ancient, agrarian past during his rule, and indeed for some time afterwards.

You can see why the Emperor liked coming to Debre Zeit to rest, read and think. The English translation of Debre Zeit is the Mount of Olives, named after the place where Jesus is recorded as weeping as he looked down over Jerusalem. Such a strong Christian resonance would have made the area extra special for a deeply religious man like the Emperor. Today the town is becoming increasingly known by its name in the language of the Oromo people, Bishoftu, which means a watery place.

The Fairfield property is perched high on the edge of the rim of Hora Lake. It

CHAPTER 9

is still peaceful, though in common with other lakes in the region, there are some sprawling resort buildings being built on some of the surrounding hills. It is not possible to enter the house today as it is a military hospital. A big air force base is situated nearby. In some ways that seems appropriate as Haile Selassie always loved aircraft. He was the first and only Solomonic king to have flown in a plane. And it was he who brought the first aircraft to Ethiopia in the 1920s.

The Emperor on the steps of Fairfield in Debre Zeit

I was able to walk on a small path by the lake shore for the princely entrance sum of four birr, the equivalent of 12 pence. The weather was warm and welcoming. After the hustle and bustle of Addis, it was like being suddenly transported to a tranquil paradise. On the opposite side of the lake, some local people were marking irecha, an important festival in local Oromo culture with much feasting and singing. The event was held under a tree, the symbol of the Oromo people, the largest ethnic group in Ethiopia. Some of the Emperor's ancestors were of Oromo origin.

The lakeside path meanders along the shore where many rushes are growing and different kinds of birds circle and hover in the azure sky. I could only catch a brief glimpse of the yellow painted stone walls of Fairfield, as it was masked by trees with sprawling branches. A couple of local men acted as impromptu guides, though they seemed to know little about the house or the Emperor's links to it. In the early days of the residence a huge neon sign was put on the outside of the property, spelling out the letters of Fairfield House. The Emperor was not only having some fun with a new-fangled electronic gadget but was keen to show to everyone around that he was proud of the name.

Princess Seble can remember coming here for weekend visits and said her grandfather loved his walks in the local area. He would often stroll to the nearby village, presumably with his latest favourite dog in tow. Prince Beede Mariam can also recall visiting here on many weekends as a young boy. He said his grandfather loved this retreat, so calling it Fairfield was something special. In this place the Emperor had a special library of much treasured books, including some written in Latin and various classics written by his favourite authors. The Emperor would hide himself away for hours carefully reading these tomes.

Relaxing at Ethiopia's Fairfield, pictured in 1972

I took a boat into the centre of the lake and could see clearly that the house dominates the landscape. The lakeside remote setting is very different to the Bath Fairfield and I wondered why the Emperor chose this specific retreat to christen with the Fairfield name. Maybe it was the gentle rolling hills of the surrounding area which reminded him of the view from his bedroom window in Bath. This in turn had reminded him of his home town of Harar. It is perhaps a little surprising that the Emperor wanted to perpetuate the name of Fairfield, given that he had often been so cold and miserable there and had received so much distressing news during his stay. However, maybe it

CHAPTER 9

was just an outward sign that he wanted to thank and honour Fairfield House in some way, given that it had provided shelter for him at one of his greatest times of need. He may have been keen to forget and bury the corrosive emotions he endured as an exile but did not want to allow his sense of gratitude to be pushed out of the way. As many people have said, he always repaid a favour. The Fairfield of Hora Lake is simply a testament to his way of paying respect.

CHAPTER TEN
THE FINAL CURTAIN CALL

The Emperor had the opportunity to resume his relationship with the city of Bath in 1954. He went there during a visit to the UK, the first since he had slipped away in secret in the summer of 1940. This time the British establishment gave him full respect as a visiting head of state. The Emperor arrived in Portsmouth on board *HMS Gambia*. He did not have to sneak in on a passenger boat. This time cannons fired royal salutes and a fly past was carried out by RAF Coastal Command. Haile Selassie then went by train to London where on this occasion he was met in person at the station by the monarch, the young Queen Elizabeth, and her husband the Duke of Edinburgh. The Emperor was dressed in full ceremonial uniform and kissed some of the hands of the female members of the Royal party, including the Queen Mother. Some of them in turn curtsied to him. The Prime Minister, Winston Churchill, the Emperor's war time ally who had effectively ended his exile, was also part of the official welcoming party.

In BBC television coverage of the event the distinguished commentator Richard Dimbleby remarked how much happier must Haile Selassie have been today than on that day 18 years ago when he came to the UK as an exile. This time there was no tampering with the Emperor's route through London. He was invited to sit with the Queen in a ceremonial horse drawn open carriage. Among the cheering crowds was a young woman, Rita Eldon, who within two years was to travel to Ethiopia to join Richard Pankhurst where she became his wife.

The Emperor attended a state banquet at Buckingham Palace in his honour. He would have been relieved that there were to be no cat-and-mouse charades, and that he was fully accepted as a person of power and importance. The Queen told him that she hoped he would always feel at home in England and referred to the special link

CHAPTER 10

between the two countries: 'We greet you as the Sovereign of an ancient Christian state which has many links with our own Church.'

The Emperor at the time of his return to Bath

In reply, the Emperor expressed his gratitude for Britain's help in liberating Ethiopia. Empress Menen was unwell back in Ethiopia and sent her apologies. Makonnen, the Duke of Harar, accompanied his father on the visit. The Duke, with his zest for life, was presumably excited to be back in the country where he had had such fun as a teenager. Tragically three years later he would be killed in that fateful car crash in Ethiopia.

BACK AT FAIRFIELD

A trip to Bath was an important part of the itinerary on the UK tour of 1954. The return visit was given extra significance because the Emperor had been invited to receive a special honour. He had been awarded the Freedom of the City to recognise his contribution to the life of Bath and the general war effort. The move had been proposed by the Mayor and was backed unanimously by the whole council. The ceremony came four years after Churchill had also been made a Freeman of Bath. Freedom of the City status is a rare honour granted by British cities to valued residents or eminent visitors, who have made a special contribution to a particular municipality. The custom dates back to medieval times when citizens were released from the constraints of serfdom.

By tradition those made a Freeman of London were entitled to some quaint privileges such as being able to drive sheep across one of the Thames bridges or carrying a sword openly in public. More dubious was the right to be hanged with a silken cord rather than a plain rope if a freeman ever committed a heinous crime and was sentenced to death. The city of Bath had no such colourful heritage. In modern times the honour is ceremonial and carries no practical privileges. In addition to Churchill, the Emperor joined other dignitaries such as Admiral Nelson and Maharao Shri Khengarji III of Cutch in 1921. He was the ruler of a princely state in western India and one of the longest serving monarchs in the world. He was also regarded as being one of the finest exponents of horsemanship anywhere.

This time the Emperor returned to Bath by road, not along the familiar railway route. He therefore did not make use of Bath Spa Station, which harboured an array of emotional memories of poignant arrivals and departures. His return after 14 years enabled the local people to show their respect. They had not forgotten him. The *Chronicle* also leapt at the chance to provide extensive coverage of their exotic royal ex-exile. The paper published photographs showing huge crowds in the streets outside the Guildhall where the ceremony took place and followed official proceedings throughout the day.

Arriving at the ceremony by the Guildhall

Inspecting the guard of honour

CHAPTER 10

An ecstatic crowd waiting in Bath Abbey Churchyard

A cheery wave during official proceedings

A chance to taste the spa waters

A visit to the Stothert and Pitt engineering firm

At the home of Mr and Mrs Rowlands. They had got out their best china to offer their royal guest a cup of tea but he was running behind schedule and so did not have time to stay

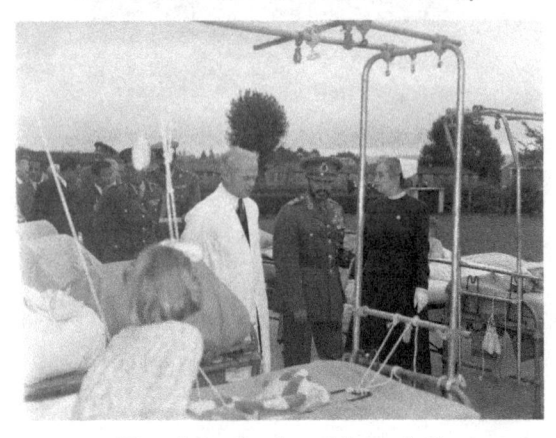

Touring the local hospital

CHAPTER 10

A chaotic visit to Moorlands School

The Bath authorities were anxious to get everything just right when the Emperor returned for lunch at the Guildhall in the centre of Bath. There was a red carpet and 750 dahlias on display. In the banqueting room were bowls of lavender, and salmon and pink cyclamen. In his formal speech the Emperor was in a reflective mood: 'Bath has a long and glorious history, back to Roman times. It was with you I bore my sorrows…It was from you that I drew strength to lead my people back on the highway of freedom and progress.'

Signing the Freedom of the City document

In the evening the ceremonies moved back to Fairfield House, the scene of so much anguish during the Emperor's exile. There he made the Mayor a commander of the order of Menelik II and said that he would never give up Fairfield. It would always be kept in order and made available for Ethiopian officials and students. The house had been made ready by Rosalind Sawyer, one of the original members of the Fairfield staff. Rosalind was still living in a property on the edge of the Fairfield grounds and had been left in charge after the last members of the royal family left.

Fairfield served briefly as a centre for babies and young children left homeless by the bombing during the war but the house had been empty for nearly a decade. Before the Emperor returned, Rosalind had been busily sprucing up the grounds and redecorating the interior to make it habitable once again. One of Rosalind's favourite memories of Fairfield in the 1930s was when one of her sons and the Emperor's grandsons had misbehaved and had been sent to bed without any supper. Later in the evening she saw the King of Kings creeping into their rooms with a secret supper so they would not go hungry.

PUTTING MATTERS IN PERSPECTIVE

As usual, the Emperor presented his normal calm exterior. Beneath the surface his emotions must have been racing back again to those testing exile years in Bath, with many more sad memories than joyful ones. Some of his thoughts would likely have turned to specific events or experiences: shivering in the cold at Fairfield with his family in the winter; wrestling desperately trying to pay the bills; hearing the news of the massacres in Addis Ababa after the attempt on Graziani's life. Other memories would have been of individuals: walking round the grounds of the Bath Spa Hotel with his beloved daughter Tsehai, now laid to rest in Addis Ababa after her death in 1942; burying his dear friend Heruy; comforting his daughter Tenagneworq after hearing of the death of her husband Ras Desta. Was he pleased to be back? Or was it difficult and awkward, throwing up a lot of emotions that would have been better to lie untouched? Despite any misgivings, there would have been some positive aspects to the trip – seeing some familiar sights and faces belonging to those who had helped him, and having a chance to express his gratitude.

After a gap of 14 years the Emperor would have been able to bring some perspective to assessing his time in Bath. The experience had been undoubtedly arduous and bleak. He had known what it was like to be violently uprooted from everything familiar. He had endured a permanent 'mind of winter.' He had been tested to the limit. But he had stubbornly come through it all. Some exiles can wallow in self pity and sulk about the setbacks they are facing. But the Emperor generally kept his nerve and his self respect. He did not succumb to playing the role of victim, a kind of silent martyr. He did not throw in the towel, though he must have come close to it on one or two occasions.

His faith in God had been strengthened and he had discovered new reserves of resolve and determination. He had received uplifting support from family and friends and had understood even more the importance of gratitude. He had no cause to regret deciding to spend his exile in England. His original calculation that the best

CHAPTER 10

chance of getting back to Ethiopia was through the British had proved to be correct. If he had gone to Switzerland or France he might still have been languishing there in 1954, descending ever further into despair and regret. The history of Ethiopia would also have been vastly different if the Emperor had not settled in Bath. In the end, Haile Selassie's policy in following his father's lead in opening up to countries outside his own had paid off. The painful decision to abandon his capital had finally borne fruit. Bath had not let him down. It had given him a secure base with enough trappings of royalty and grandeur to keep up his spirits.

For Bathonians, seeing the Emperor again was certainly a pleasure. He had given them an example of how to meet suffering and setbacks in a polite, calm and respectful way. He had been a perfect gentleman while a guest in the city. There had been no scandal or unpleasantness. He had also given them some insight into a completely different culture and way of life. They could never really fully understand the world he came from and the political dark arts he had needed to rise to the top in his own country. But Bathonians had done their best to offer support, gladly going out of their way to help an underdog.

As war approached, they did forget him to some extent. But they had been glad and proud to have had him in their midst. In some ways the people of Bath and Haile Selassie formed a kind of early twinning arrangement, so popular between cities after World War II. The Emperor and his family had learned a lot about the culture, history and character of the British. In return Bathonians had learned about the intricacies of the Orthodox Church, Ethiopian kings and had the chance to discover that African nations too had their special histories and identities. Both Bath and the Emperor had a humanising effect on each other. They had much in common. Both were regal and reserved with a hinterland stretching back centuries. It was a genteel and orderly relationship, which suited one another.

On the other hand, it is unlikely whether deep down the Emperor ever really felt at home in Bath. As Dante put it, Haile Selassie had had to taste the salty bread and trudge up stairs he was unfamiliar with. He was always a stranger and outsider, a reluctant sojourner desperate to be back home ruling his kingdom. For him Fairfield was just an enforced staging post, albeit a dignified one. So the relationship was never one of strong feeling and attachment. It was more of a courteous working relationship, based on mutual respect. In that sense it was out of keeping with the turbulent 1930s, which gave vent to uncontrolled rage and prejudice in a terrifying way. Bath and the Emperor were something of an odd couple but they took solace from each other at a time when the civilised world was being turned on its head.

The story of the Emperor in his wilderness years had thrown up some delicious ironies and contradictions. He was the first Ethiopian leader to flee from his own country in the face of an aggressive enemy, though he was later to be restored to his throne in glory. He was an implacable enemy of the Italians yet settled in Bath, a city which was founded by the Romans. He came to a country having involuntarily given up his throne but found himself in a nation where the ruling monarch, Edward VIII, willingly gave up his crown for the love of a woman. And he came to a city where Britain's war time leader Churchill received loud applause when he delivered his first political speech as a young aspiring Conservative, and would later be a major factor in restoring the Emperor to his throne.

THE EMPEROR'S OPPONENTS

A reminder of the Emperor's previous diplomatic sparring with the British government came when he visited Oxford University during his UK trip in 1954. At a special ceremony he was awarded an honorary degree by the university's chancellor Lord Halifax, who had been so flinty in his attitude towards the Emperor's plight in the late thirties. Now it was the African leader who was having the last laugh. Halifax had retired from politics, his reputation sullied by being an arch supporter of the failed policy of appeasement. In contrast, the Emperor was now firmly back in power and in full control of his country and his people.

In the end Haile Selassie outlasted all the people who had been in power in the 1930s during his darkest moments. The urbane Duke of Aosta, the last Italian Viceroy of Ethiopia, died while being held in detention in Kenya in 1942. The first commander of the Italian invasion forces into Ethiopia, Emilio de Bono, was executed by firing squad in January 1944 after Mussolini had him convicted of treason in a show trial. Mussolini himself survived only until 1945 when he was summarily executed by Italian partisans and his body hung upside down on a meat hook. Both of the ruthless Italian generals prominent during the later stages of the Abyssinian campaign, Badoglio and Graziani, endured years of turmoil after the Second World War trying to defend their records. They both died of natural causes in the mid 1950s. The Emperor's words to his granddaughter Princess Seble had finally come home to roost. God had now seen off those Italians.

Pierre Laval, the French Prime Minister, who wanted to carve up Ethiopia in a shoddy deal, was found guilty of treason at the end of the Second World War for serving in the Vichy regime, Germany's puppet government in France. He was executed by firing squad. Two British prime ministers, who favoured Italy over Ethiopia, both died in the 1940s. Neville Chamberlain, who had forced the pro-Ethiopian Eden out of office, succumbed to cancer only six months after resigning in 1940. Stanley Baldwin, who had dived under a table to avoid meeting the Emperor in the Houses of Parliament, died in his sleep in 1947.

Another perspective on the exile years was provided by the Emperor himself on a fascinating trip he made to Rome in 1970. The visit revealed that, although his

CHAPTER 10

attitude to the British remained cordial, he was emotionally more at home with the culture of the French and, maybe somewhat bizarrely, the Italians. Relations with Italy had ebbed and flowed ever since the war in a series of recriminations over reparations, the Axum obelisk and the issue of Eritrea. However, Haile Selassie wanted to repair the breach with Italy. He believed in the merits of the Italian people, respected their artistic achievements, and blamed the war on the fascist madness of Mussolini. Italy was a republic by 1970 and had no great enthusiasm for receiving an African monarch, though it did acknowledge that the Emperor had probably saved a lot of Italian blood in his appeal for no reprisals to be made after his return to Addis Ababa.

After his official tour of Rome, the Emperor was given use of the presidential train to go on a private visit to several Italian cities where he was showed great warmth and respect. The Italian people were saying sorry. Haile Selassie achieved one of his childhood dreams when in Milan he saw Leonardo da Vinci's famous painting *The Last Supper*. He also slept in a bed at the Palazzo Monforte that used to belong to King Victor Emmanuel II, who had been the first king after the unification of Italy. While he was approaching Venice, the Emperor made an extraordinary confession to Ambassador Pasucci-Righi, his fellow traveller. This was his comment, as quoted in Del Boca's book *The Negus*.

> 'I owe nearly everything to Great Britain. The British gave me a place to live when I went into exile, and they brought me back to my homeland. All the same, strange as it may seem, the Ethiopian people have no love for Britain. Only two countries are our friends and understand us. Those countries are France and Italy. I hope that my successors will keep faith with this two-fold constant."

If this quote is accurate, it shows that the actions of Britain, in trying to interfere in Ethiopia after the war, did take their toll on its reputation there. It may well give further credence to the view that the Emperor's relationship with the British people, including those in Bath, was primarily of the head and not of the heart. He gave the people of Bath a tremendous amount of respect and gratitude but one cannot imagine the Emperor giving any of them an affectionate hug, as he did to his grandchildren. In any case, the whole experience in the city had been tainted by the intense estrangement and loneliness he had undergone there.

THE END OF THE AFFAIR?

The Freedom of the City ceremony in 1954 was to be the last time the Emperor ever set foot in Bath. He did return to London as an ageing leader on another state visit in 1972 and there was some talk of his travelling out of the capital to visit his former place of exile. The plan fizzled out and so he was never to see Bath Abbey or the Royal Crescent again. However, he did not sever his links completely. In 1958 he decided to make a gift of Fairfield House to the people of Bath. It was his way of saying a formal thank you. He made it known that he especially wanted the elderly residents of Bath to benefit.

Over the years the house once owned by a Solomonic king has become like a microcosm of the United Nations. It has played host to a variety of groups of different faiths and ethnic backgrounds. These include Rastafarian organisations, a Caribbean elderly residents group and some Ethiopians in the area, who use the house for special feast days and holidays. For a while it was a residential care home for the elderly. In a poignant co-incidence the mother of Ruth Haskins, the assistant governess to the children of the Emperor's family back in the 1930s, was a resident in the home in later life. She died in the same room that had been used as an Imperial nursery all those years before.

The running of the house has not always been smooth. On at least two occasions the local council considered getting rid of the building. Like the Emperor before them, they were finding it too costly to heat and to maintain. However, the future of Fairfield looks more settled. A community management committee now runs the property, though the council still retains ownership. Fairfield is a Grade 2 listed building, meaning it is worthy of preservation. Many hundreds of people from Bath and the surrounding area have enthusiastically taken part in a variety of activities and there is a real determination to keep the legacy of Haile Selassie alive. A big appeal fund to raise a quarter of a million pounds to repair Fairfield House was launched in October 2014. The formation of the Teferi museum in the house is a focal point in the bid to open up the house to a wider range of visitors. Clearly, Bathonians are determined not to lose an important part of their history when a family residence was turned into an adjunct of an Ethiopian Emperor's royal court.

The spirit of the Lion of Judah lives on in Bath.

CHAPTER 10

CHAPTER TEN EYEWITNESS INSIDE THE GUILDHALL

The central part of the current Guildhall building in Bath has proudly stood in Bath since the mid 1770s. The building was designed by the city architect Thomas Baldwin and occupies a prominent position next to Bath Abbey. It is near the River Avon and the old east gate, one of four entrances into the city when Bath boasted a medieval wall. The Emperor first went to the Guildhall on his second full day in Bath during his first visit in that faraway summer of 1936. The mayors who gave him much moral support during his exile were all based here. I suppose you could describe the Guildhall as the gebbi of Bath, the centre of ceremonial and administrative power for the region.

The crowning glory of the municipal Guildhall is the banqueting room, which always rivalled both the private Upper and Lower Assembly Rooms in terms of splendour and elegance. The room contains several Corinthian columns, ornate cornices and a number of large, glittering chandeliers. This is the sort of grandeur that Haile Selassie would have appreciated. The Mayor of Bath said that the Emperor's visit in 1954 was one of the greatest days the city had seen. The council chamber was packed and a special overflow relay was arranged in the banqueting room. For the first time the proceedings of the council were recorded by BBC engineers so the event could be rebroadcast in Ethiopia.

In the basement of the Guildhall is the Bath Record Office where various archives are kept. I had heard that some information about Haile Selassie was based there so went to have a look for myself. The council still keeps an album displaying photographs from his visit to Bath in 1954. During the Freedom of the City ceremonies the council presented the Emperor with an illuminated parchment scroll in a custom made leather case. The council, ever keen to show off the architectural splendours of the city, also gave him a handsomely bound volume of Walter Ison's *Georgian Buildings of Bath*.

IMPERIAL EXILE

The Record Office still had in its possession an Ethiopian rug, presented to the city by the Emperor. The gold, green and scarlet carpet was kept rolled up on top of a cupboard, though there was talk that it could be displayed one day at the museum at Fairfield House. Two magnificent elephant tusks had also been presented to the city by Haile Selassie. They were worth £4,000 and were five feet long. Unfortunately, the tusks were stolen in 1987 by thieves with no sense of history or understanding of the arduous experience of exile. They smashed a glass case in the south side entrance hall and tore the tusks from their mount.

The ill-fated elephant tusks

In the Record Office there were also some account books from the spa baths in the city in the 1930s. A number of entries mention visits by the Emperor and some of his family. They also display the amount of money he spent each time in the former currency of pounds, shillings and pence. The books smell musty, and the spidery but neat handwriting in ink seems to be incongruous with the modern computer age. One entry under the Emperor's name is for four children to go swimming in August 1936. There are also various entries for different types of mud treatments such as Vichy and Tivoli. All the accounts were settled by cheque. It is the kind of detailed record keeping that the Emperor would have liked – functional, accurate, yet without any fuss or emotion.

The Victoria Art Gallery adjoins the Guildhall and on the gallery's outside wall on Bridge Street is a carved stone figure of Queen Victoria, installed to celebrate her Diamond Jubilee in 1897. If Haile Selassie had looked up to notice the sculpture, he might have wondered whether he too would enjoy 60 years in power. At the time of the Freedom of the City ceremony in 1954, he had been, in effect, ruling his country for 38 years after being appointed to the highly influential role of regent in 1916. In the end the Emperor was to be deposed in the revolution of 1974 so he fell just short of the 60 year mark. In the year after being made a freeman, he did though fully celebrate the silver jubilee of his ascension to the throne as Emperor in 1930.

EPILOGUE

For someone who lived such a tumultuous life there is perhaps no surprise that it ended in dramatic and tragic style. In 1974 Haile Selassie was deposed in a revolution led by the military and left-wing intellectuals who attempted to stir up public anger against the Emperor for his extravagant style while so many Ethiopians lived in poverty and hunger. The previous year they had used extracts from a British television documentary as propaganda, repeatedly showing the Emperor feeding his pet chihuahuas, intercut with pictures of a widespread famine. The revolutionaries also resurrected the issue of the Emperor's escape to Djibouti in 1936 to evade the invading Italians, accusing him of abandoning his country.

After he was removed from power by a disgruntled military, Haile Selassie was taken to the great gebbi, established by Menelik. He was to fester there under house arrest for several months. This was the first time since his stay at Fairfield House that the Lion of Judah had lost his freedom of movement and control over his life. After 33 years it must have been a bitter blow to once again not be the master of his own destiny.

The Emperor was effectively now in internal exile. But, unlike in Bath, he had no loyal advisers to support him, no young children to lift his spirits, no solid English folk offering their help and sympathy, and also no loyal wife – Empress Menen had died several years previously. At the age of 82 the Emperor was facing an even bigger test of his faith and character than he had in Bath all those years before. He was confronted by an adversary with the cruelty and barbarity to match that of Mussolini. After the coup the hard-line Colonel Mengistu Haile Mariam emerged as leader of the revolutionary movement, which came to be known as the Derg or committee. Mengistu was as fearsome as Goliath but, on this occasion, he was not defeated by a weaker David. This time the Emperor's rule had been decisively rejected by many of his own people. He was seen as an anachronism in the modern world. No-one was able to help him, not individuals, groups nor governments. There would be no crazy escape, no mad dash to Egypt by seaplane.

IMPERIAL EXILE

Haile Selassie spent much of his time under house arrest cooped up in a small residence, christened the inkulal bet or egg house. It was so called because of an oval shaped dome on the roof. The Emperor was very restricted in his movements, though he was able to stroll around the small garden and admire the flowers. However, he was still greeted with a bow whenever he was seen by his staff. Even some of the Derg soldiers guarding him showed him similar respect.

During his house arrest, the Emperor read many international newspapers, something he had not had time to do since his time in Bath. The spiritual writings of Thomas à Kempis, one of his favourite authors, were especially relevant to a man contemplating his own mortality. As time progressed, the area round the egg house was surrounded by a tall fence made of corrugated tin to keep him out of sight. He became increasingly isolated with only the occasional visitor allowed. One of them reported that the Emperor had been thinking a lot about the past. How often did his mind stray back to his tribulations in Bath? Did he draw strength from remembering that, despite many dark days there, he had overcome them in the end? His exile only formed around five per cent of his life but the experience and its effect on the rest of his life were of disproportionate significance.

The Menelik-era church of Our Lady Covenant of Mercy

Some of the Emperor's family were allowed to visit him. His grandsons Prince Micheal and Prince Beede Mariam, the sons of his favourite son Makonnen, were beckoned into his room at the inkulal bet. The ageing monarch was keen to show them how he was putting crumbs out to feed the birds just outside his window. He may have been separated from his beloved dogs but to the end he still found a way of expressing his affection for the animal kingdom. Prince Micheal also has vivid memories of that visit to this day. He says he asked the Emperor what he was missing

EPILOGUE

most about being in captivity. Sharing a meal with the family, came the response. The two grandsons were so moved by this they tried to persuade the guards to allow them to bring in some food on a future occasion. But their request was waved away and they were never to see their grandfather again.

The inkulal bet overlooked the church of Se-el Bet Kidane Mehret or Our Lady Covenant of Mercy. The church was established in Menelik's reign and was built outside the walls of the gebbi palace compound. The building was circular as was the fashion at that time and had a corrugated tin roof. Although the Emperor was not allowed to attend services there during his imprisonment, he could still hear the spoken or sung liturgy of the priest and had the opportunity of joining in the responses of the congregation.

A MOVING VISIT

On a visit to Addis Ababa in February 2015 I stumbled by chance across crowds of worshippers spilling out in the streets surrounding the Kidane Mehret church. The women were dressed in their distinctive white shawls worn on religious occasions. Some had traditional white dresses embroidered at the edges with flashes of green, gold and other colours. It turned out that the pilgrims were marking the feast day of the Virgin Mary, a very holy occasion. Intrigued, I decided to make my way up a track alongside the gebbi compound to the church itself.

Hundreds of people were still making their way from the church, past the groups of beggars and sellers of church icons and CDs of religious music, which was blaring out everywhere. The gebbi's guards were in full evidence, doing their bit to ensure the safety of the prime minister, who is based on the compound. However, it was still possible to see some of the official buildings and gardens through some decorative, circular holes cut into the ceremonial stone walls when they were built. Some of these gaps are flanked by two spears crossing over each other, a sign of Imperial power. On different sections of the wall other gaps are shaped like a cross, reflecting divine power. Other sections contain crowns, a symbol of the royal power that Menelik wielded.

As I continued to make my way up the crowded bumpy, stony track, I kept nonchalantly stealing some glances into the official gebbi. Suddenly I caught a glimpse nearby of a brown and weathered egg shaped roof. It was the inkulal bet where the former refugee in Bath had been restrained once again. What I had not realised was that next to the Church of St Mary is an impressive stone building, the mausoleum of Emperor Menelik or the Ba'ata Mariam. His body was laid to rest there along with that of his daughter Empress Zewditu. Haile Selassie's daughter Tsehai, who so captivated the people of Bath in 1936, is also buried there in the underground vault, accessed through a large metal trapdoor. She died before the completion of Holy Trinity Cathedral where many of the rest of the Imperial family are buried.

One of the majestic stone lions standing guard

The mausoleum is square in shape and eight stone lions, two on each side, stand guard. The large stone crown at the top of the church, removed by the Italians during their occupation, is now back in its pride of place.

The imperious final resting place of Menelik, complete with crown

While the Emperor was cooped up in his egg house, he could just about see the resting place of a man he greatly admired and loved, Menelik, and of his special daughter, Tsehai. It is hard not to be moved by what fate dealt out to the Emperor in what turned out to be his final days on earth.

EPILOGUE

FINAL DAYS

The Emperor's mind must have been tortured by his fall from power. Before ending up in the inkulal bet, he had been ignominiously removed from office by being bundled into an ordinary Volkswagen beetle car and paraded through the city in shame. Several of the crowd hurled abuse at him, yelling 'leba, leba, leba' or 'thief, thief, thief.' The Derg was obsessed with gaining access to the supposed existence of a fund of billions of dollars which they claimed the Emperor had stashed away in a bank deposit box in Switzerland. However, despite investigating many different leads, they could find no evidence of such a fortune.

In November 1974 the ruthlessness of the Derg was becoming all too apparent. Sixty members of the Imperial military and other organs of state were executed. The victims were lined up against a wall in pairs and mowed down. Among them was a former inhabitant of Fairfield House, Rear Admiral Iskender, one of Princess Tenagneworq's sons and the Emperor's grandson. The Derg also killed Asserate Kassa, Ras Kassa's remaining son, who had also lived at Fairfield and had been the Emperor's camping companion near Swansea just before the start of the Second World War. The news was greeted with a deep sense of shock and sadness by the Bible College of Wales. Another victim of the mass killings was Abebe Retta who had assisted the Emperor while he was in Bath.

In March 1975 the Derg abolished the monarchy. They had prepared for the move by publicly undermining the Emperor and ruthlessly seeking to destroy his reputation. Towards the end of his exile in Bath, Haile Selassie had been described by the British press and officials as the ex-Emperor. Now the Derg ensured that he actually was in reality. Their character assassination was very successful then and since. Among many Ethiopians today, the Emperor's image is still very negative. He is being judged on what he was at the end of his life, not on the whole of it.

As the scholar and translator Ullendorf so memorably once surmised, the real tragedy of the Emperor is that he spent the first two thirds of his life ahead of his people in trying to modernise them and then spent the last third trying to catch up with them. He tried to be the mediator between the old and the new but in the end it proved too much. The Emperor's attempts to bring his country into the 20th century had contributed to his own downfall. He had always been an evolutionist, moving along cautiously, but now the intellectual elite and military wanted dramatic revolutionary action. The creation of Haile Selassie I University at his former palace allowed students to read about revolutionary political and economic ideologies, giving a clear alternative to the Imperial system.

Several African countries made attempts to free the Emperor by suggesting to the Derg that he could leave Ethiopia and live under their jurisdiction. Even if these proposals had ever gained any traction, the Emperor wanted nothing to do with them. He apparently made it be known that he was an old man who had been in exile once and had no wish to repeat the experience.

In August 1975 the Derg announced that the Emperor had died. The official cause of death was given as complications arising from a prostate operation he had undergone three months earlier. However, he was murdered, smothered on Mengistu's orders. The Derg had not one ounce of respect for Haile Selassie. His body was callously buried under a toilet on the gebbi compound. Teferi Makonnen had come into the world 83 years earlier at a time of great famine. And it was another tragic outbreak of hunger which led to his departure from this world. Some maybe recalled the curse given by Menelik to anyone who would raise a hand against his designated successor Lij Iyasu. They could point to the uncanny echo of the prophecy which said that such a man would die a miserable death and nobody would know his grave.

The Derg also dealt ruthlessly with many other members of the royal family. All of them still living in Ethiopia were rounded up and thrown in jail. They were detained at a notorious and desolate prison in the suburbs of Addis Ababa. It was known as 'alem bekagn,' which translates as 'I have had enough of this world.' All the females were held in one group, the males in another. Among the female captives were the Emperor's daughter Princess Tenagneworq, who had lived at Fairfield. With her in jail were all her four daughters: Princess Aida, who had gone to school in Penzance; Princesses Ruth and Seble, who used to play happily together at Fairfield; and Princess Sophia, who stayed in Jerusalem during the family's exile. They were held together in one room in dreadful conditions for about 14 years. Philippa, the daughter of Colonel Sandford, told me how her mother would faithfully take food to the female prisoners. Philippa took on the duty after her mother died. She recalls that the guards would not let her get close to the women and she had to shout greetings and news to them from about 50 yards away.

The male members of the royal family were held in even rougher surroundings and for an extra year longer than the female relatives. Among them were Prince Beede Mariam and Prince Micheal, the sons of the Emperor's son Makonnen. Prince Beede now runs the Wabe Shebelle Hotel, which was returned into the ownership of the royal family in 2011. He was a mere 17 years old when he was imprisoned.

I have met the Prince a few times in recent years. He seems so calm and alert that you would never guess that he spent the cream of his youth in captivity. The same is true of Princess Seble and Princess Sophia, who displayed similar inner strength when I met them. They had obviously watched or heard how their grandfather had remained steadfast at times of extreme adversity. Supporters of the Ethiopian royal family in western England gave their public support to a campaign to release them. They included staff of the schools in Bath, Penzance, and Malvern, attended by some of the Emperor's family.

ACKNOWLEDGEMENTS

As well as the royal family, many ordinary Ethiopians suffered under the despotic rule of the Derg. Tens of thousands were later killed in the Red Terror launched by Mengistu to purge the party of those whom he deemed as being against the revolution. The peaceful home of the Pankhursts was commandeered by local left-wing authorities and was used to brutally imprison some opponents of the revolution. Hundreds of thousands of Ethiopians fled for their lives to escape the slaughter. Like their ruler before them, they were forced to taste the bitter fruits of exile. Crown Prince Asfa-Wossen was already out of Ethiopia, undergoing medical treatment in Switzerland following a stroke. Although he was offered the chance to return as a puppet ruler, he refused and once again became an exile. He eventually died in 1997.

Mengistu, in turn, was deposed by a coup in 1991 and fled to Zimbabwe where he was granted sanctuary. Like his predecessor, he became an exile, though the reason for his absence from his country was being a fugitive from justice and not being a victim of colonial aggression. He simply fled to save his skin.

A year later, Haile Selassie's body was exhumed and transferred next door to the crypt of the Ba'ata Mariam. The new government came under pressure to provide a proper burial for Haile Selassie. After a series of delays the Emperor and Empress Menen were interred in November 2000 in Holy Trinity Cathedral, the church he started to build before his exile in Bath and completed after his triumphant reappearance. Both of them are buried in large tombs made of marble.

Haile Selassie's final resting place

On the top of the tombs is a symbol of the Axum obelisks and, in the middle, is a symbol of the rock-hewn churches of Lalibela. On one of the ceilings overhead is the painting depicting Haile Selassie's famous speech at the League of Nations in 1936, one of the greatest achievements of his life.

It seems fitting that the Solomonic king was finally laid to rest in the place he had dedicated to his victory over the Italians after his return from exile in Bath.

ACKNOWLEDGEMENTS

Many people have helped me while I have been writing this book. It has been a fantastic journey during which I have met such a wide range of people across three continents. They have all been so generous with their time.

In Addis Ababa I have visited the home several times of Rita and Richard Pankhurst, who have been generous hosts in Ethiopia for nearly 60 years. I have drunk their coffee and eaten their cake, and feel privileged to have benefitted from their support and wisdom. I am grateful to them and their publisher, Elias Wondimu of Tsehai Publishing, for supplying me with some photographs from their collection. One of the Emperor's granddaughters Princess Mary has been a continued source of support and encouragement. So too has the Emperor's grandson Prince Beede Mariam. We have had many discussions about past and present events and also shared our joy at the way Arsenal play their attacking football when on top form.

I have visited the home of the author Ian Campbell a few times in the Wollo Sefer area of Addis Ababa. His collection of books, papers and photographs is an extraordinary treasure trove. I am also deeply grateful for his insights and his willingness to share his considerable knowledge so freely. Arabella Stewart, who is based in Addis Ababa, helped me with a number of contacts and passed on her wisdom about how the city operates.

I have interviewed Ellene Mocria, the granddaughter of Charles Martin or Hakim Workeneh, and she also provided me with two great photographs of her grandfather with the Emperor in London. I have also debated the intricacies of Ethiopian history with Bekoure Sirak, the grandson of the foreign minister, Heruy Wolde Selassie. His sister Askale Sirak also first alerted me to the existence of Captain Morgan's astonishing diary aboard *HMS Enterprise*, which picked up the royal party from Djibouti. Another of Heruy's grandchildren, Emeyou Tekle Mariam, passed on some important information about her grandfather. She also took me to see his former residence on the northern outskirts of Addis Ababa. The Ethiopian historian Bahru Zewde, who has written several

ACKNOWLEDGEMENTS

authoritative books about the country's modern history, granted me an interview at his office near the Imperial Hotel in the south of Addis Ababa. Professor Shiferaw Bekele passed on valuable contacts at Addis Ababa University as well as sharing his own perspectives about the Emperor's rule. Daniel Mamo, the Head Librarian of the Institute of Ethiopian Studies, paved the way for me to access the Institute's written and visual archives. Messay Tagesse patiently tracked down several key images from the Institute's collection. Heruy Arefine and Jonathan Niehaus also helped me find the photograph of the Emperor and his family at Fairfield House.

In London I have interviewed the Emperor's granddaughter Princess Sophia and also met with another of the Emperor's grandsons, Prince Micheal. I have had several captivating exchanges with the Emperor's great nephew Asfa-Wossen Asserate after meeting him in London in November 2015 at the launch of his biography of Haile Selassie. I also travelled by train from Bath to Tiverton in Devon to hear the vivid memories of Philippa Langdon, the granddaughter of Daniel Sandford.

One especially joyful experience was being able to meet the assistant governess at Fairfield House, Ruth Haskins, at the age of 96. Her respect for the Emperor was undimmed even after all these years. Dr Shawn-Naphtali Sobers, who produced the HTV documentary about the Emperor's time in Bath is a fount of knowledge about Fairfield House. He also was my guide in finding Heruy's grave in the sprawling grounds of Locksbrook Cemetery. I met Kenah McConnell, known as 'Tim,' in Bath and she passed on her memories of meeting the Imperial family during their exile. Hilary King, whose parents began the Little Theatre in Bath, helped me set the record straight about several aspects of life in Fairfield House.

Another of the highlights in researching this book has been my two meetings with Princess Seble in Virginia, who gave me her vivid recollections at the time of Fairfield. Her daughter Laly was very patient in answering my emails with a host of follow up questions. We also had another chance to meet at a cafe in Chelsea when she was with Yeshi, another of her daughters.

David Retta, who lives in Washington DC, gave me some very helpful information about the life of his father Abebe Retta, who was an assistant to the Emperor during his exile.

I am very grateful to those people who have read various drafts of the book and passed on their very useful advice. In the UK: my daughter Bridget Bowers, Ezra Tsegaye, Philip Rayner, Mary Sugden and Kate Ashcroft. In Addis Ababa: Solomon Hailemariam, Yemane Tsegaye, Judy Gifford, Ian Campbell and Carola Frenzen.

There are many other people who have helped me organise my research trips and have pointed me in the right direction. In the UK: the photographer and fashion designer Addishiwot Asfawosen; the staff at Bath Central Library; Jean Broadbent of the Anglo-Ethiopian Society; John Cooper, a fellow Mayor's Guide in Bath; Stephen and Vera Constant; Wainam Masai; Steven Nightingale, Hayley Porter, and Pauline Wallace from Fairfield House; Kifle Derege from Bristol; the research staff at the Bath Record Office and the Imperial War Museum; Lesley Telford, the secretary of the Ventnor and District Local History Society; Kevin Bacon at the Royal Pavilion & Museum, Brighton & Hove and Adrian Imms from the Argus newspaper in Brighton; Harry Hall from Haus, the publishers of *King of Kings*; Councillor Martin Veal, who interrupted his busy council duties to talk about his mother's recollections of the Emperor. Prince Asfa-Wossen's sister Rebecca Grove-Stephensen helped me to double-check some family details and also track down some photographs.

In Ethiopia, Roman Demeke was my guide and translator when I travelled to Debre Libanos, and to Hora Lake in Debre Zeit to find Haile Selassie's other Fairfield House. Dénis Gerard, who now lives in Debre Zeit, was very generous with his time when I went to ask him about the minefield of ascertaining the copyright of photographs of the Emperor. Heranie Berhane-Meskel and her husband Betru Dimberu explained about the activities of her grandfather Ras Kassa in Jerusalem. She also gave me permission to use several family photographs. Abiye Abebe, who has the same name as his father, told me some details about his father's experiences at the Bible College of Wales.

It was a great pleasure to work with Shama Books to produce an edition of this book for the Ethiopian market. From the outset Gassan Bagersh was an enthusiastic supporter of the project and Asfeha Tesfaye ensured all the business ran smoothly. I am deeply grateful to Amare Mamo for keeping me on the straight and narrow about various facts and the correct spelling of many Ethiopian names.

I am very thankful to George Steer's son, also called George, for permission to quote from his father's books. Sophie Petros in London helped in making this arrangement. B. Macklin kindly forwarded to me his well-researched essay *No Power on Earth can Remove his Liability*, on the British government's deliberations about providing funds for the Emperor. This put me on the track of the relevant cabinet papers.

Dan Brown at Bath in Time kindly arranged for me to publish so many wonderful pictures from the Emperor's time in Bath. I am grateful too to Lynne Fernquest, the Editor of the *Bath Chronicle*, for permission to quote so much of the paper's reporting about Haile Selassie in Bath.

Tom Rankin did an excellent job in designing the four maps included in the book and thanks to my son Tim Bowers for arranging the whole process.

Finally a special thanks to all at The Self-Publishing Partnership in Bath who helped bring this project to fruition. Douglas and Heather for their invaluable guidance, Kate for her excellent proof-reading and to the designers Kevin and Andrew for their great work.

PHOTOGRAPHS

LIST OF PHOTOGRAPHS (WITH CREDITS)

I have made every effort to track down the copyright owner of the photographs I have used in the book. I will gladly make any updates to this list should further information come to light.

Bath Abbey (author) 18
Stained glass window of King Solomon and the Queen of Sheba (author) 19
Ras Kassa Hailu (courtesy of Heranie Berhane-Meskel) 26
The hunting group by the train (courtesy of IES collection) 28
Addressing the League of Nations (courtesy of IES collection) 42
Bath Spa Station (author) 44
Pulteney Bridge (author) 44
Bath Spa Hotel Gardens (author) 45
On the steps of the Bath Spa Hotel (Bath in Time) 46
The Royal Crescent in Bath (author) 48
Greeted by the crowds (Bath in Time) 50
Tour of Roman Baths (Bath in Time) 52
The sacred spring (author) 53
Octagon Chapel exhibition (Bath in Time) 55
Another welcome by the crowds (Bath in Time) 56
Canal in Bath (author) 63
Ras Teferi as a boy (courtesy of Dénis Gerard collection) 67
Menelik on his horse (author) 77
Crowned as Emperor (courtesy of IES collection) 78
The Kissing Pool (author) 81
Lion statue in Bath (author) 86

Holburne Museum (author) 87
Fairfield House (Bath in Time) 89
Arriving at Bath Spa Station (Bath in Time) 90
Marlborough buildings (author) 92
Family portrait (thanks to Princess Sophia) 98
Duke of Harar doing gymnastics (Bath in Time) 102
Duke of Harar in a car (Bath in Time) 103
The Emperor at an official function (Bath in Time) 104
Haile Selassie tour of Bath (Bath in Time) 105
The Emperor in unfamiliar surroundings (Bath in Time) 106
The Royal couple in grounds (Bath in Time) 107
Group photo with Princess Seble (courtesy of Menah McConnell) 112
The Gennete Leul (author) 115
Casa Littoria (author) 118
Memorial to Graziani victims (author) 119
Emperor attends memorial service in London (courtesy of Pankhursts and Tsehai Publishing) 121
Little Theatre (author) 131
Roseries garden party (Bath in Time) 132
Copy of Sebastopol gun (author) 140
Dr Charles Martin with Emperor (courtesy of Dr Martin's family) 141
The Pankhursts' home (author) 143
Tapestry of Fairfield photograph (author) 144
Pankhursts' wedding (courtesy of the Pankhursts and Tsehai Publishing. Photo by Afewerk) 146
Bath Horse Show (Bath in Time) 147
Bath Dog Show (Bath in Time) 150
The Imperial family (Shama Books) 154
Sitting on the West Pier in Brighton (Royal Pavilion & Museums, Brighton & Hove) 161
Walking past the Royal Pavilion in Brighton (Royal Pavilion & Museums, Brighton & Hove) 162
Boat trip in Isle of Wight (Ventnor and District Local History Society) 165
Fry's visit (Bath in Time) 169
Fairfield House today (author) 171
Lion carvings at Fairfield (author) 172
Camp at Penllergaer School (courtesy of ByFaithMedia) 180
Delivery of Morris car (Bath in Time) 182
Outside a tent in Sudan (courtesy of IES collection) 190

PHOTOGRAPHS

Stepping off a plane (courtesy of IES collection) 191
Emperor back in Addis Ababa (courtesy of Dénis Gerard collection) 194
George Steer with the Emperor (courtesy of Nicholas Rankin and George Steer, son of George Steer) 201
Winding steps at Gennete Leul (author) 202
Holy Trinity Cathedral (author) 204
Church of the Saviour of Exiles (author) 204
Churchill Road (author) 207
Sylvia Pankhurst's grave (author) 208
The Emperor with Ras Kassa (courtesy of Heranie Berhane-Meskel) 214
Haile Selassie outside Fairfield in Debre Zeit (courtesy of Dénis Gerard collection) 217
Haile Selassie playing with his dogs (courtesy of Corbis Images) 218
Haile Selassie portrait (Bath in Time) 221
Arrival at ceremony (Bath in Time) 222
Inspecting the guard (Bath in Time) 222
Outside Bath Abbey (Bath in Time) 223
Cheery wave outside Guildhall (Bath Record Office) 223
Pump Room (Bath Record Office) 223
Visiting Stothert and Pitt (Bath in Time) 224
The home of Mrs Rowlands (Bath in Time) 224
Hospital visit (Bath in Time) 224
Visiting Moorlands School (Bath Record Office) 225
Signing ceremony (Bath Record Office) 225
Elephant tusks (Bath in Time) 232
Menelik's church (author) 234
Stone lion (author) 236
Ba'ata Mariam (author) 236
Haile Selassie's coffin (author) 239
Old photograph of Fairfield House (courtesy of Dénis Gerard collection) 260

CHAPTER SOURCES

There is a range of brilliant books written about the Emperor. A full bibliography is provided in the next section of the book. The works I have found particularly helpful are written by authors who knew the Emperor and so have special firsthand insights, which I have reflected throughout this book. *The Negus* by Angelo del Boca is an authoritative account of the whole of the Emperor's life and is based on many Italian as well as Ethiopian sources. He generously has given me permission to quote freely from his book. Harold Marcus wrote a breathtaking study of the early life of the Emperor, *Haile Sellassie 1: The Formative Years 1892-1936*.

George Steer's books, *Caesar in Abyssinia* and *Sealed and Delivered*, are not only beautifully written but convey the urgency and immediacy of Ethiopia and Britain in the 1930s. Leonard Mosley's *Haile Selassie* has some revealing eyewitness accounts of the life and times of the Emperor. *King of Kings* by the Emperor's great-nephew Asfa-Wossen Asserate provides a rounded account of the whole of the Emperor's life and is a judicious mix of detached observation mixed with special insider knowledge.

The two volumes of the Emperor's autobiography, *Emperor Haile Sellassie I: 'My Life and Ethiopia's Progress,'* provide some source material straight from the horse's mouth.

On the general history of Ethiopia I have been helped greatly by the book by the leading Ethiopian historian Bahru Zewde, *A History of Modern Ethiopia*. From the British perspective, The *Eden Memoirs* give a top-level insider's account of the diplomatic mood and conflicts during the thirties. I have also relied heavily on the official British government records at the National Archives in Kew in south-west London to understand the diplomatic and political climate in the exile period. Precise references can be found at the end of the bibliography section.

The archives of the *Bath and Wilts Chronicle and Herald* have provided a wealth of information, not just about the activities of the Emperor during his time in Bath but also about the social and political scene, both in the city and the UK as a whole. In the

CHAPTER SOURCES

1930s regional and local newspapers in the UK were widely read and often carried items of national and international news. Many of them avidly published stories about the Emperor and many entries can be found in the extensive online British Newspaper archive, which I have searched in detail and unearthed some enthralling snippets which have been buried for years.

I have consulted all the editions of Sylvia Pankhurst's weekly newspaper *New Times* and *Ethiopia News* between 1936 and 1940. Bound copies are held at the British Library's underground storage facility at Wetherby near the northern city of Leeds. With notice they can be transported down to the inspirational surroundings of the British Library next to St Pancras Station in central London.

Wikipedia is sometimes derided as an unreliable source of information but I believe it has helped greatly in disseminating knowledge across the world. I happily make regular donations to it. I found Wikipedia to be invaluable as one of the first ports of call to try to find vital leads and specific references about key people and events. I have endeavoured to double-check all the information I discovered via the written sources quoted above. However, I accept full responsibility for any factual errors.

In addition to the written word, this book has been greatly enriched by interviews with some of the families of the Emperor and his co-exiles. Full details can be found in the Acknowledgements section. Many people in Bath have a range of anecdotes about the Emperor handed down to them across the generations. I am grateful to all those who have given permission for the various photographs to be used, giving a unique flavour of the turbulent times during which Haile Selassie lived.

I quote many of the relevant sources during the body of the main text. However, I believe it will be helpful to list below the main sources I relied upon for each chapter.

PROLOGUE

Most of these comments are based on my own experiences and observations. However, Edward Said's essay *Reflections on Exile* provides an expert and moving analysis of the experience of being separated from home. Paul Tabori's book *The Anatomy of Exile* contains a sobering and incisive poem about the state of exile. John Simpson's anthology *The Oxford Book of Exile* also throws up some revealing attitudes about separation and banishment.

The celebrated Nigerian writer Chinua Achebe offers some telling insights into dispossession. In *Home and Exile* he says that one of the commonest symptoms of this condition is a lack of self-esteem.

CHAPTER ONE

The Western Daily Press on 3 August 1936 claimed it was exclusively revealing that Haile Selassie was to visit Bath, on the recommendation of the Duke of Connaught.

IMPERIAL EXILE

The English translation of the *Kibra Negest* is a fascinating read about the story of Solomon and the Queen of Sheba. The accounts of the battles between Ethiopia and Italy are based on a number of sources, including Anthony Mockler's magisterial book *Haile Selassie's Wars*. *The Negus* provides details of Haile Selassie's own disturbing accounts of the effects of yperite gas. Other accounts of the fighting and Haile Selassie's escape from Ethiopia include *Haile Sellassie 1: The Formative Years 1892-1936* by Harold Marcus; Steer's *Caesar in Abyssinia*; *Mussolini: A New Life* by Nicholas Farrell; and Paul Henze's *A Layer of Time*.

For the Italian perspective I turned to *The War in Abyssinia* by Badoglio, the Italian commander. *Class and Revolution in Ethiopia* by John Markakis paints an incredible picture of the chaos and pillaging in Addis Ababa after the Emperor left. Richard Greenfield's political history of Ethiopia provides a colourful account of the Emperor's exploits on the battlefield, and of the special council meeting summoned to discuss the evacuation to Djibouti.

Most of the detail about the voyage of *HMS Enterprise* is gleaned from the highly readable official report provided by Captain Morgan. This is contained in a file held at the National Archives with a reference of 116/3045. The cabinet meeting at CAB/23/84 also contains some relevant information.

Time magazine edition on 11 May 1936 has a detailed article about Haile Selassie's flight from the battlefield, including the reference to one of his arms being bandaged after a mustard gas attack. It also suggests that some disgruntled Ethiopians made an attempt on his life as he was retreating. *Time's* despatch on 16 December 1935 has a vivid description of an Italian air raid on the northern town of Dessie.

CHAPTER TWO

The account of the Emperor's arrival at Waterloo station draws partly on the *Time* magazine report of 6 June 1936, though it was also reported in several British regional newspapers. The online subscription archive of *Time* contains many despatches about the Emperor throughout his long reign, including a vivid account of his speech before the League of Nations. Mockler's book also gives considerable space to the Emperor's arrival in the UK.

In the second volume of his autobiography the Emperor himself gives more details about Switzerland's rejection of his request to live there. Martelli's eyewitness account of seeing Haile Selassie in London is contained in his book *Italy against the World*. Much of the information about Haile Selassie's first few weeks in Bath comes from a variety of reports in the *Chronicle* newspaper. An analytical essay by Lutz Haber, *The Emperor Haile Selassie I in Bath 1936 – 1940*, provides a very helpful summary of events. In a file at Bath Central Library there are also some useful notes drawn up by Haber, citing many specific date references to Haile Selassie's appearances in the

CHAPTER SOURCES

Chronicle. Leonard Mosley in *Haile Selassie* makes some reference to the Emperor's spa treatments and the special trips organised from London to see him.

The background about the mood and appearance of Bath in the 1930s comes from a number of local history books, including *A History of Bath: Image and Reality* by Graham and Penny Bonsall, and *Bath* by J. Haddon.

CHAPTER THREE

The early years of the young Ras Teferi and his activities until he came to the UK are covered superbly in the core books I mention at the start of this section. These include works by George Steer, Angelo del Boca, and Bahru Zewde. Harold Marcus's biography and Paul Henze's book, cited in the sources for Chapter One, also flesh out the Emperor's early life.

The description of Father Jarosseau as having the appearance of a primitive Italian saint is contained in *Chapman-Andrews and the Emperor*. The book referred to a comment by Geoffrey Harmsworth, a member of the Northcliffe-Rothermere family. Harold Marcus gives some captivating detail about the Emperor's grand tour in his biography *Haile Sellassie 1: The Formative Years 1892-1936*. The Emperor's own autobiography, as mentioned earlier in the book, has a wealth of eyewitness information and observations about his trip. Greenfield typically has some descriptive and entertaining stories about the early life of Haile Selassie.

Wilfred Thesiger's *The Life of My Choice* has some fascinating detail about the Emperor's coronation, as does Evelyn Waugh's *The Coronation of Haile Selassie*. Del Boca's *The Negus* is as usual the source of a range of riveting material as is Harold Marcus's biography of the Emperor. *Ethiopia* by John Markakis has a masterly summary on pages 244-45 of the Emperor's complex and contradictory character at the time of his coronation. For example, he said the Emperor had profound ambition pursued with judicious caution. The notice boards in the entrance of the Institute for Ethiopian Studies contain much information about the development of the Gennete Leul Palace and other palaces at Siddist Kilo.

CHAPTER FOUR

The insights into the Emperor's reading habits are contained in *The Mission* by Hans Wilhelm Lockot. More details about the exile of Kaiser Wilhelm II can found in *Kaiser Wilhelm II: Germany's Last Emperor* by John Van der Kiste.

Some of the eyewitness accounts and anecdotes of daily life at Fairfield are provided by interviewees on the HTV documentary, *Footsteps of the Emperor*, narrated by Benjamin Zephaniah and produced by Shawn Sobers in 1999. It is available on YouTube. Some eye witnesses also appear on an entertaining Radio Four documentary, *The Emperor in Bath*. This was transmitted on 6 June 1987 and a copy can be found at the Imperial War Museum. Princess Seble's interview for this book is obviously of vital relevance to these events. The incredulous reaction to the Emperor playing billiards in Eritrea was recounted by Asfa-Wossen Asserate at the launch of his book in London in November 2015.

Details of the Emperor's financial position are contained in two Foreign Office documents, 371/20196 and 371/20198. The estimates of the Emperor's financial position drawn up by Charles St John Collier, the governor of the Bank of Ethiopia, are backed up by figures given by Captain Morgan of the *HMS Enterprise*. He told his superiors at the Admiralty in his report of the evacuation from Djibouti that the Emperor's luggage contained between 250,000 and 300,000 Maria Theresa thalers.

For further information about comparing purchasing power in different eras consult websites such as www.measuringworth.com. For information about the purchasing power of the old French franc see http://www.insee.fr/en/indicateurs/indic_cons/guide-lecture-tableaux-2012-english.pdf

CHAPTER FIVE

The Plot to Kill Graziani by Ian Campbell is an invaluable source of material about the massacres of the innocents in Addis Ababa. The accounts by the Hungarian doctor known as Doctor Sava were later published weekly in several editions of the *New Times and Ethiopia News* from July 1940 to the early part of 1941. The paper also reported details of the raping of Ethiopian women. Several of the core books on Ethiopian history have gripping detail about the massacres and their aftermath.

Another of Campbell's books *The Massacre of Debre Libanos* also provides a wealth of new information about the chilling operation launched by Graziani and his henchmen to exterminate the community at the monastery. The obituary of Ras Desta was contained on page 18 of the *Times* on Friday 26 February 1937.

CHAPTER SIX

The Life of My Choice again provides some good background to Thesiger's view of the Emperor. George Steer's books reveal a lot about himself as well as about the personalities and places around him. The biography of Steer, *Telegram from Guernica,* is teeming with anecdotes and astute observations, especially about the rivalry between Steer and Evelyn Waugh. It is written by Nicholas Rankin, a fellow exile from the BBC.

Richard Pankhurst is a prolific writer about Ethiopian history and gives some memorable insights into two books about his mother. They are *Sylvia Pankhurst: Artist and Crusader: An intimate portrait by Richard Pankhurst* and *Sylvia Pankhurst: Counsel for Ethiopia.*

Richard and Rita Pankhurst's recent book *Ethiopian Reminiscences* contains many

CHAPTER SOURCES

memories of the life and works of Sylvia Pankhurst. Her secret service file is stored at the Kew Records Office under the reference SV2/1570 2. There is also an excellent BBC radio programme about Sylvia Pankhurst called *The Radical and the Emperor*, broadcast on 13 December 2006. D. Mitchell's *The Fighting Pankhursts* provides the wider context of the Pankhurst family.

Peter Garretson's biography of Dr Charles Martin is a very authoritative and comprehensive assessment of his life. The full title is *A Victorian Gentleman and Ethiopian Nationalist: The Life and Times of Hakim Warqenah, Dr Charles Martin*.

CHAPTER SEVEN

B. Macklin's essay *No Power on Earth can Remove his Liability* gives some revealing pointers about the various official British government papers about the Emperor, especially those dealing with his lack of money and the anonymous benefactor who came forward to help him. The relevant documents include FO1093/83, FO1093/82 and FO1093/83.

Halifax's account of his meeting with Haile Selassie can be found in PREM 1.275 at the Kew Records Office. Emmanuel Abraham's autobiography *Reminiscences of My Life* is a helpful guide to how the Ethiopian Legation continued to function in various places in London against the odds in the late 1930s and the early part of the war. Leonard Mosley's *Haile Selassie* has some intriguing insights into the Emperor's decline in Bath, following his car accident. He also quotes some observations by a local policeman on the beat outside Fairfield House, giving more insight into the low-key security arrangements made for the Emperor.

The *Chronicle* is as usual a mine of information on the royal family's life in Bath. Lutz Haber's essay on the Emperor's exile contains some detailed references to the Emperor's court actions. In his paper in the *Ethiopia Observer* Richard Pankhurst is once again on the ball about the legal action concerning the Bank of Ethiopia.

More information about Dunham Massey can be found on the website of the National Trust, which held a well attended special event in 2012 called the Earl and the Emperor. The Ethiopian coffee ceremony was performed and there were some special readings by the poet Lemn Sissay, whose Ethiopian mother arrived in the UK shortly before he was born.

Details about the Emperor's trips to Brighton and Worthing can be found in the *Brighton Argus* at http://www.theargus.co.uk/news/yesterdays/features/13897918. Haile_Selassie_s_visit_to_Sussex_remembered/

Special thanks to Bekoure Heruy, who told me some revealing anecdotes about the exiles in Bath and the funeral of his grandfather, Blattengeta Heruy. John Spencer's discussion of secret peace negotiations between Italy and Ethiopia can be found on page 84 of his memoir *Ethiopia at Bay*.

CHAPTER EIGHT

The detailed feature article on life in Fairfield appeared in the *Sunday Post* on 12 February 1940. Mary Lishman's first-hand recollections appeared in the *Yorkshire Post* on 17 April 1941. The *Chronicle* in Bath is essential reading as usual about the Emperor's movements. *Sealed and Delivered* gives Steer's own hair-raising account of his role in the dramatic escape to Sudan and then his part in the campaign to liberate Addis Ababa. Other engaging insights are provided by *Telegram from Guernica*. A special correspondent for *New Times* and *Ethiopia News*, Alexander Clifford, also filed a vivid despatch about the Emperor's impromptu party in Alexandria. The wonderful story of Ayatollah Khomeini's reaction to returning home from exile is contained in John Simpson's *The Oxford Book of Exile*.

The core Ethiopian history books by Del Boca, Bahru Zewde, and Leonard Mosley come into their own in telling the story of the Emperor's sojourn in Sudan and the eventual triumphant entry into Addis Ababa. The British press also followed these events in detail. I am indebted to David Sheriff for his explanation of the meaning of Mission 101 in his book *Bare Feet and Bandoliers*.

CHAPTER NINE

Details of the celebratory telegram from the Emperor to the Bible College of Wales and his relationship with its founder Rees Howell can be found at www.byfaith.co.uk.

The core Ethiopian history books provide a wealth of detail about the Emperor's remaining decades in power. These include *Layers of Time*, *The Mission*, *The Negus*, *Haile Selassie* and *A History of Modern Ethiopia*. Edward Ullendorf's paper in the *Journal of Semitic Studies* in 1979 provides the detail about the Emperor paying back the money proffered to him by the British Government. John Spencer's *Ethiopia at Bay* contains an authoritative analysis of the way the Emperor's mind and character operated in the post-liberation years. On page 269 of *Ethiopia* John Markakis compared Haile Selassie to Menelik, who saw no difference between his own money and the public treasury. Asfa-Wossen Asserate's *King of Kings* is packed with detail about the Emperor's policy initiatives and his approach to governing. He also includes the story about the Governor of the Bank of England revealing that the Emperor no longer trusted any bank after his return from exile (page 305).

This chapter draws heavily on oral sources, including Prince Beede Mariam, Philippa Langford and Princess Mary. My own travels and experiences in Addis Ababa and Bishoftu (Debre Zeit) also helped greatly to compose this chapter.

CHAPTER TEN

The *Chronicle* is by far and away the best source of information on the Emperor's return to Bath. The Record Office of the Bath and North East Somerset Council

CHAPTER SOURCES

also holds a splendid photo album of the events surrounding the Freeman of the City ceremony. The Foreign Office paper, FO371/108283, provides some information on the preparations for the Emperor's visit.

EPILOGUE

The Negus by Angelo del Boca contains a moving opening chapter about the Emperor's imprisonment at the great gebbi. John Spencer's memories of seeing the Emperor for the last time are illuminating, especially his observations about how he was losing his powers of recall of names, faces and incidents. I am grateful to Princes Micheal and Beede for their anecdotes about when they last saw their grandfather. *Time* magazine has some vivid accounts of the Emperor's downfall.

BIBLIOGRAPHY AND OTHER WRITTEN SOURCES

Abraham, E. (1995) *Reminiscences of My Life*, Oslo: Lunde Forlag.

Achebe, C. (2003) *Home and Exile*, Edinburgh: Canongate Books.

Asfa Yilma, Princess (1936) *Haile Selassie*, London: Marston & Co. Ltd.

Asher, M. (1994) *Thesiger*, London: Viking.

Asserate, Asfa-Wossen (2015) *King of Kings: The Triumph and Tragedy of Emperor Haile Selassie 1 of Ethiopia*, London: Haus Publishing.

Badoglio, P. (1937) *The War in Abyssinia*, London: Methuen.

Barriagober, A. (2006) *Conflict and the Refuge Experience*, Aldershot: Ashgate Publishing.

Bernstein, H. (1994) *The Rift: The Exile Experience Of South Africans*, London: Jonathan Cape.

Blackwell, D. (2005) *Counselling and Psychotherapy*, London: Jessica Kingsley Publishers.

Brooks, M. (2000) (Editor and translator) *Kebra Nagast*, Asmara: The Red Sea Press.

Campbell, I. (2014) *The Massacre of Debre Libanos*, Addis Ababa: Addis Ababa University Press.

Campbell, I. (2010) *The Plot to Kill Graziani*, Addis Ababa: Addis Ababa University Press.

Churchill, W. (1941) *My Early Life: A Roving Commission*, London: Macmillan.

Churchill, R. (1966) *Winston S Churchill 1 Youth 1874-1900*, London: Heinemann.

Clapham, C. (1969) *Haile Selassie's Government*, London: Longman.

Cline, S and Gillies, M. (2012) *The Arvon book of literary non-fiction*, London: Bloomsbury.

Cunliffe, B. (1986) *The City of Bath,* Gloucester: Alan Sutton Publishing.

Davis, G and Bonsall, P. (2006) *A History of Bath: image and reality*, Lancaster: Carnegie Publishing.

Davis, M. (1999) *Sylvia Pankhurst: A Life in Radical Politics*, London: Pluto Press.

Del Boca, A. (1969) *The Ethiopian War 1935-41*, Chicago: University of Chicago.

Del Boca, A. (2012) *The Negus*, Addis Ababa: Arada Books.

Duggan, C. (2012) *Fascist Voices*, London: Bodley Head.

Earl of Avon (1962) *The Eden Memoirs: Facing the Dictators*, London: Cassell & Company.

Farrell, N. (2003) *Mussolini: A New Life*, London: Weidenfeld & Nicolson.

Garretson, P. (2012) *A Victorian Gentleman and Ethiopian nationalist: The Life and Times*

BIBLIOGRAPHY

of Hakim Warqenah, Dr Charles Martin, Woodbridge: James Currey.

Gerard, D. (2009) *Ras Tafari*: L'Archange Minotaure.

Getachew, I. (2001) *Beyond the Throne*, Addis Ababa: Shama Books.

Gilbert, M. (2000) *Churchill – A Life*, London: Pimlico.

Gilbert, M. (1976) *Winston S Churchill Vol 5*, London, Heinemann.

Gooch, J. (2007) *Mussolini and his Generals*, Cambridge: Cambridge University Press.

Greenfield, R. (1965) *Ethiopia: A New Political History*, USA: Praeger.

Haber, L. (1992) *The Emperor Haile Selassie I in Bath 1936 – 1940*, London: Occasional paper published by The Anglo-Ethiopian Society.

Haddon, J. (1973) *Bath*, London: Batsford.

Hardy, D. (2013) *Haile Selassie Remembered in Shropshire*, London: Anglo-Ethiopian Society News File.

Henze, P.B. (2004) *Layers of Time*, Addis Ababa: Shama Books.

Hess, R.L. (1970) *Ethiopia: The Modernisation of Autocracy*, London: Cornell University Press.

Hibbert, C. (1986) *The Rise and Fall of Il Duce*, Harmonsworth: Penguin.

Judah D. (2015) *Revelation of an Emperor*, Bath.

Kapuscinski, R. (2006) *The Emperor: Downfall of an Autocrat*, London: Penguin.

Kettler, D.T (2011) *The Liquidation of Exile: Studies in the Intellectual Emigration of the 1930s*, London: Anthem Press.

Khama, R. (2003) *Dark Continents: Psychoanalysis and Colonialism*, London: Duke University Press.

Leslie, P. (2005) *Chapman-Andrews and the Emperor*, Barnsley: Pen and Sword.

Lockot, W.H. (1992) *The Mission: The Life, Reign and Character of Haile Sellassie*, London: Frontline Distribution International.

Macklin, B. (2007) *'No Power on Earth can Remove his Liability': Emperor Haile Selassie and the Foreign Office, a Documentary Essay' Immigrants & Minorities Vol. 25, No. 1, March 2007, pp 73-93*: Routledge.

Marcus, H. (1987) *Haile Sellassie 1: The Formative Years 1892-1936*, New Jersey: The Red Sea Press.

Markakis, J. (2006) *Ethiopia: Anatomy of a Traditional Polity*, Addis Ababa: Shama Books.

Markakis, J. (1986) *Class and Revolution in Ethiopia*, New Jersey: The Red Sea Press.

Martelli, G. (1937) *Italy against the World*, London: Chatto and Windus.

Mikes, G. (1946) *How To Be An Alien*, London: Penguin.

Milosz. C. (10 December 1980) *Speech at Nobel Banquet.*

Mitchell, D. (1967) *The Fighting Pankhursts*, London: Jonathan Cape.

Mockler, A. (2003) *Haile Selassie's Wars*, Oxford: Signal Books.

Mosley, L. (1964) *Haile Selassie*, London: Weidenfeld and Nicolson.

O'Kelly, S. (2003) *Amedeo: The True Story of an Italian's War in Abyssinia*, London: Harper Collins.

Pankhurst, R. and R. (2013) *Ethiopian Reminiscences: Early Days*, Los Angeles: Tsehai Publishers.

Pankhurst, R. (1999) *Italian Fascist War Crimes in Ethiopia: A history of their Discussion, from the League of Nations to the United Nations (1936-1939)*: North East African Studies 6.1-2 83-140.

Pankhurst, R. (1971) *Emperor Haile Selassie's Litigation in England to Reassert the Independence of Ethiopia during the Italian Occupation in 1937 and 1938*: Ethiopia Observer, Vol XIV Pages 46-67.

Pankhurst, R. (1979) *Sylvia Pankhurst: Artist and Crusader: An intimate portrait by Richard Pankhurst*, London: Paddington Press.

Pankhurst, R. (2003) *Sylvia Pankhurst: Counsel for Ethiopia*, Hollywood: Tsehai Publishers.

Papadopoulos, R.K. (ed) (2002) *Therapeutic Care for Refugees*, London: Karnac.

Payne, J. (2012) *Bath*, Oxford: Signal Books.

Pearce, J. (2014) *Prevail: The Inspiring Story of Ethiopia's Victory over Mussolini's Invasion*, New York: Skyhorse Publishing.

Pelling, H. (1979) *Churchill*, Great Britain: Macmillan.

Perham, M. (1969) *Government of Ethiopia*, London: Faber and Faber.

Ponting, C. (1994) *Churchill*, London: Sinclair-Stevenson.

Pugh, M. (2001) *The Pankhursts*, London: Penguin.

Rankin, N. (2003) *Telegram from Guernica*, London: Faber and Faber.

Rhodes James, R. (1970) *Churchill: A Study in Failure*, London: Weidenfeld and Nicolson.

Robertson, E.M. (1977) *Mussolini as Empire Builder*, London: Macmillan.

Romero, P. (1987) *Sylvia Pankhurst Portrait of a Radical*, Avon: Bath Press.

BIBLIOGRAPHY

Rose, N. (1994) *Churchill: An Unruly Life*, London: Simon and Schuster.

Rose, P. (ed) (2005) *The Dispossessed: An Anatomy of Exile*, Northampton: University of Massachusetts.

Said, E. (2002) *Reflections on Exile and other essays*, Cambridge, Massachusetts: Harvard University.

Sandford, C. (1946) *Ethiopia Under Haile Selassie*, London: J.M. Dent & Sons.

Sandford, C. (1955) *The Lion of Judah Hath Prevailed*, London: J.M. Dent & Sons.

Schwab, P. (1979) *Haile Selassie I Ethiopia's Lion of Judah*, Chicago: Nelson-Hall.

Sellassie, H. (1976) *Emperor Haile Sellassie I: 'My Life and Ethiopia's Progress' volume 1 1892-1937: Translated and annotated by Edward Ullendorff*, London: Oxford University Press.

Sellassie, H. (1999) *Emperor Haile Sellassie I: 'My Life and Ethiopia's Progress' volume 2, 1936-42: Translated by Ezekiel Gebissa*, edited and annotated by Harold Marcus, London: Frontline Books (4th Edition).

Sellassie, H. (1967) *Selected Speeches of his Imperial Majesty Haile Sellassie 1*, Addis Ababa: Published by Imperial Ethiopian Ministry of Information.

Seyoum, A. (2013) *The Bureaucratic Empire*, New Jersey: Red Sea Press.

Shirref, D. (1995) *Bare Feet and Bandoliers*, London: The Radcliffe Press.

Simpson, J. (ed) (1995) *The Oxford Book of Exile*, Oxford: Oxford University Press.

Smith, D.M. (1984) *Mussolini*, London: Phoenix.

Smith, D.M. (1976) *Mussolini's Roman Empire*, London: Longman.

Spencer, J.H. (1984) *Ethiopia at Bay*, Algonac, MI: Reference Publications.

Steer, G.L. (2009) *Caesar in Abyssinia*, London: Faber and Faber.

Steer, G.L. (2009) *Sealed and Delivered*, London: Faber and Faber.

Tabori, P. (1972) *The Anatomy of Exile*, London: Harrap.

Tames, R. and S.(2009) *A Travellers History of Bath*, Moreton-in-Marsh: Chastleton Travel.

Thesiger, W. (1996) *The Danakil Diary*, London: Flamingo.

Thesiger, W. (1987) *The Life of My Choice*, London: William Collins and Co.

Ullendorff, E. (1977) *Haile Selassie in Bath – Journal of Semitic Studies no 2 v 24 251-264*: Manchester.

Ullendorff, E. (1960) *The Ethiopians: An Introduction to the Country and its People*, London: Oxford University Press.

Van der Kiste, J. (1999) *Kaiser Wilhelm II: Germany's Last Emperor*, Stroud: Sutton Publishing.

Van der Veer, G. (1992) *Counselling and Therapy of Refugees*, Chichester: John Willey and Sons.

Waugh, E. (1931) *The Coronation of Haile Selassie*, London: Penguin.

Waugh, E. (1976) *The Diaries of Evelyn Waugh*, London: Book Club Associates.

Wrong, M. (2005) *I Didn't Do It For You*, London: Fourth Estate.

Zegeye, A. and Puasewaris, S. (eds) (1999) *Peasantry, Nationalism and Democracy*, London: British Academic Press.

Zewde, B. (2001) *A History of Modern Ethiopia*, 1855-1991, Oxford: James Currey.

Zewde, B. (2002) *Pioneers of Change*, Oxford: James Currey.

BATH AND WILTS CHRONICLE AND HERALD

A series of articles written in both the daily and weekly versions of the newspaper between 1936 and 1941.

Several articles were published during Haile Selassie's visit to Bath in October 1954.

NEW TIMES AND ETHIOPIA NEWS

A series of articles from the editions dated between May 1936 and May 1941. (Paper copies available via British Library.) Permission to use quotations from the papers was given by Richard Pankhurst.

TIME MAGAZINE

The magazine has many articles about the Italian invasion of Ethiopia, the Emperor's position and relevant international diplomacy between 1935 and 1941.

ECONOMIST MAGAZINE

Edition of 9 May 1936.

CABINET AND FOREIGN OFFICE MINUTES – THE NATIONAL RECORDS OFFICE IN LONDON

ADM 116/3045 (accounts of Haile Selassie's departure from Djibouti)

CAB/23/84 (discussion about Haile Selassie leaving Djibouti)

CAB 66/8/36 1940 (discussions about return of Haile Selassie to Ethiopia)

CAB 65/17/11 January 1941 (discussions about the recognition of Haile Selassie's claim to the throne)

BIBLIOGRAPHY

CAB 65/17/9 January 1941 (another discussion about the recognition of Haile Selassie's claim to the throne)

CAB 65/17/12 February 1941 (further discussion about emergence of independent Ethiopia. Decided it would be 'premature to recognise Abyssinia as an ally of this country.')

CAB 65/17/10 (discussion about future of the white population in Ethiopia)

CAB 65/17/5 February 1941 (discussions about a revived Ethiopian state)

FO1093/82 (discussion about providing a gift to Haile Selassie)

FO1093/83 (exchanges about the mysterious benefactor)

FO3711/23375 (discussions about the Emperor's restoration to the throne)

FO/854/6A (early discussions about sanctions against Italy)

FO371/20197 (1936)

FO371/108283 (1954 visit)

FO1093/332 (discussions about finance in Sudan)

PREM 1.275 (Halifax reports on discussions with Haile Selassie)

IR 83/281 (Haile Selassie's tax file)

SV2/1570 2 (Sylvia Pankhurst secret service file)

Plus other online documents during Haile Selassie's time in Bath, including: Cabinet meetings in 1935:
  8, 15, 17, May
  17, 26 June
  3, 10, 23, 24, 31 July
  1936 30 May
  1937 8 September
  1940 16 June War Cabinet
  1941 23 Jan War Cabinet
Foreign Office discussions on 7, 13, 27, 29 Jan and 3 Feb 1941

WHAT HAPPENED TO FAIRFIELD HOUSE'S PRINCIPAL RESIDENTS POST-EXILE

Imperial couple

Emperor Haile Selassie — Left Bath in June 1940 for Sudan. Entered Addis Ababa on 5 May 1941. Reigned until 1974 and murdered by Derg in 1975 at the age of 83.

Empress Menen — Left Bath in spring 1941. Back in Ethiopia focused on church matters and issues affecting women. Died aged 70 in 1962 after a long illness.

Children

Princess Tenagneworq — Remained in Bath until 1943. Returned home and remarried in 1944. Imprisoned by Derg. Died in 2001 at the age of 91.

Crown Prince Asfa-Wossen — Returned to Ethiopia with his father in 1941. Became Governor of Wollo. Lived abroad after 1973. Died in US in 1997 after long illness, aged 80.

Princess Tsehai — Left Bath in 1941 with her mother and returned to Ethiopia. Died in pregnancy in 1942 at the age of 23.

Makonnen, Duke of Harar — Left Bath in June 1940 with his father. Travelled to Sudan and then Ethiopia. Killed in a car crash in 1957, aged 33.

Prince Sahle Selassie — Left Bath in 1943 and returned to Ethiopia. Died in 1962 after a short illness, aged 31.

FAIRFIELD RESIDENTS

Grandchildren

Princess Aida	Stayed in England to continue her studies. Returned later to Ethiopia and was imprisoned by Derg. Died in 2013, aged 85.
Princess Hirut	Stayed in England to continue her studies. Returned later to Ethiopia and was imprisoned by Derg. Died in 2014, aged 84.
Princess Seble	Stayed in England to continue her studies. Returned later to Ethiopia and was imprisoned by Derg. In 2015 was living in US with her family.
Admiral Iskender Desta	Returned to Ethiopia in 1943 and later became head of Ethiopian Navy after federation with Eritrea. Murdered by Derg in 1974, aged 40.
Prince Amaha	Returned to Ethiopia in 1943 with his mother Princess Tenagneworq. Died shortly afterwards in Harar after a long illness, aged 16.

Emperor's other family members and advisers

Ras Kassa	Left Bath in January 1938 for Jerusalem. Returned to Ethiopia in 1941. Remained as Emperor's closest adviser. Died in 1956, aged 75.
Asserate Kassa	Remained in England to study. Later returned to Ethiopia and was President of the Crown Council. Murdered by Derg in 1974, aged 52.
Lorenzo Taezaz	Left Bath in 1940 with the Emperor for Sudan and then Ethiopia. Held various government posts. Died in Stockholm in the mid-1940s.
Sirak Heruy	After returning to Addis Ababa he worked for the Ethiopian foreign ministry. Translated Rasselas. Died in 1982, aged 72.